New York University Studies in
French Culture and Civilization

General Editors:
Tom Bishop and Nicholas Wahl

D1002831

Medieval Narrative and Modern Narratology

Subjects and Objects of Desire

Evelyn Birge Vitz

New York University Press

NEW YORK AND LONDON

Library of Congress Cataloging-in-Publication Data

Vitz, Evelyn Birge.
    Medieval narrative and modern narratology: subjects and objects
of desire/Evelyn Birge Vitz.
        p.   cm.—(New York University studies in French culture and
civilization)
    Bibliography: p.
    Includes index.
    ISBN 0-8147-8761-4 (alk. paper)   ISBN 0-8147-8766-5 (pbk.)
    1. French literature—To 1500—History and criticism. 2. Desire
in literature. 3. Narration (Rhetoric) 4. Rhetoric, Medieval.
5. Self in literature. 6. Autobiography. I. Title. II. Series.
PQ155.D47V58 1989
940'.9'23—dc19   88-36509
                                                                      CIP

p 10 9 8 7 6 5 4 3 2 1

New York University Press books are printed on acid-free paper, and
their binding materials are chosen for strength and durability.

Book design by Ken Venezio

For Paul with love

Contents

Acknowledgments

I wish to express here my gratitude for the NEH Younger Humanist Research award that allowed me to launch this research. I am also deeply grateful to several of my colleagues at New York University from whom I have learned so much and whose collegiality I have so greatly enjoyed. In particular, without the encouragement and invaluable critical readings of Michel Beaujour, Nancy Freeman Regalado, and Kathryn Talarico this book would never have been written. Over the years that I have worked on these texts and ideas, I have found it exceedingly rewarding (and pleasant) to talk about them with my husband—and many of my insights derive from our conversations. My children too have contributed to this volume, albeit often unwittingly!—and it was while reading "The Little Gingerbread Man" to one of them that my eyes were opened to some of the deficiencies of the Greimasian system (see chapter 5).

Earlier versions of chapters included here appeared, in French or in English, in the following journals: *Genre, Modern Language Notes, Publications of the Modern Language Association, Poétique, Romantic Review*, and *Yale French Studies*. Permission to revise them here is gratefully acknowledged:

A somewhat different form of chapter 1 appeared in French in *Poétique*, no. 24 (1975) with the title "Type et individu dans l' 'autobiographie médievale.' "

An earlier version of chapter 2 (originally presented in French) first appeared, translated into English by Barbara DiStefano, in *Genre* 6, no. 1 (March 1973): 49–75. Copyright 1973 by Donald E. Billiar, Edward F. Heuston, and Robert L. Vales.

An earlier version of the second part of chapter 3 appeared in *Yale French Studies* 58 (1979): 148–64 under the title "Inside/Outside: First-Person Narrative in Guillaume de Lorris' *Roman de la Rose*.

A somewhat different version of chapter 4 was published in *Modern Language Notes*, 92 (4): 645–75 as "Narrative Analysis of Medieval Texts: *La Fille du comte de Ponthieu*."Reprinted by permission of The Johns Hopkins University Press.

Chapter 5, in a somewhat different form, was published in *PMLA* 93, no. 2 (May 1978): 396–408.

Chapter 6, originally given as a paper in 1977 at a colloquium on language and style at the City University of New York in a section devoted to modern approaches to medieval stylistics, appeared, in an earlier version, in *Romanic Review* 74, no. 4 (Nov. 1983): 383–404. Copyright by the Trustees of Columbia University in the City of New York.

In an earlier form, chapter 7 appeared in *Romanic Review* 71, no. 3 (May 1980): 213–43 under the title "Desire and Causality in Medieval Narrative." Copyright by the Trustees of Columbia University in the City of New York.

I am also grateful for permission to quote from the following:

The Story of Abelard's Adversities, trans. J. T. Muckle, pp. 11–79, by permission of the publisher; © 1964 by the Pontifical Institute of Mediaeval Studies, Toronto.

Le Roman de la Rose, ed. Félix Lecoy, vol. 1 (Paris: Champion, 1965).

La Fille du comte de Ponthieu, ed. Clovis Brunel (Paris: Champion, 1926).

Lais, by Marie de France, ed. A. Ewert (Oxford: Basil Blackwell, 1965), with permission of Basil Blackwell, Oxford.

Tristan et Yseut, ed. J. C. Payen, Les Classiques Garnier (Paris: Bordas, 1974).

Introduction

This book brings together seven essays. In each one I have dealt closely with a single text, or a small group of texts, of medieval narrative, drawing from this detailed analysis a theoretical reflection of a more general kind. The first three chapters focus on aspects of the representation of the self in medieval autobiographical and first-person narrative—and point out some of the ways in which our modern understandings of the self and autobiography have tended to obscure for us the meaning of medieval texts.

In the chapter on Abelard's *Historia calamitatum*, I elaborate a vertical axis of self-comparison and self-definition—that is, an axis (or set of axes) on which one defines oneself with respect both to God and to models of human greatness. This axis is vertical, then, in two senses: both in that it speaks of the individual's relationship with God—with the transcendent—and that it is centrally preoccupied with notions of greatness or magnitude on any of a number of dimensions. In the Middle Ages this axis is very common, far more so than today—and indeed, insofar as there is any modern autobiographical axiology, it tends to be horizontal: the individual subject is apt to compare himself to the common run of men, with issues of "normalcy" rather than "greatness" or transcendence in mind.

Chapter 2 focuses on the representation of the self—the "I"—in Guillaume de Lorris's *Roman de la Rose*. One of the striking features of this work is that whereas in one sense it offers a highly analytical representation of the subject—compartmentalized into four distinct entities with respect to the experience of love and the act of narration—still the four selves are ultimately harmonized, synthesized: essentially, they agree. There is here remarkably little irony —and its lack is perhaps particularly surprising to us as we have gotten used to thinking that irony is intrinsic to the autobiographical task, if not to *all* narrative.[1]

Chapter 3 focuses on a central, and obsessive, dichotomy of Guillaume's *Rose*—that between inside and outside—and the ways in which this dichotomy is structured in the text. The terms in which the dichotomy is conceived in the *Rose* (and in many other medieval works) are significantly different from its typically modern conceptualizations.[2] Whereas the *Rose* associated the self with the "outside" (what was "inside" being the object of desire, of value), the modern period and modern texts tend to think of the self as being "inside," as constituting a self-contained, adequate whole— the world and others being "outside." This major shift in the structuring of the inside/outside dichotomy is of considerable importance for the history of Western culture, for it points up among other things the progressive shift from an objective to a subjective (or psychological) concept of value.

These first few chapters which focus on the self-representation and self-narration by the subject raise a number of broader issues, revolving essentially around the general concept of the subject in medieval narrative and culture, the striking paradox being this: on the one hand, the individual subject (such as the hero, the protagonist) receives immense predominance in medieval *récits* (the centrality of the hero is far greater in medieval than in modern narrative), and yet, on the other hand, there is a fundamental decentering of the subject. Not only is the subject represented as the outside, as a void, but we are frequently reminded (though not in quite these terms) that the narrative subject is one subjected, both to a discourse of which he is not the master, and to the will and intentions of other subjects, including not merely other characters but God and the narrator as well. It is to an elaboration of such issues that the remaining chapters are devoted: to the ways in which subjects are shown in action and in relation to other subjects in medieval narrative.

The primary way in which the subjects of medieval narrative are represented in relation to other people and things in the medieval *récit* is—as was already apparent in the Abelard and the *Rose*—through desire, which is an extraordinarily pervasive preoccupation in medieval narrative. Desire is certainly a preoccupation of *all* literature, but it has a peculiarly intense and central role in medieval works, because it is virtually the *sole* characterological principle. We are always told—and in general we are *only* told—what a character wants: what he (or she) loves, desires, intends. He generally wants whatever it is (and the things vary enormously) with great intensity and single-mindedness. By contrast, we are hardly ever told what someone *thinks* (rare is the character who does more than very occasionally "*se purpenser*" [reflect]). Insofar as a central character is described more generally, and physically, the details only go to prove superiority and desirability—thereby motivating the desire of another character for him or her as an object of value.

In focusing on the narrative representation of desire and of the relations among various desiring subjects, I take up that short and curious thirteenth-century *conte*, *La Fille du comte de Pontieu*. I attempt to show how the different protagonists, all characterized by strong and divergent desires, are used by the narrator. Each of them interests us, but not one of them provides a central focus for the plot, whose coherence (such as there is) is provided at a higher level, first that of family, or dynasty, and finally that of God, who is understood to be both the author and the central protagonist of history. The analysis of *La Vie de saint Alexis*, in chapter 5, shows that although Alexis is clearly the central human subject—and the hero—the very nature of hagiography requires that we consider God as the foremost subject, and that the desires and needs of the Christian public itself be taken into consideration as well. All of which suggests, among other things, that we cannot discuss medieval plots as simple watertight units, but must be willing to encompass in our analyses both those to whom the discourse is addressed, and transcendent characters. By this term I mean characters such as God or the saints, or occasionally Love, who are not physically

present, not visible, not obviously identifiable as dramatis personae
—but who are nonetheless represented as existing, as motivated by
some intentionality, and as active or having a significant stake in
the narrative events.

In the sorts of narrative analysis done in chapters 4 and 5, the
trail had, of course, already been heavily blazed by various structural narratologists, such as Greimas, Todorov, and others. Their
work was hard to ignore. First, such theories generally claimed to
be applicable to all narrative works, and they took up several of the
questions that were of central concern to me, such as the structure
of relations—through antagonism and hierarchization—among the
various characters (the subject and other actants), narrative closure as provided by the satisfaction of desire, and so forth.[3]

Greimas's actantial system was particularly attractive because it
highlighted the Subject, and his relation, by desire, to an Object, as
well as relations among all the various characters in narrative.
Basing himself on the work of Propp and others, Greimas established
a set of basic functions or roles (which do not necessarily correspond to particular characters) found in all narratives:[4] the *Sujet* is
the desirer; the *Objet*, the desired, that which or the person whom
the Subject desires; the *Adjuvant*, the Helper; the *Opposant*, the
Obstacle; the *Destinateur*, the Dispatcher, who gives to the Subject
his mission; the *Destinataire*, the Beneficiary.

Chapters 4 and 5 make considerable use of Greimasian terminology. But in a good many ways—spelled out in some detail in those
chapters—Greimas's work is seen as presenting serious deficiencies.
To begin with, he never reflects carefully on just what it is that his
system is applicable *to*. Now this broad (and fuzzy) applicability is
in fact a fundamental characteristic of structuralism, deriving no
doubt from its mixed roots in linguistics, folklore, and semiology.
Structuralists have tended to have very large ambitions, extending
to nothing less than the *sciences totales* of all language and meaning—and therefore not only extending well beyond, but also frequently bypassing, the mere domain of literature, seen as nothing
more than an instance. Structuralism has had other, bigger fish to
fry than literary analysis. Whatever the advantages of these mixed
origins and broad ambitions of structuralism, one distinct disadvan-
tage of them is that structuralism thereby fails to help us grasp

those things that are peculiar to works of narrative as distinct from other phenomena. Greimas's system in particular seems applicable to a good many things other than narrative literature[5]—among them, our attitudes toward each other. We all surely share, though to varying degrees, a human tendency to see ourselves as the Subject and to cast others in the roles of Objects of, Adjuvants and Opposants to, our desires. (We may or may not work this basic actantial scheme into complex imaginary scenarios.) But in a word, Greimas's actantial system is at least as applicable to many people's fantasy life as it is to narrative literature.

As to Greimas's presentation of the Subect/Object relationship, it is conceptually extremely deficient, leaving all manner of fundamental questions unasked. For example, what exactly does Greimas mean by "desire" (which he tends to represent, *tout simplement*, by an arrow)? Is this really so simple and invariant an idea—even in its structural implications alone? Is the Subject/Object relationship universal and immutable, or to some degree culturally determined and bound up with problems of intellectual history? Is it equally relevant to all literary genres and texts? And, within a given text, how do we go about determining who is—who is to be thought of as—the Subject? Does a text have only one Subject, or can it have several? How is the notion of Subject related to the concepts of "hero" and "protagonist"? What levels of the text can be appropriately analyzed in terms of Subject and Object? More specifically, is the plot to be thought of and analyzed as a self-contained and watertight unit with respect to its Subject-Object structures? Chapter 5 is largely devoted to such problems.

It is obvious (see the discussion of *La Fille du comte de Pontieu*, chapter 4) that Greimasian analysis works only on certain kinds of plot structures. One might have anticipated that such a system would work best on such simple compositions as children's stories that are in the oral folk tradition, in principle the forte of Greimas and other Proppians. But my analysis of "The Little Gingerbread Man" (chapter 5) shows that a strict Greimasian analysis is too ham-handed and unsubtle even for so "simple" a tale as this. Still, the actantial system, when carefully refined, has enough usefulness to make it worth retaining. In particular it allows us to highlight one of the most extraordinary features of medieval narrative: its glorification of the role of the Helper—especially the divine Helper —at once Adjuvant and Subject. And in other ways as well, it proves useful for distinguishing among medieval genres: to a striking degree each narrative genre specializes in certain relations among potential Subjects, and in certain kinds of desire as providing motivation and closure to the narrative.[6]

Chapter 6 turns to the kinds of "intelligibility" offered to us by such works as the *Lais* of Marie de France, the central point being that they are only very modestly intelligible at what Todorov (and other narratologists) would call the "syntactic" level. It is largely at other levels—poetic, thematic, rhetorical—that such works have their meaning, their intelligibility; their narrative closure as well, for Marie like many other medieval storytellers is far from committed to making textual closure coincide with the satisfaction of Subjects,—protagonists,—desires.

Ultimately, I think we must begin to question the very usefulness of the grammatical, or syntactical, model as used as a metaphor and guide for our comprehension of narrative structures. We must be wary of thinking of the *récit* as a sentence writ large, and of thinking of our experience of the two—the *récit*, the sentence— and of our psychological methods of processing them as identical. For example, in narrative works we frequently do not have just one Subject (or even some fairly simple if compound Subject), but rather we must view the actions of the story (even a short children's story) with respect to the desires of two or more different Subjects, either simultaneously or retroactively. This *no* ordinary sentence asks of us. That is, as we hear or read a sentence, we know who is the Subject: we know whose action (or being) we are to follow. We may occasionally be kept in the dark until the very end of the sentence as to the identity of the subject: the Subject may be the final word in the sentence. But in narrative literature, not only do we not necessarily know until the end who was—who turns out to have been—the Subject, but we may have more than *one* Subject whose interests must be kept in mind. To put it differently: a sentence offers us a single frame of reference, whereas a piece of narrative is not required to do so. Moreover, there are *récits*—such as some of the *Lais* or *La Fille du comte de Pontieu*—that never really make sense syntactically. And, as I point out (in chapter 4) with respect to the distinctions between *chronique* and *histoire*, that sentence that is the *récit* may not have much of a "period" in narrative works of the chronicle variety.

These observations are all the more significant since from the beginning narratology has bought heavily into concepts and ambitions borrowed from linguistics, from sentence-structure analysis in particular. It is worth reminding ourselves that, however useful such linguistic terms may be in narrative analysis—and I do not altogether deplore their use—the relation between linguistic and narrative phenomena is one of metonymy, not identity. But, in fact, perhaps the time is ripe to envision the deconstruction of this analogy: the concept of the sentence is a highly *literate* one—one that is primarily relevant both literally and by analogy to *texts*. But how universal a concept, an entity, is the sentence with respect to works that are still strongly rooted in the *oral* tradition? It is far from clear in many a medieval work (and in oral and semioral works in general) that the primary unit of expression and thought is the sentence at all. The poetic line has at least as strong a claim to primacy. (I shall return to this matter of the dominance of ultraliterary, as opposed to oral, concepts in modern approaches to literature in the Conclusions.) At any rate it is simply not the case that (as Barthes declared, and so many other structuralists have implied): "le récit est une grande phrase" (the narrative is a large sentence).[7]

In the final chapter, I suggest some of the major ways in which causality—a fundamental narrative (and narratological) principle —is represented in medieval literature, and spell out some of the differences between medieval understandings of causation and those of today, including those articulated or embedded in narratological theories such as those of Todorov. Modern views, on the whole positivistic, assume that we (the author and/or the reader) understand in narrative why things happen—how they are caused— whereas many medieval narrative works of different genres are mysterious, leaving both the workings and the comprehension of causality to God.

In several chapters, then, I apply narratological models and also provide a critique of these models and of their fundamental assumptions. I have been, I confess, at least as interested in seeing how various models *do not* work, and why, as how they do. I set models up in comparison—even virtually casting them in debate—with the medieval texts themselves, and with concepts provided by medieval theoreticians, as in chapter 5 where Bernard of Clairvaux takes on (as it were) Greimas. The assumptions of medieval narrative and culture are examined—but so are those of modern critical theory.

One besetting sin of virtually all modern narrative analysis—and a particularly acute problem in structuralist narratology—is the tendency to bracket off as irrelevant all *but* the narrative elements in a *récit*. It has totally ignored the relation of the narrative elements—the *histoire*—to the broader rhetorical *discours* of a text. This bracketing-off procedure is especially impoverishing with respect to medieval literature, where *why* the story is being told—for what purpose, to what audience—is often so crucial an element that, without due consideration of it, we cannot properly make sense of the text.

This volume by no means attempts to explore exhaustively or systematically structuralist approaches to medieval narrative, and various important theories and theorists of contemporary narratological analysis remain unmentioned here; nor have I made a systematic attempt to update the references, many of which go back a decade or so. But it is not so much the detailed setting out of the contents of modern narrative analysis (all the various paradigms, models, and so forth that are currently popular, and were even more so in the late 1960s and 1970s) that has interested me, as an examination of the *structure* of such analyses in general, and of the ideological *content* often implicit in those structures. (Unlike most structuralists, I am concerned with content as well as with structure.)

It is—to be more candid, it gradually became—one of the basic contentions of this volume that narrative analysis is profoundly if unwittingly ideological, and that its ideology—as we might say, its fundamental "mythology"—is at the very antipodes from the basic ideology of the Middle Ages. Thus, a number of crucial medieval views and mental structures turn out to be largely unconceptualizable—unthinkable—for modern critical theory. (Prime examples would be the wide implications for medieval narrative of belief in the existence and omnipotence of God, on the one hand, and of the related conviction that life largely defies human comprehension, on the other.) But then, the superficiality with which so much of the narratology has been thought through, the arbitrariness with which it has been set forth, and the rigidity with which it has often been applied have not made things any easier.

One major problem with structuralism as so commonly practiced —in particular, in narratological analysis—is this: despite its claim to universality, to a status of timelessness in the elaboration of its general models, it has all too often failed to be *above* historical and cultural differences; it has tended simply to *ignore* them—while being itself very time- and culture-bound. Thus, a good many structures and paradigms that have been presented as operative everywhere and at all times, turn out to be largely expressions of the worldview of modern Western—secularized, highly rationalistic— culture. Although modern structuralist paradigms and distinctions (for example, among different kinds of sequences or causality) generally provide an intrinsic plausibility, *not* all works of narrative, by any means, allow themselves to be analyzed—dissected—in these terms.

It is true that my own approach here has been in this sense structuralist: rather than to offer yet another round of readings of medieval literary works, my purpose has been to elucidate fundamental structures of medieval literature and, indeed, insofar as possible, structures of medieval thought. And the works selected were often chosen partly to provide cases in point and not merely in and of themselves. (I have, however, attempted to analyze the texts carefully and thoughtfully. Whether I have succeeded is, as always, for the reader to judge.)

Such readings have, to some degree, the defect of all structural(ist) analyses: they tend to be reductionistic, to deny or at least minimize variation. But my purpose is by no means to claim that every medieval work corresponds perfectly to these paradigms or to deny historical change. I can certainly imagine works that, for any of a number of historical reasons—including the individual artist's temperament and choices—might not conform to these models. But I suggest that these paradigms are far more useful to us —that they account for more of the medieval literary "data"— than the ones we tend to accept, unexamined, today. These paradigms should also serve to make us recognize more readily those periods and works in which we see paradigm shifts, as, for example, in the representation of the self in Charles d'Orléans's poetry and in Montaigne, discussed briefly in my third chapter.

At any rate, it has been my desire to provide an analysis both structurally powerful and faithful to historical realities, and it is to such major problematics that this book is devoted: the self, or subject, and his definitions (and self-definitions) in medieval narrative; medieval representations of desire and its relation to narrative closure; concepts of time, causality, and unity in medieval plots; attitudes toward literature and its pleasures. Finally, this book is largely concerned with the role of the transcendent—of God —in medieval narrative.

NOTES

1. See, e.g., Stephen A. Shapiro, "The Dark Continent of Literature," *Comparative Literature Studies* V, no. 4 (December 1968)p: 437; Robert Scholes and Robert Kellogg, *The Nature of Narrative* (Oxford: Oxford University Press, 1966), 240. This tendency toward a nonironic compartmentalization of present and past selves is also present in the Abelard—though there the various selves remain, as it were, in their separate compartments and are not brought together into a synthetic harmony: the lover and the penitent monk cannot be made to see eye to eye. (But then Abelard's past was indeed a hard one to reconcile!) At any rate, there is remarkably little irony in the *Historia.*

2. As articulated by Jacques Ehrmann in "Le Dedans et le dehors," *Poétique,* no. 9 (1972): 35, 37.

3. These theories presented a particular lure to young scholars, such as I was then, of dispensing them from knowing anything much about history or literary tradition: one had only to master the theory and read the text, and apply the former to the latter; no knowledge of historical context was required. I was drawn by— if (I like to think) skeptical of—such claims.

4. Greimas elaborated the actantial system in *Sémantique structurale* (Paris: Larousse, 1966); he has refined his concepts somewhat in later writings, such as *Du sens* (Paris: Seuil, 1970), and "Les Actants, les acteurs et les figures," in *Sémiotique narrative et textuelle* (Paris: Larousse, 1973).

5. See, for example, my "Ronsard's *Sonnets pour Hélène:* Narrative Structures and Poetic Language," *Romanic Review* 68, no. 4 (November 1976).

6. I will return to this issue in the Conclusions of this volume.

7. Roland Barthes, "Introduction à l'analyse structurale des récits," *Communications* 8 (1966): 4.

Abelard's *Historia calamitatum* and Medieval Autobiography

Medieval "autobiography": according to various modern theoreticians, including some medievalists, it barely exists, and the few texts that appear to claim such status tend to be relegated to that literary limbo we all have found useful: the "prehistory of the genre." What I should like to do in these pages is pose some of the large questions raised by one such work: the *Historia calamitatum* (or *Abaelardi amicum suum consolatoria*), written apparently by Peter Abelard around 1130.[1] These are questions concerning the representation of self and comparisons of the self to other selves; the structure of the work; and its function, as Abelard presents it. In asking these questions—and in attempting a response to them—I shall also be reflecting upon aspects of medieval narrative in general. In particular, upon medieval portrait (and self-portrait) and characterology, as I believe that modern ways of viewing these issues (for example, modern characterological axes) have made it hard for us to grasp the ways in which medieval men viewed themselves and others—just as modern narrative analysis, overly preoccupied with the narrative component of narrative works, has often made it difficult for us to understand *why* people in the past chose to write about themselves.

Now Abelard is in many ways an extraordinary figure, a source of fascination not only for us but also for many men and women of the medieval period itself; dialectician and philosopher; seducer, lover, husband, and castrate; monk, whose fellows hated him; master of a school, whose students adulated him; theologian, whose book was burned; and finally abbot, whose monks tried to poison and stab him.

My first question is this: In what terms, on what dimensions, does Abelard present himself, in the text, as extraordinary, unusual, unique? (Or if this text should be spurious, how does the "pseudo-Abelard" present Abelard? I will postulate this caveat henceforth.)

Abelard's self-definitions, his self-portraits, his self-evaluations, all bear primarily on the *size*—or greatness or height—of his gifts, qualities, achievements. The image of himself that Abelard projects into this work is that of a "superior" man—and indeed this word occurs frequently. He has a great and powerful mind. God has given him "no less favor in profane than in sacred letters" (42).[2]

> Cum autem in divina scriptura not minorem mihi gratiam quam seculari Dominus contulisse videretur. (82)[3]

He is the "winner" (12)—"superior in disputanto" (64)—in various of his discussions with his master, William of Champeaux. Then, after frequent challenges to debate, he forced William "by clear proofs from reasoning to change, yes, to abandon his old stand on universals" (16)[4]

> de universalibus sententiam patentissimis argumentorum rationibus ipsum commutare, immo destruere compuli. (65)

He explains, later, that most people's reaction to his book on the Unity and Trinity of God was that they were

> very pleased with it as it appeared to answer all questions alike on the subject. And since these questions seemed especially difficult, the subtlety of their solution appeared the greater. (43)

> Quem quidem tractatum cum vidissent et legissent plurimi, cepit in commune omnibus plurimum placere, quod in eo pariter omnibus satisfieri super hoc questionibus videbantur. Et quoniam questiones iste per omnibus difficiles videbantur, quanto earum major extiterat gravitas, tanto solutionis earum censebatur major subtilitas. (83)

And so on.

Abelard never presents his philosophical or theological arguments as being original, unusual, and different—only *better*; better in the sense of stronger, more subtle, and irrefutable. It is possible that Abelard was doing, or thought he was doing, radical new things in philosophy; such is the popular image of Abelard's philosophical position.[5] But he consistently presents his accomplishments as the result of the sheer magnitude of his talents and arguments. His mind, his logic are not different, only greater than those of his adversaries.

And as a lover, Abelard is the "compleat" lover. He is the quintessential philosopher turned fool, like Aristotle in the *Lai d'Aristote*.

No sign of love was omitted by us in our ardor and whatever unusual love could devise, that was added too. And the more such delights were new to us, the more ardently we indulged in them, and the less did we experience satiety. And the more these pleasures engaged me, the less time I had for philosophy and the less attention I gave to my school. (28)

Nullus a cupidis intermissus est gradus amoris, et si quid insolitum amor excogitare potuit, est additum; et quo minus ista fueramus experti gaudia, ardentius illis insistebamus, et minus in fastidium vertebantur.
     Et quo me amplius hec voluptas occuparaverat, minus philosophie vaccare poteram et scolis operam dare. (73)

The word *insolitum* (unusual) requires further commentary: the lovers' search for ever-new pleasures in love is not I think to be construed as a desire to be, as it were, "original" in their lovemaking, by finding strange new *voluptés*; these pleasures are, presumably, new to them, not to the human race. They are attempting, rather, to "exhaust" love, as an experience; to be "great lovers"; to fulfill completely the term "lover" by continually adding to, heaping ever higher the amount of love enjoyed.

In short, Abelard's faculties and accomplishments are not presented as peculiar to him, or special. They are, rather, superlative examples of normal faculties and accomplishments; indeed it is consistently in extravagant terms—and frequently in grammatical superlatives—that Abelard discusses himself and his situation. For instance, speaking of the attacks on him by William, he says:

And the more openly he attacked me in his jealousy, the more prestige he gave me, as the poet says: "What is highest is envy's mark: winds sweep the summits." (18–19)

Et quanto manifestius ejus me persequebatur invidia tanto mihi auctori-
tatis amplius conferebat juxta illud poeticum,
  Summa petit livor, perflant altissima venti. (66)

Perhaps to avoid charges of immodesty, Abelard often puts these various superlatives in the mouths of others. He tells us that the scholarly Heloise refrained from presenting arguments to him say-ing: "less I appear to teach Minerva herself" (35) / "ne Minervam ipsam videar docere" (78). Geoffrey, bishop of Chartres, defending Abelard at the Council of Soissons, is quoted as saying of Abelard that "his vine extends its branches from sea to sea" (47) / "ejus vineam a mari usque ad mare palmites suos extendisse" (85), and as citing St. Jerome who wrote:

> courage when displayed always arouses jealousy and it is the mountain peaks which the lightning strikes. (47)

Semper in propatulo fortitudo emulos habet,
                              Feriuntque summos

          Fulgura montes, . . . (85–86)

As the first quotation of the preceding page suggests, it is not only Abelard's frequent superlatives that reveal his preoccupation with size—greatness, height, the more versus the less—but even his sentence structure is based on such considerations: here *quanto/ tanto amplius* (so much/all the more). And many of the other sentences quoted above are also constructed by considerations of quantity or size: *autem/non minorem* (however/no less) or *quanto major/tanto major* (the more/all the more) for example commonly constitute the syntactical framework for Abelard's sentences. To give another example: he tells us that Heloise

> was a lady of *no mean appearance* while in literary excellence she was the *first [supreme]*. And as gift of letters is rare among women, so it had gained favor for her and made her *the most renowned woman* on the whole kingdom. I considered all the qualities which usually inspire lov-ers and decided she was just the one for me to join in love. I felt that this would be very easy to accomplish; I then enjoyed *such renown* and was *so outstanding* for my charm of youth that I feared no repulse by any woman whom I should deign to favor with my love. And I felt that this maiden would *all the more readily* yield to me as I knew she possessed and cherished a knowledge of letters . . . (26–27; my emphasis)

Que cum per faciem *non esset infima*, per habundantiam litterarum erat *suprema*. Nam quo bonum hoc litteratorie scilicet scientie in mulieribus est rarius, eo *amplius* puellam commendabat et in toto regno *nominatissimam* fecerat. Hanc igitur, omnibus circunspectis que amantes allicere solent, commodiorem censui en amorem mihi copulare, et me id facillime credidi posse. *Tante* quippe tunc nominis eram et juventutis et forme gratie *preminebam*, ut quamcunque feminarum nostro dignarer amore nullam vererer repulsam. *Tanto* autem facilius hanc mihi puellam consensuram credidi, *quanto amplius* eam litterarum scientiam et habere et diligere noveram; . . . (71; my emphasis)

Abelard's constant use of superlatives like *supreme* and *nominatissimam* (the most famous), verbs like *preminebam* (I was the foremost), constructions like *tanto/ut* (so much/that) and *tanto/ quanto amplius* (the more/all the more) indicates that he is continually *measuring* himself and the events of his life (and, here, Heloise) against other men (and women) and their lives.

Abelard certainly did not invent such constructions or such considerations: far from it. Indeed, it is impressive how common—in fact, how dominant—differentiation by magnification (by size, or height) is in medieval art. At any rate, Abelard's use of such terms and structures is so massive, and they so utterly pervade his work that one can only conclude that, as well as constituting one of the chief features of his literary style, they reveal what is perhaps the major element in Abelard's self-definition: size.

Abelard is also unusually broad in the range of qualities and gifts that he possesses superlatively: he is a great dialectician *and* philosopher *and* poet *and* lover *and* sinner *and* monk *and* theologian *and* master *and* spiritual director.[6] He is great—successively if not simultaneously—according to the flesh, the intellect, and the soul. This very multiplicity will present Abelard with a basic problem, both literary and human: how to reconcile all these rather contradictory superlatives, all these different dimensions of excellence. It is not easy to be—or even to have been—*both* a great lover (or sensualist) *and* a great theologian![7]

Let us speak of the portrait in terms of a coordinate system, and establish two axes. The first, the vertical axis—the hierarchical or evaluative axis—has to do with the range between superiority and inferiority. On this axis, position is measured quantitatively: how *much* of any given quality the character in question is presented as possessing. This axis has to do with being "very" something-or-other.

(We should note, a propos of this notion of character, the etymology of the words "virtue" and "vice." Virtue—*virtus*, from the word *vis*: "force, power, strength" (and metonymically "a large number or quantity")—originally meant "manly excellence" or "power"—and then "goodness," "worth." And vice, *vitium*: "fault, defect, blemish, imperfection." Virtue is, thus, strongly associated with the idea of "great-ness," "power"—and vice with a falling away from the power and excellence of virtue; with the notion of an im-perfection. But there is another notion of character—in its more extreme form rather "Manichaean"—in which vice is not associated with weakness or lack but with an aggressive and diabolical strength. These two notions seem to have coexisted all through Christian thought—and are indeed present even in Baudelaire's *Fleurs du Mal*—but particularly in the Middle Ages. Sometimes evil is weak and sickly, and "faulty." But sometimes it is the true and energetic *rival* of the good; sometimes villains are "very bad" indeed.)

The horizontal axis would bear on what is *like* or *unlike*, on the particular mode or form in which the quality in question exists within the character. Here "zero" would again represent that which is normal or average, but here it would mean normal as opposed to unusual, unlike. Let us call this the axis of differentiation.

My contention is that the medieval period[8] was almost exclusively concerned with the placement of characters—especially but not only heroes—on the vertical axis: with what set them *above* or *below*—but not *apart from*—the common run of men. Medieval heroes—protagonists—are defined by the *quantity* of their "qualities," not by the *quality* of their "qualities"—not by the particular form that these qualities take. Heroes possess, either in an absolute sense, or specifically, in superlative terms, certain characteristics—and they possess them without further refinement or differentiation. Heroines—female characters—either have a great deal of beauty—along very standard and typical lines—or very little beauty; but they never have an *unusual* kind of beauty, a beauty unlike that found in other women.[9]

Of course, it is possible to have competing vertical systems or axes: spiritual excellence and worldly glory may be presented as incompatible. This is of course a particularly common dichotomy in religious literature—the thirteenth-century *Queste du saint Graal*, for example.

At any rate, most of what passes for "character development" in medieval literature can be translated into the notion of a rising or falling on one or several of these vertical axes. Frequently the hero falls on one axis, subsequently to reedem himself. He may simply rise higher and higher on one axis, or he may fall on one and rise on another. (As Abelard *rises* as lover, he clearly *falls* as philosopher.)

Character, in the medieval period, appears to have been conceived more as a list than as a *gestalt*, or pattern: it was a set of juxtaposed traits—vices and virtues—which were among themselves, either compatible or incompatible, either at war or at peace[10] with each other, but which did not have complex inner connections or constitute an organic whole, with some mysterious unity. Hence, though a given trait may come increasingly to dominate a hero's character—may become relatively stronger, greater than the others (which may in fact go into eclipse)—there has been, ordinarily, only a "transformation" in quantity, not in mode or quality. Indeed there has often been no *irreversible* development: medieval protagonists with character defects are exceedingly prone to relapse, even after "repenting," for example Tristan and Lancelot. (Even the castrated Abelard will be accused of relapse.) This is, of course, one of the features of medieval characterology which permitted and encouraged the practice of "continuations": the basic *stability* not of character itself, but of the elements which constitute a given protagonist's character and situation.

This way of presenting character[11] is typical throughout much of the medieval period—that is, again, roughly between the eleventh and fifteenth centuries—and to a considerable degree well before and well after. To attempt to pin down at least a few of the main terms and stages in the rise of this form of characterology, I should like to compare very schematically Suetonius's early second century *Lives of the Caesars* and Einhard's early ninth century *Life of Charlemagne* with the *Historia calamitatum*.

Suetonius writes about twelve different men—all reliably "great" only in that they were famous, historically important figures. Some he generally praises (for example, Augustus), some he generally condemns (for example, Nero)—but often his portraits and accounts are nonjudgmental and morally neutral. He gives many details about the tastes, habits, and general characteristics of his subjects. It is true that the "ideal man," in Suetonius's eyes—as in those of Cicero *(De Officiis: On Duties)*—is the moderate man, the man who disciplines his appetites to conform to a norm of behavior; but Suetonius has no trouble distinguishing between the "ideal" and the "real"—and he does not hide from us even Augustus's weaknesses and vices.

Einhard, when he set out to write his biography of Charlemagne, copied Suetonius, but—significant choice—he modeled himself only on the "Divine Augustus": the most encomiastic of Suetonius's *Lives*; further, he almost totally eliminated from his portrait of Charlemagne any unfavorable details. In short, he is writing not so much *history* (or realistic portraiture) as *eulogy*.[12] He does very occasionally note features and characteristics of Charlemagne that were mildly unusual (as opposed to great): "his belly was prominent," "his neck thick and somewhat short" —though, significantly, "the symmetry of the rest of his body concealed these defects" (50). He does speak rather neutrally[13] of some of the emperor's habits and tastes. But taken as a whole it is clearly and almost exclusively the *greatness* of Charlemagne that stands out in Einhard's work. This is perhaps not surprising: Carolus Magnus lent himself to such treatment. But this encomiastic sort of handling was very important for the history of historiography;[14] it tended to narrow the notion of character depiction, the very function of historical writing. One described only what was great, or superlative, about one's subject. And, correlatively, one passed over in silence that which was deviant, or mediocre, or decidedly base.[15] And one made up "great" characteristics and features where their presence might seem desirable. (This is particularly the case with saints' lives.)

By the time we reach Abelard, this narrowness has become very extreme indeed: only "greatness" has survived as a consideration. Abelard's self-portrait gives very few details which particularize him—as opposed to the many which aggrandize him. He has no specific tastes,[16] no specific—even conventional—build or features (no hair color, no size, and so forth). He is, for example, simply, abstractly, attractive: "so outstanding for my charm of youth" (27)/ "Tanti quippe tunc nominis eram et juventutis et forme gratia preminebam" (71).

This narrowness, which belongs essentially to the rhetorical tradition of praise (and blame), is definitely one of the most striking features of medieval autobiography, in the modern sense of the word, and surely became possible only as self-portraiture and self-narrative became disengaged from demonstrative rhetoric.

How are we to account for the emergence and dominance in the Middle Ages of this vertically oriented structure? It is, of course, only one manifestation of a broad cultural and historical phenomenon, further manifestations of which are the very structure of medieval society, the dominance of Platonic philosophy, and many others.

At any rate, the roots of this medieval characterology in antiquity are, as we have seen, very real. But obviously, something profound has happened to the classical portrait on its way into the Middle Ages.

The influence of Christianity is, without any doubt, significant. In particular, psychology in this period is not yet secularized; it is hardly distinct from theology. Indeed, the men who write about "psychology"—that is, human nature, the faculties, the appetites—are primarily theologians. And their basic concern is not with individuation—horizontal differentiation among individuals—but with salvation and damnation, the rise and fall of souls, their vertical movement in relation to God. And this basic orientation seems to have pervaded almost all of medieval thinking about human character and change: psychological movement is either exaltation or abasement (and abasement—humiliation—on *one* axis can be directly tied to exaltation on *another*); it is progress or regress: "super-gress" or "sub-gress."

Hagiographical narrative also appears to have exerted a strong influence on narrative: it provided some of the more important models for medieval narrative; and in its general disdain for the fleshly and concrete details of human existence may well have contributed to this "narrowing" phenomenon that we have been describing. The authors of saints' lives are interested, not in the "breadth" of the *humanity* of their heroes, but rather in the "degree" of their *super*-humanity. The emphasis in such works is *intensive*, not *extensive*. Even when a young *sainte* is described—and always in vague terms—as being very beautiful, it is only so that she will then have the opportunity to reject, to sacrifice this part of her being: for example, St. Lucy who, when a suitor admired her beautiful eyes, is said to have offered them to him. It must be said that hagiography provided a problematic model for medieval autobiography.

Whatever its causes, this way of presenting character—this extreme flattening or narrowing in along the vertical axis (or axes) which we find so well exemplified in the *Historia*—is common throughout most of the medieval period. It is only since the Renaissance that there has arisen a real interest in—and then cultivation of—what distinguishes one man from all others; a real interest in what we call the "individual"—an interest in the unusual, the different, the bizarre, the deviant.[17] In other words, to look at definitions of the word "individual"[18] given by the *Oxford English Dictionary*, medieval narrative (historical and hagiographical as well as fictional) knew and cultivated these:

> A single object or thing, . . . ; a single member of a class, group, or number . . . a single member of a species, a single specimen of an animal or plant.

But definitions such as the following do not express accurately what one finds in medieval texts:

> Distinguished from others by attributes of its own . . . An object which is determined by properties peculiar to itself and cannot be subdivided into others of the same kind.[19]

It is true that medieval philosophy in this period was much involved precisely with the definition of the individual—this was indeed one of the major issues of the "nominalist-realist" controversy. And Peter Abelard is famous for his nominalist position. The degree of his nominalism has apparently often been exaggerated: he was in fact a "moderate"[20] in his stance. But at any rate he did argue that *only* "individuals" exist—that terms such as "species" and "genus" are not realities but (however valid) only intellectual constructs, abstractions *from* individual cases.[21] It is no doubt surprising that Abelard should display, in his autobiographical narrative, so little interest in or willingness to discuss the "accidents" of his being: everything concrete and particular—and peculiar—about the individual man that he was. Indeed this silence might even be construed as a further indication that it was not he who wrote the *Historia*, that the text is only a *pseudo*autobiography. Perhaps. But it seems to me altogether possible that Abelard may have been much more conservative[22] as a man of letters—as the author of an autobiographical work with strong moral preoccupations—than as a philosopher and logician. (It is surely a common phenomenon that philosophers and theoreticians fail to carry out fully in their lives, and in their nonphilosophical writings, the consequences of their theories; it may be just as well!) Indeed, he may not even have *seen* the implications and the literary possibilities of his interest in the notion of individuation.

There is one moment in Abelard's life—and story—which drastically shakes up his self-concept on the vertical axis (axes) and even introduces the horizontal—the notion of being *un*like other men. This event is, of course, his castration.[23] Abelard's initial reaction is one of humiliation—that is of being cast down from his glory. He tells us that he remembered the "law" that eunuchs are in abomination before the Lord, and cannot enter his church, nor can a damaged or imperfect male animal be offered in sacrifice.[24] In short, he felt diminished; he felt *less* than a man; imperfect. He later uses the word "diminutio" (71/102) to refer to the effect of castration. And he felt mortified—like a freak; as he says, he is afraid of being a "monstruosum spectaculum" (80) that people will laugh at.

There is in this passage where he discusses his reactions to this calamity—the first of many calamities—the potential for a development of self-awareness along the horizontal axis of differentiation, deviancy; for him to say with Rousseau,[25] "Je suis autre" (I am other).[26] But this potential remains largely unrealized and Abelard shifts his point of view toward his castration. First he abandons the concept that God hates eunuchs: he quotes his friends as telling him that:

I should realize that the hand of the Lord has touched me especially, that, being freed from the allurements of the flesh and the tumult of the world, I might devote myself to the study of letters and become a true philosopher not of the world but of God. (41)

. . . et ob hoc maxime dominica manu me nunc tactum esse cognoscerem, quo liberius a carnalibus illecebris et tumultuosa vita seculi abstractus studio litterarum vaccarem, nec tam mundi quam Dei vere philosophus fierem. (81)

He becomes a monk, then an abbot (the latter rather reluctantly). And this initial feeling of being "monstrous"—or even inferior—never recurs in the text; there is never any explicit indication that others treat him, or that he is, peculiar, or unlike other men. There is no discussion here of what it means, or what it feels like, to be a castrate.

In short, the horizontal dimension fades quickly; and indeed Abelard soon—almost immediately—seems to take the attitude that he has been called to new heights of spiritual excellence; called to rise, as it were, on new vertical dimensions both of suffering and accomplishment.

There is no explicit discussion of the consequences of castration. But how *does* Abelard react to it—on a human and on a literary plane? How does it—consciously or unconsciously—affect his thinking? The first interesting feature about Abelard's reaction to his castration is that he presents it as by no means the *worst* of his calamities: He constantly uses his castration as a measure by which to judge the greatness of his other, subsequent, calamities—and the others always prove *more* painful: he says of his humiliation after his book was condemned and burned:

I considered my former betrayal of little moment when compared to this injustice and I bemoaned the damage to my reputation far more than that to my body; the latter was the result of some sin while a sincere intention and love of our faith which compelled me to write had brought this open violence upon me. (52)

Parvam illam ducebam proditionem in comparatione hujus injurie, et longe amplius fame quam corporis detrimentum plangebam, cum ad illam ex aliqua culpa devenerim, ad hanc me tam patentem violentiam sincera intentio amorque fidei nostre induxissent, que me ad scribendum compulerant. (89)

One aspect of the parallel that he sets up between these two catas-
trophes is very interesting indeed: his (sinful) love for Heloise resulted in his castration/ his (sinless) love of the faith resulted in a
new "wound"—the condemnation of his "pen," the destruction
(not total: he will write again) of his intellectual manhood. And
he was even forced this time to maim himself—to throw his own
book into fire (50/187). Abelard's pen does indeed seem to constitute a partial replacement for his lost virility—indeed he did not
even begin to write until after the castration; before, he only lec-
tured.

When, later—despite his castration!—he is accused of lewdness
in his relations with Heloise, he compares himself to Origen, who
castrated himself "when he undertook the instruction of women in
holy doctrine," and asserts:

> I considered that on this point God in His mercy was kinder to me in this,
> that what Origen did through imprudence, thereby incurring grievous
> censure, that He accomplished in me through no fault of my own. He
> thereby prepared me and made me free for a little work, and with less
> suffering for they laid hands on me quickly and suddenly when I was
> asleep and so felt little pain.
>
> But the less I endured then, as it happened, from my mutilation, the
> longer am I now afflicted by their detraction and am tortured by the loss
> of my reputation than I was from the mutilation of my body, for as it is
> written: Better is a good name than great riches. (71)

> Ad quam quidem penitus removendam maximum illum Christianorum
> philosophum Origenem, cum mulierum quoque sancte doctrine inten-
> deret, sibi ipsi manus intulisse Ecclesiastice historie lib. VI continet.
>
> Putabam tamen in hoc mihi magis quam illi divinam misericordiam
> propitiam fuisse, ut quod ille minus provide creditur egisse atque inde
> non modicum crimen incurisse, id aliena culpa in me ageret, ut ad simile
> opus me liberum prepararet, ac tanto minore pena quanto breviore ac
> subita, ut oppressus sompno cum mihi manus inicerent nichil pene fere
> sentirem; sed quod tunc forte minus pertuli ex vulnere, nunc ex detrac-
> tione diutius plector, et plus ex detrimento fame quam ex corporis cru-
> cior diminutione, sicut enim scriptum est: "Melius est nomen bonum
> quam divitie multe." (102)

Still later, Abelard had a fall from a horse—"the hand of God
struck him." And of this accident he says:

> This fracture afflicted and weakened me more grievously than the former injury. (77)

> Et multo me amplius hec fractura afflixit et debilitavit quam prior plaga. (106–7)

Two points about these comparisons. First, Abelard *does* consistently present his castration as the least of his calamities: because he was asleep, and did not suffer greatly—either at the time or afterward; because the punishment was one that he could understand and in a sense accept; because he cares less about his body than his reputation; because his castration prepared him for a holy life. But, second, it is striking how the castration presents a sort of model for all his subsequent griefs: they are all violent blows, bringing pain and loss. His life is like a series of mutilations. And—as we will see more clearly later—he does not know whether to interpret them, negatively, as cruel punishments, or, positively, as cures. *Whose* hand has struck him? God's or man's? And if God's, is it a loving hand? The hand of God is mysterious . . . Is he being freed *from*, as well as wounded *in*—and deprived *of*—his flesh? At any rate, it is not surprising that the language of martyrdom—of the cross—should become increasingly predominant in this text.

But the word "mutilations" is mine, and Muckle's: Abelard never, interestingly enough, uses this word, nor does he use "castrate" or "castration." In the section where he narrates the event of his castration, he refers to the latter by this circumlocution:

> They cut off the organs by which I has committed the deed which they deplored. (38)

> eis videlicet corporis mei partibus amputatis quibus id quod plangebant commiseram. (79)

Subsequently, speaking of what befell his flesh, his book, and his reputation, he most commonly uses the words *plaga* or *vulnus*[27] (wound): thus rendering his calamities in "noble" terms (let us not forget that he is, by class, a knight)—and thus diminishing the degradation and the irreversible nature of the original calamity.

To return to our horizontal/vertical axes: Abelard does not present himself as set apart from others. Insofar as, in the latter portions of the *Historia*, he sees himself as isolated, it is because he towers *above* others, by virtue and intellect. Abelard's is essentially the loneliness of maligned superiority.

But Abelard never sees himself as maligned, hated by *everyone*. His relation to others takes one of two modes, and is always defined by their reaction to his superiority. Some are envious, and envy— *invidia*—is consistently given as the sole motivation of his dialectical and theological enemies. This is strangely parallel to what one finds in medieval romance: an enemy (that is, a domestic enemy) of the hero—even a hero of dubious moral stature like Tristan— *cannot* have a "good" reason for his hatred.

Those who do not envy, hate, and persecute Abelard admire and love him—like his many students, disciples, and partisans (and Abelard is almost always confident of having many supporters). These are virtually the only two modes according to which Abelard conceives of his relation to others.

Abelard, then, does present himself as extraordinary, in a sense unique, on a vertical scale; he is solitary in his excellence—like the knight of romance who is alone in his wanderings and questings rather than the epic hero who fights among friends and comrades. But in his own eyes he is not *incomparable*. Abelard's *Historia* is heavily larded with comparisons—and they are all positive, as it were, rather than negative; he is *like*, rather than *un*like, the figures to whom he compares himself. He presents himself as like the victorious Ajax (20/67), like Mars caught in adultery with Venus (30/74), like the persecuted St. Jerome (70/101), like St. Anthony despairing of God's absence (52/89), and so forth.

In short, he aligns himself continually with historical, biblical, and literary figures—models of verticality—from the past. And often he quotes to us not what he said on any given occasion, but his own quotation of some warrior, saint, or philosopher.

We can perhaps on one level dismiss all this as mere reference to *auctoritas*. But this literary habit reveals a profound mental habit. Abelard does not, I think, see himself—his life, his series of calamities—as *unique*, but precisely, as (at least one by one, if not globally) *comparable* to what other great men have been through; and as interesting precisely because of this "comparability." This is another expression of the fascinating tendency of the Middle Ages —and even, paradoxically, of medieval autobiography—to be much less interested in the individual and his experiences and reactions, than in the time-honored experiences of all men—or rather, of the great men and models from the past. The individual seeks to align himself with these old models—these embodiments of vertical excellence on the various dimensions of human experience—these old truths; not to feel or say new and different things, or distinguish, for example, between *his* experience of pain and that of the martyrs.

Abelard, as we have seen, compares himself to quite a disparate collection of types on different vertical axes. And the coordination among them proves very problematic. Indeed, I see this text as composed of self-contained sections, rather at odds with each other, with no overview providing a true coherence.[28]

Let us look at the initial episode. Within this passage, which deals with Abelard's success as a dialectical *bellator* (metaphors of war abound: of challenge, attack, counterattack, pitching camp, and so forth) there is at *no* point any self-criticism or self-condemnation.

But, suddenly, after he has reached great heights of renown, a new attitude toward himself emerges: suddenly he refers to himself, retroactively, as having been (or having become) proud and arrogant. And he defines, in advance, his relation with Heloise as lustful and sinful. His speaks of the "unclean life" (25) *("immunditia vita"* [70]) and "lechery" *("luxuria")* of the episode to come—that is, of his affair with Heloise.

He then relates their liaison and marriage. What is striking here is that once he is in the *thick* of his narration of their love affair the language of condemnation which characterized the introduction *to* the episode disappears entirely. And this moving and seductive passage is characterized by a feeling of the intensity of their passion. It is the spontaneous naturalness, and not the sinfulness, of erotic love which predominates here.

> What was the result? We were first together in one house and then one in mind. Under the pretext of work we made ourselves entirely free for love and the pursuit of her studies provided the secret privacy which love desired. We opened our books but more words of love than of the lesson asserted themselves. There was more kissing than teaching; my hands found themselves at her breasts more often than on the book. (28)

> Quid plura? Primum domo una conjungimur, postmodum animo. Sub occasione itaque discipline, amori penitus vaccabamus, et secretos reces-

sus, quos amor optabat, studium lectionis offerebat. Apertis itaque libris, plura de amore quam de lectione verba se ingerebant, plura erant oscula quam sententie; sepius ad sinus quam ad libros reducebantur manus. (72–73)

Augustine tells us, in his *Confessions*, that "amabam amare"—"I loved to love"—but he is not prepared to offer such descriptions as Abelard; there is clearly a process of auto-censure at work.

In other words, once Abelard is in the heart of his narration of his love and of his worldly success he has—or expresses—virtually no sense of sin. It is as if he is once again caught up in the immediacy of the lived phenomenon. Reflection and moralization are possible only at a distance—not only in life itself, but even in the telling of his life.

As concerns both his success as logician and his experience as a lover, Abelard appears caught between two conflicting typologies. In speaking of his career he is torn between the language of war and victory, and that of the moral life—of sin and virtue—as conceived by the Church. The Christian life condemns as pride *("superbia")* what the warrior praises as boldness. (I do not want to oversimplify the conflict; there were grounds for reconciliation between the two: the "Christian soldier," for example.) In his affair with Heloise, he is using, on the one hand, a typology borrowed—again—from the Church: its only words for carnal love outside of marriage were negative: *luxuria, concupiscentia, libido.* But on the other hand, he was heir to the classical (Ovidian) literature of love—of *voluptas* —part of the newly emerging literary and cultural phenomenon of love (Abelard was himself a love poet) in his fascination not only with the pleasures of love, but also with the value of the lady in question (Heloise was beautiful, learned—famous, indeed, for her learning [26/71]). And both of these typologies—these basic attitudes and sets of terminology—are contradictorily present,[29] although it is the ecclesiastical typology that will dominate the second half of the work.

There are moments of clear contrast between the two—especially as concerns Abelard's initial interpretation of his castration. He is torn between a worldly definition and a spiritual or Christian one —the former stressing his fall from glory, the bitterness of this betrayal by fortune, the latter God's loving and saving grace.

Perverse fortune as the saying goes, by her blandishments, found an easier way to cast me down from the height of my glory, or rather God in his goodness claimed me for Himself, a humbled man instead of one most proud and forgetful of the grace he had received. (26)

Fortuna blandiens commodiorem nacta est occasionem, qua me facilius de sublimitatis hujus fastigio prosterneret, imo superbissimum nec accepte gratie memorem divina pietas humiliatum sibi vendicaret. (71)

I see these two passages—that dealing with his career as dialectician and that dealing with his love affair—as subsections of the first part of the *Historia*. These two sections are in an important sense incompatible: Abelard found that he could not be both *libidinosus* and *philosophus:*

The more these pleasures engaged me, the less time I had for philosophy and the less attention I gave to my school. It became wearisome for me to go there and equally hard to stay when I was using nightly vigils for love and the days for study. I became negligent and indifferent in my lectures so that nothing I said stemmed from my talent but I repeated everything from rote. I came simply to say again what had been said long ago and, if I composed any verses, the theme was of love and not of the secrets of philosophy. (29)

Et quo me amplius hec voluptas occupaverat, minus philosophie vaccare poteram et scolis operam dare. Tediosum mihi vehementer erat ad scolas procedere vel in eis morari; pariter et laboriosum, cum nocturnas amori vigilias et diurnas studio conservarem. Quem etiam ita negligentem et tepidum lectio tunc habebat, ut jam nichil ex ingenio sed ex usu cuncta proferrem, nec jam nisi recitator pristinorum essem inventorum, et si qua invenire liceret, carmina essent amatoria, non philosophie secreta. (73)

What is important here is not so much that Abelard found these two modes incompatible in his *life*, but that he does not manage to make them compatible *narratively:* he does not succeed in ordering them, hierarchically; they remain purely sequential and indeed antagonistic, unharmonized by an ordering overview.

But however incompatible these two types and episodes may remain, they both treat of his life in the world, his life before that basic turning point, his castration. It is his castration which provided the cure *("remedium")* [70]) for each of his two worldly sins —pride and lust—and which functions structurally like a conversion (however reluctant it may have been). For this work has an essentially bipartite structure with conversion as the pivot, the (irreversible?) turning point.[30] Part 2 treats the series of calamities that have befallen Abelard since his castration—since he first became a monk.

It is interesting to note that, starting from the time of his castration up to the present, Abelard never accuses himself of any sin. He sees pride—for example—in himself only in the abstract, that is, as characterizing a whole period of his life, and in the past; not in any particular action or statement, and not in the present. The image of the martyr—of suffering innocence—thus dominates the entire section.

The various sections of this work are self-contained and do not illuminate each other. To give an example: Abelard experienced with Heloise desire (or lust), concern, shame, the anguish of an irregular life, and so forth. But in no way does this experience make him empathize with—make him understand better or be tolerant of—his undisciplined monks at St. Gildas, with their concubines and their bastards. Once he is abbot, he is pure abbot, as it were,[31] scandalized by the turpitude of his monks. The same is true of his experience as a monk: he is horrified by the worldliness and irregularity of the monks at St. Denis—only two pages after being castrated for his own lust! The psychology of each of the different types that he fulfills in the successive periods of his life is like a watertight compartment: it is incompatible with that of the others, and remains isolated to that type and that period.

What are we to make of Abelard's failure to "homogenize" his text, as it were—to unify it, to organize his picture from one consistent perspective? Should we—taking this lack of unity as an expression of incapacity—read this fragmented work as the very metaphor of Abelard's loss of virility, of the capacity to carry through the work of his "pen" (pun intended)? To put it syllogistically: If man is a grammatical being,[32] an orderer of words into coherent propositions, a "copulator"[33] of verbs to subjects; and if Abelard's *Historia* is his intended proposition—then Abelard has perhaps revealed himself to be less than a man, to be a literary castrate. He has not succeeded in making the raw material of his life—its various moments—into a cohesive or unified story; this work remains a mere sequence of episodes. But is this failure Abelard's alone—

and is it truly the result and visible sign of his castrated state? Is it not in fact a common weakness of autobiographical narrative (not to mention quite a common feature in medieval narrative)? Our lives, after all, are not served up to us with the interpretation—or even the narrative structure—attached. We are obliged, humanly if not literarily, to supply the meaning ourselves. Abelard is one of the first autobiographers, but he is by no means the last, to have failed in his attempt to get hold of his life in its entirety, to make, of the moments and days and years of his existence, a story.

And there is a something rather appealing—surely something human—in Abelard's willingness to be, or inability to avoid being, "faithful" narratively speaking to his love for Heloise; to show us his passion in technicolor.

Finally, to accuse this work of being an "unsuccessful narrative" may well be (as we shall see more clearly shortly) to miss the point: it is far from clear that Abelard really conceived of his work as primarily narrative in function.[34]

There have long been rumors that Abelard's *Historia* was written by someone else. In a sense, it would not change much—except, of course, that it is fascinating and revealing in itself of medieval mentalities that someone, in this period, would have been tempted by such an endeavor, and would have thought it possible! There is in this work almost no attempt at individualized, personalized analysis in the modern sense. Almost everything that Abelard tells us about himself someone else could have told us. For example: at one point—when he is an abbot, she an abbess—Abelard tells us that he began to see a good deal of Heloise, in order to give her and her nuns spiritual direction. He is accused by some of being "still in the power of a lingering delight in carnal lust" and of being unable to "endure the absence of my old lover" (70).

> In quo nec invidie mihi murmur defuit, et quod me facere sincera karitas compellebat, solita derogantium pravitas impudentissime accusabat, dicens me adhuc quadam carnalis concupiscentiae oblectatione teneri, qua pristine dilecte sustinere absentiam vix aut numquam paterer. (101)[35]

A rather interesting charge! And how does Abelard parry it? In purely objective terms: he does not discuss how he *did* feel toward Heloise. In explaining why he went to her, he had referred to

Heloise merely as "now my sister in Christ rather than wife" (68)/ "jam in Christo soror potius quam uxor" (100). And he answers the calumny on the one hand by pointing out that he is now, literally, incapable of sin:

> but now that God in His mercy has freed me from any cause for such suspicion by taking away from me the power to commit base acts, how is it that suspicion remains? (70)

> Nunc vero mihi divina misericordia ab hac suspitione liberato, quomodo, hujus perpetrande turpitudinis facultate ablata, suspitio remanet? (101–2)

And then he cites examples of saints who lived in close but innocent association with women, and who were—or could have been—falsely accused of sin. The personal, subjective question is begged here; or rather, Abelard presumably does not see his feelings as relevant, only his acts are of interest, and the parallelism of his case to that of the saints.

Even when he does deal with motivation, it is in a very peculiarly medieval way: in terms of *topoi:* of commonplaces. Abelard—like the period in which he lived—seems to have felt that there were certain basic motivations for all fundamental human behaviors: to understand why someone behaved in a certain way, one defined the category to which he belonged, and that provided the explanation. Man or woman; young, mature, or old, rich or poor; high or low on Fortuna's wheel; belonging to a particular class or estate, and so forth. People who belonged to a certain set or group could be expected—and could expect themselves—to behave in a certain way. As Abelard says,

> Success always puffs up fools and worldly repose weakens the strength of one's mind and readily loosens its fiber through carnal allurements. (25)

> Sed quoniam prosperitas stultos semper inflat et mundana tranquillitas vigorem enervat animi et per carnales illecebras facile resolvit. (70)

Only then does he go on to tell of his relationship with Heloise and his fall from glory. The general rule precedes and explains the individual case.

The only sense in which this period conceived—literarily if not philosophically—of the "individual" was in the sense of the single case of a universal principle or idea. Not that the individual denied, in any way—or deviated from—the general or universal, but only that it constituted a concrete and single embodiment of that universal.[36] There is, in medieval literature, virtually no exploration of the "accidents" of individual being—of the *esse* of individuals; authors (artists as well) [37] give only the minimum number of details to make it possible to "tell"—to distinguish—one hero from another, and do not indulge in dilation upon differentness.

Why did Abelard write the *Historia?* What is its function, as he presents it? He does not, of course, present it as an "autobiography." And this is not—despite the word *historia*—really the "story of his life." This is obvious from the very fact that the text is very short— only 46 pages in the Monfrin Latin edition—and very schematic and cursory indeed. Moreover, Abelard makes it clear at several points that he assumes that his reader will already *know* the story of his life.

This work is of course, to a substantial degree, narrative. Indeed it typifies in many ways medieval narrative in general, and even prefigures in some provocative ways the structures of medieval romance. But it is often narrative in what one might call the "second degree": it is not the telling of a story, but the retelling. And this is not that kind of collective commemoration of past events that one finds in epics, but rather a *corrective* retelling: Abelard wants to set the record straight, on various points:

> I would have you know correctly the story of each cure [of his pride and of his lust] just as it occurred, from the facts and not from hearsay. (25)

> Cujus nunc rei utramque historiam verius ex ipsa re quam ex auditu cognoscere te volo, ordine quidem quo processerunt. (71)

The "topos of truth"? It is hard to say what is artifice and figure in medieval literature! At any rate the much-maligned Abelard had ample cause to fear *Fama* and her thousand mouths. But, still more important: the narrative itself is subordinated to purposes that are not essentially narrative,[38] but belong to the world of discourse.

Abelard is not primarily narrating, in this work; he is speaking to others. This work, in terms of its explicit purpose, is not egocentric or centripetal. The *Historia* is not—as has been said[39]—about the "quest for the self." Abelard, at least at the time when he is writing, raises no questions, no doubts about his past or present motivations, or his nature. This is not a soul-searching book, and there is here no discovery of "who I am" through writing.

Abelard is writing to have *impact on* his reader. This is literature not of *expression*, but of *impression*. The very fact that this is a letter of consolation suggests the importance of the recipient or *destinataire* (in the Jakobsonian sense) —as opposed to the *destinateur* or sender of the message. And the richly rhetorical character of this text makes it clear that it is not conceived as a private and intimate act of articulation or communication. This work is by no means spontaneous, sincere, natural—*whatever* those words mean.

Abelard's explicit purpose in writing, as he announced in the prologue and reiterated at the end, is this: he tells his (nameless) friend that he is writing so that

> when you compare your trials with mine you may consider them of little or no account and be stronger to endure them. (11)

> ut in comparatione mearum tuas aut nullas aut modicas temptationes recognoscas et tolerabilius feras. (63)

Abelard is thus making of himself a sort of type, or *exemplum*, of suffering and the events of his life are given as a list of calamities. As measured, quantitatively, against this list of Abelard's calamities, his friend's sufferings will be found less great, and therefore more tolerable. Abelard, in thus pushing himself into a typological model, is voluntarily narrowing, schematizing, and hyperbolizing himself to fit his topic. He is delivering a sermon with his own life as the *exemplum* from which the lesson is to be learned.

There is, to be sure, a good deal of self-justification in this work: Abelard defends himself against various criticisms. But his discourse always has a tendency to be curiously impersonal and self-effacing —didactic in a general sense. For example, his several-page defense of why he named his oratory the Paraclete (60–63; 94–97) is basically a theological argument, not a personal explanation.

But there is one sense in which Abelard himself learns through this narrative discourse; one sense in which he is trying, not only to teach his friend—and us—something, but to learn something himself. Abelard is seeking not to understand *himself*, but to understand the *meaning*—in an allegorical, or figural sense—of his life. As he reviews the lives and the words of figures from the past, setting them up (as we saw earlier) in parallel to his own, and as he repeats lessons from the Bible, he is seeking peace, acceptance on his own part of his grandiose but disastrous life—and the ability to go on.

After reflecting on the words of "blessed Jerome, whose heir in calumny and detraction I see I am" (78)/ "cujus me precipue in contumeliis detractionum heredem conspicio" (108), he says in his final paragraph:

> And so fortified by this evidence and these examples, let us endure our crosses with greater resignation as they are the more unjust. Let us not hesitate, if not to gain merit, at any rate to make some progress in the purification of our soul. And since everything occurs by divine ordinance, let every faithful soul under every affliction find consolation in the thought that God in His great goodness never permits anything to occur outside His plan and that no matter what wrongdoing is done, He makes it work to the best issue. (79)

He speaks of the necessity of learning to say: "Thy will be done."

> His itaque documentis atque exemplis animati, tanto securius ista toleremus quanto injuriosius accidunt. Que si non ad meritum nobis, saltem ad purgationem aliquam proficere non dubitemus; et quoniam omnia divina dispositione geruntur, in hoc se saltem quisque fidelium in omni pressura consoletur, quod nichil inordinate fieri umquam summa Dei bonitas permittit, et quod quecumque perverse fiunt optimo fine ipse terminat; unde et ei de omnibus recte dicitur: "Fiat voluntas tua". (108)

Here Abelard himself contemplates his *own* life, along with the other *exempla* that he has evoked. And he associates himself with his reader as the *destinataire* of his own sermon.

NOTES

1. The authenticity of this text has, over the centuries, often been contested—though, for the time being at least, this issue seems to have been put to rest. We should no doubt for prudence's sake continue to consider the autobiographical authenticity of this text as uncertain. Perhaps I should refer to the author as

"Abelard" (that is, in quotation marks) to distinguish him from Abelard, the man, the subject matter of the book, but that possibility seems a bit ponderous . . .

2. English quotations are taken from *The Story of Abelard's Adversities*, trans. J. T. Muckle (Toronto: Pontifical Institute of Medieval Studies, 1964).

3. Latin quotations are taken from the J. Monfrin edition of the *Historia calamitatum* (Paris: Vrin, 1959).

4. In his behavior as a dialectician, Abelard is behaving like a young "knight," which by class he *was;* more on this later.

5. The degree of his originality is a difficult issue—and one on which scholars are in disagreement (on occasion even with themselves: for example Etienne Gilson, *La Philosophie au moyen âge* [Paris: Payot, 1962], 280 vs. 288). There seems to be agreement that Abelard is less of a "rationalist," less of a "radical"—indeed less "original"—than used to be thought; and that the techniques he used had been used before. Beyond that some scholars (such as Frederick Copleston, *A History of Philosophy*, vol. 2: *Medieval Philosophy* [Garden City, N.Y.: Doubleday/Image, 1962], 170–73) speak primarily—like Abelard himself—in terms of "greatness" and "power" when speaking of Abelard's gifts and achievements: of his mastery of complex issues, of his dominance, etc. Others (such as David Knowles, *The Evolution of Medieval Thought* [New York: Vintage Books, 1962], 107–31; and Gilson) are impressed by the originality of his positions.

6. He makes some of these claims more fully than others. For example, while he finds that he has been *irreproachable* as an abbot, he does not present himself as a particularly effective one; he is "perfect" in one sense, not in the other.

7. St. Augustine of course also had this "problem." One could, somewhat simplistically, say he coped with it primarily by *condemning* the sensualist—and, narratively, by refusing to render, to "relive," his experiences as an erotic lover.

8. By the term "medieval period" I mean, roughly speaking from the eleventh to the fifteenth century; but in many cases what I am saying would be true, I think, for several centuries both before and after that time segment. I am voluntarily riding roughshod here over all the differences between the eleventh and fifteenth—and even the twelfth and thirteenth—centuries. What I am trying to get at is what works of this period have in common.

9. See Alice Colby, *The Portrait in Twelfth Century French Literature* (Geneva: Droz, 1965).

10. Prudentius's influential late fourth century *Psychomachia* provided an early model for this.

11. I am not distinguishing here between nouns and adjectives (what or how a character *is)* and verbs (what he *does).* Medieval verbs *reflect* what characters are—rather than *make* them what they are; hence, this nondistinction is justifiable.

12. Indeed, Einhard himself speaks of his work thus. See *The Life of Charlemagne* (Ann Arbor, Mich.: University of Michigan Press, 1960),17.

13. He is surprisingly neutral sometimes: he speaks without any apparent criticism (and without noting the possible conflict with Charlemagne's extreme piety) of the emperor's various concubines and illegitimate children.

14. Einhard's work was very popular: approximately eighty manuscripts are extant.

15. As had Einhard, about Charlemagne's scandalous daughters. He only referred to them in veiled and cryptic terms (48).

16. A rare exception: Abelard tells us that he had "always detested unclean harlots" (23) / "Quia igitur scortorum immunditiam semper abhorrebam" (71).
17. It must be conceded that there is something of this interest in Suetonius: although his ideal is clearly the moderate—and un-original—man, still he is interested in *everything* "*notabilis*" about the Caesars.
18. From medieval Latin *individuus* (indiviisible, inseparable).
19. Definitions from the *Shorter Oxford English Dictionary* (Oxford: Clarendon, 1933), 993.
20. See, for example, Copleston, 170–73.
21. On this general question, see Copleston; Knowles, 112–13; Gilson, 284–89.
22. The "realist" position was that of the "ancients," the "nominalist" that of the "moderns"; in Abelard's own terms the ultrarealist position was the *antiqua doctrina* (quoted by Copleston, 181).
23. It is so common, in modern literature and psychology, to read about "castration obsessions" that it is almost a relief to find a man who *was* castrated: to confront reality rather than fantasy. (What are the fantasies of a castrate?)
24. (39–40/80). (The first number refers to the Muckle English edition; the second to the Monfrin Latin edition.)
25. To whom Mary McLaughlin has compared him: each a "lonely individual at variance with himself and his world": "Abelard as Autobiographer: The Motives and Meaning of His Story of Calamities" *Speculum*, XLII, no. 3 (1967): 463–88) especially 473.
26. Moi seul. Je sens mon coeur et je connois les hommes. Je ne suis fait comme aucun de ceux que j'ai vus; j'ose croire n'être fait comme aucun de ceux qui existent. Si je ne vaux pas mieux, au moins je suis autre. Si la nature a bien ou mal fait de briser le moule dans lequel elle m'a jetté. c'est ce dont on ne peut juger qu'après m'avoir lu.

    I alone. I feel my own heart and I know men. I am made like none of those whom I have seen; I dare to believe that I am made like no one else who exists. If I am not better, at least I am other. If nature did well or badly to break the mold in which she cast me, that is what one can judge only after having read me. *(Confessions,* livre 1, p. 5, in the Pléiade edition, Rousseau's *Œuvres complètes* vol. 1. My translation)

27. He also, on occasion, uses *detrimentum* and *diminutio*.
28. I would therefore have to disagree with Mary McLaughlin, who considers that Abelard "was able to achieve the unified comprehension of [his] life" (486).
29. William J. Brandt has discussed, in *The Shape of Medieval History: Studies in Modes of Perception* (New York: Schocken 1973—originally New Haven, Conn.: Yale University Press, 1966), the problem of "incoherence" in medieval narrative and character depiction (162–70 in particular).
30. One could see Augustine's "conversion" as a figurative—and of course voluntary —"castration," symbolized by his circumcision, and by his subsequent chastity.
31. See Muckle, 41, 66; Monfrin, 81, 99.
32. See Jean Jolivet *(Arts du langage et théologie chez Abélard* [Paris: 1969]), on the central importance of grammar—language—in the philosophy of Abelard.
33. Ibid., 57.
34. There are, moreover, *many* other medieval works of literature and painting which present this same segmented or fragmentary quality. The Middle Ages clearly did not value as highly as we "unity" in a work of art.
35. Interestingly enough, Abelard's definition of sin in his *Ethics (Scito teipsum)* —

written later than the *Historia*—is far more subjectivistic: he defines sin not as a "bad deed" but as a "consent to evil," as "contempt for the Creator." (See "Quid sit animi uicium et quid proprie dicatur peccatum.")

36. Colin Morris has studied what he calls *The Discovery of the Individual*, 1050–1200 (New York: Harper Torchbooks, 1972). Although he does not make the same distinctions as I with respect to the meanings of "individual," his remarks and examples would seem to corroborate my viewpoint.

37. See religious iconography, for example the emblems and objects by which one tells the saints apart.

38. To writers of this period, the idea of telling one's life story just to tell it—even because one was famous—would have seemed odd indeed, and perhaps even rather perverse.

39. McLaughlin, 464.

CHAPTER 2

The "I" of the *Roman de la Rose* of Guillaume de Lorris

Inherent in the literary—and linguistic—existence of autobiography is a paradox, for autobiography is a genre based on two mutually contradictory uses of language—discourse versus history. As Benveniste puts it: "Discourse excludes the simple past *[aoriste]*, but historical narrative, which uses it constantly, retains only its third-person forms."[1] Autobiography is thus a genre characterized by an underlying tension, for the "I was" on which it is based means that the I who speaks, speaks of himself as another. The *me* to whom the *I* refers is someone else: a past self, someone who no longer exists.

This underlying split in the identity of the hero-narrator, who is both the subject and object of his own verb, suggests that autobiography is a literary form with a definite potential for irony. Of course, to a certain extent, all narrative, as opposed to lyric poetry and theater, is ironic by the very fact that there are differences in viewpoint between the characters, the narrator, and the reader[2]— though the word *distance* might express more appropriately than irony this impression of a separation among points of view. In autobiographical works, at any rate, the narrator's attitudes toward and judgments regarding the facts he is recounting seem to play an exceptionally important part. The narrator does not just tell his story: he interprets himself, explains himself, criticizes or defends his past, his alter ego. (We saw all this clearly enough in Abelard's *Historia*.)

As Shapiro puts it:

> Autobiography is primarily an art of perspective, an art of juxtaposed perspectives: the present commenting upon the past, the past commenting on the present. It is an art of contrast and integration. The time of autobiography tends to be ironic and comic, because it usually represents experience gazing backward at the innocent illusions of the child that fathered the man and because it reflects the individual's ability to rise above circumstances, if only through retrospective analysis. Autobiographies of course contain tragic scenes, but never the death of the protagonist. The Götterdämmerung theme is strong in autobiography but it is elegiac and ironic rather than starkly tragic.[3]

Obviously, this fundamental split in the central identity of autobiographical narrative can be developed in any of a number of ways, in different works. Fully exploited, it may culminate in the articulation of two radically and irreconcilably alienated identities. At the other extreme, the narrator may achieve a synthesis, a reunification of these dichotomized perspectives. As concerns Abelard: while he is, in the *Historia*, long on self-condemnation at various points—as with respect to his lustful relationship with Heloise—his work is remarkably short on irony; this perhaps for the simple reason that when speaking of his past selves, Abelard can condemn himself only by means of general moral pronouncements, but not narratively: when he recounts the past, he is once again in it; he is *there*. As was pointed out in chapter 1, his work is strongly compartmentalized, and we do not find it in that blend of self-condemnation (distance) and self-justification (identity) that irony entails.

If Abelard's *Historia* was one of the first—and only—works of autobiographical literature of the medieval period,[4] Guillaume de Lorris's *Roman de la Rose* is the first autobiographical novel, or romance, in French literature. This short (apparently incomplete) verse romance offers in many respects a fertile domain for a study of Old French autobiographical writing.

I will make virtually no distinction here between autobiography as such and the first-person novel, or between autobiography and pseudo- or semiautobiography. I will opt for Shapiro's view[5] that a writer's formalization of a "life" given as his own calls upon a full range of artistic resources, whether the contents of that life are real or imaginary: he must organize and structure his narrative material to give it shape and meaning. Even when a work deals exclusively with the actual events of the author's life, it would be naive to assume that he never has recourse to *inventio* (consciously or unconsciously) as well as to *dispositio*[6] in his narrative. If we assume that any writer has an esthetic or moral purpose in relating his life, it is clear that the image offered us will always be a mask rather than "mon coeur mis à nu." The mask, the image created, cannot fail to be influenced by literary tradition. Then, too, writers attempt to enhance the coherence and beauty of their literary creations by the use of rhetorical figures. From a purely literary standpoint—and this is our focus here—there is little difference between the two.

All this is especially true since—as I pointed out with respect to Abelard—in the medieval period, the notion of writing "naturally" or "spontaneously," without recourse to art or rhetoric, was far more inconceivable than today. When speaking of himself, the writer was always expected to transform himself, esthetically and morally, into a symbol of humanity as a whole, or at least of an entire class of men. When, then, should we make an elaborate effort to draw a firm line between fact and fiction?

From the very outset, Guillaume's *Roman de la Rose* offers an intriguing particularity: the story is not just an account of what happened to the hero-narrator, but rather of certain events dreamed by him in symbolic form and actualized only later, after the dream (ll. 1–30).[7] In typical medieval fashion, human experience is presented in its archetypal aspect, not as an individualized sequence of actual events. From both the ontological and chronological standpoints, the symbolic, exemplary side of things takes precedence over the specific case, which, indeed, is not even represented narratively.

The first consequence of such a structure is that the narrative has a double claim to truthfulness, since it recounts an actual dream, and since this dream later came true, thus proving that it was not *mençongier* (deceitful) (ll.4; 19–20; 28–30).

The structure of the narrative—which may seem odd at first—

has the effect of making it plausible or *vraisemblable*. The fact that it is a dream that Guillaume is describing justifies, so to speak, the use of symbolic allegory in the narrative. In a dream, there is nothing strange about meeting the God of Love, joining a round led by Déduit—Pleasure—or shedding tears of anguish over not being able to pick a rose; such happenings seem normal and natural in the strangeness of a dreamworld; and thus the allegory loses much of its artificiality. But on the other hand, the fact that all of this "came true" afterwards heightens the emotional intensity, which, as we shall see, is characteristic of the poem: in the sequence of "real" events, this experience brought about a permanent transformation in the hero-narrator. It is largely due to this twofold emphasis on its "true-to-life" quality that the *Roman de la Rose* avoids, on the one hand, the dry pedantry which is the weak point of so many medieval allegories and, on the other hand, the tendency to irony inherent in autobiography.

As presented by its author, the narrative purports to be not only doubly *true* but also doubly *meaningful*. As Scholes and Kellogg put it,[8] the text aims to be, at one and the same time, perfectly *illustrative*—through the symbolic allegory which gives it its exemplary, didactic quality and which makes of it an "art of Love" (1. 38); and perfectly *imitative*—through the insistence on its real-life dimension.

Finally—and this is the aspect we are most interested in—we are dealing here not just with the two identities basic to autobiography in general,[9] but rather with *four* identities, four more or less distinct, discontinuous selves, all of which exist in relation to the dream, each in a way which is qualitatively different from that of the others.

The first *I* is that of the Dreamer (D), the person to whom the dream manifested itself, who "had" the dream. He tells us he is twenty—an age both exact and, by its "roundness," vague; a symbolic, mythical age, at which (at least in the medieval mind) a young man's fancy "typically" turns to love. This indication immediately broadens the meaning, the implications of this autobiographical text: our hero is already becoming a symbol, if not of every man, at least of every young nobleman.

Apart from his dream experience, D has only an iterative[10] existence (ll. 23–25: *aloie, souloie, dormoie* [I was going] [I used to], [I was sleeping]); an existence of habit rather than of action. But on this particular night he "sees" a dream which he finds pleasing and "beautiful" (1. 27). These last two indications are highly interesting inasmuch as they suggest that the dream is not to be for D a moving experience in which he will be emotionally involved; D's identity is not going to fuse completely with that of the hero of the dream. Rather, the dream is to be a spectacle, with D acting as an uninvolved spectator. Moreover, the dream is—already—like a work of art: the dream is "beautiful" and the dreamer experiences an esthetic delight in contemplating and/or recalling it (with the verb *plot* (it pleased) it is impossible to tell whether the pleasure is simultaneous with the dream, as in the case of a book or a film, or whether it is felt only after D has awakened and begun to reflect on what he has just dreamed and seen).

The second *I* is the Hero of the Dream (HD). The separation between D and HD is not immediate—and is perhaps never complete.[11] At the beginning of the dream, the two still seem closely linked, as in lines 45 and 86: "Avis m'iere qu'en may estoie" (It seemed to me that I was in May) and "Songai une nuit que j'estoie . . ." (I dreamed one night that I was . . .). No clear-cut distinction is as yet apparent. At the beginning of the dream, D seems to share and take part in the actions and the thoughts of HD, to be living this illusion, this vision. We shall reserve for later the problem of verb tenses, but it is of interest here that the momentary fluctuation from *passé simple*[12] to present in verses 94 to 107 suggests D's emotional involvement in these events. The distance between D and HD becomes apparent for the first time when HD is described in line 103 as being "Jolis, gais et pleins de leesce" (Pretty, gay and full of happiness), for at the time Guillaume was writing, the adjective "jolis" had already begun to take on its modern meanings of "beautiful," "charming," and "graceful" in addition to its earlier senses of "joyful," and "well adorned."[13] Thus it is that D now *sees* and *perceives* HD, instead of merely identifying with him. D thus steps "outside," in a sense, and, from the next line on, the narrative continues in the preterite, a tense ideally adapted to objective narration,[14] and in the imperfect.

As concerns the Hero of the Dream, we known implicitly that he is the same age as the Dreamer, that he is "joli" and "gai" (according to the Dreamer), that he is to go through a profound emotional experience in the course of the dream. This experience begins in May: this detail, like the age of the hero, is precise yet primarily symbolic in value. And, even though the time of year and the sequence of events are clearly indicated, the experience undergone by the hero is, in many respects, extratemporal. The dream is devoid of exact duration; the day never passes, night never comes, there is never any mention of meals to mark time. Thus, although at the outset rooted in time, the dream unfolds along an indefinite and unreal time axis.

The third *I*, whom we shall designate as the Real-life Hero, RH,[15] is he for whom and to whom all the dream events happen afterwards, in reality (ll. 28–30). This *I* plays practically no part in the narrative; his existence is postulated rather than developed. He is always implicitly present, though, for everything that happens to HD happens also to RH, by definition. More precisely:

Mes en ce songe onques riens n'ot
qui tretot avenu ne soit
si com li songes recensoit. (ll. 28–30)

But there was nothing in this dream
that did not happen soon
just as the dream related it.

All the dream events also take place in reality, although presumably in a manner that is "realistic" and *ouvert* (open) rather than allegorical and *couvert* (closed, covered).[16] Another detail significant from the stylistic standpoint: as the lines quoted above suggest, events regarding HD are expressed by the preterite and, to a lesser extent, by the imperfect; but it is the *passé composé* ("qui tretot avenu* ne *soit"*—"that hasn't happened soon after") which is used in a brief allusion to RH's experience, and to the nature of the temporal and emotional relationship between RH and the voice of the Narrator. The *passé composé* refers to past events "whose consequences are still present."[17]

The last *I* is the Narrator (N), whose identity is complex. For one thing, he remembers all these past events (ll. 129–38). (It is interesting to note that for any given event, N has three sources of recall:

D, who witnessed the dream and saw himself take part in it; and HD and RH, each of whom takes part in the events in a different way). Like so many other medieval storytellers recounting narratives they had read or heard, N recognizes that his memory may be faulty; he promises to tell his story, "com moi vient a remenbrance" (as it comes to my memory). And he frequently proposes to relate these events "si com je recors" (as I recall; l. 339) To a certain extent, of course, such examples of *dubitatio* (stylistic "doubt") are nothing more than a literary topos. At the same time, though, they indicate a refusal on the part of the Narrator (and no doubt of medieval writers in general) to draw a sharp line between imagination and memory as sources of narrative material—or, for that matter, between "art" and "reality," fiction and autobiography. N proposes to relate, to describe the "semblance" of the portraits on the wall surrounding the garden. (ll. 136–38), providing us with a verbal equivalent of what was initially a visual image: in order to do so, he must transpose the image into another medium without affecting its nature and its quality. This operation is not without its difficulties, to which the Narrator alludes frequently—again using the conventional expressions of *dubitatio:* "ne vos en sai que deviser" (I don't know what to tell you; l. 770); "mes de sa robe deviser/ crien durement qu'encombré soie" (but to describe her dress/ I greatly fear that I will be overwhelmed; ll. 874–75). Although he stresses the autobiographical aspect of his story, N makes no distinction between his literary problems and those of any other storyteller: both are at grips with the problem of providing an adequate verbal expression of an inner vision which is stable, certain, and objective. The literary problems confronting the Narrator are therefore—at least as he presents them—of a purely formal and esthetic nature. There is not the slightest notion that the task of the autobiographer is in any way unique or even special.

All narrators, of course, exist in time as they compose their work, but the Narrator of the *Roman de la Rose*—unlike most—constantly calls our attention to the unfolding of his literary project. He informs us of what he is *going* to do, for example, "tot vos conteré par ordre" (I will tell you everything in order; l. 699); "Des or mes, si con je savrai,/tot l'afeire vos conterai" (From now on, as I know it,/I will relate to you the entire affair; ll. 689–90). The reader is thus waiting to hear what N will have to say and N promises that it will be fascinating (ll. 2061–74).

Often, while narrating or describing, N calls our attention to what he *is* saying: for example "Jalousie a garnison mis/ ou chastel que je vos devise" (Jealousy has put a garrison/ in the castle that I am describing to you; ll. 3849–50; also 659–60). He reminds us of what he has just *said*, of what we have just seen—and heard— before continuing:

La bele Oiseuse vint aprés,
qui se tint de moi assez pres.
De cele vos ai ge sanz faille
la façon dite et la taille. (ll. 1249–52)

Beautiful Idleness came next,
who stood quite near me.
About her I have, without fail,
told you the appearance and the size.

When referring to his own efforts, N employs the present, the *passé composé*, and the future, the tenses characteristic of discourse.[18] The "estoire" told by the Narrator is composed of the following elements: (1) the narrative as such, which is mainly divided into scenes, recapitulations being made only to remind the reader of what he has already read or heard; (2) the innumerable descriptions of places and persons seen by HD; (3) direct quotations, which account for a sizable proportion of the whole (1418 verses out of 4028); it is worth noting that there are no indirect quotations.

N is continually reacting to and commenting on his narration. At times his remarks—also a form of discourse—are introduced by expressions such as "je cuit" (I believe), "ce me semble" (it seems to me), and "au mien cuider" (in my opinion); these seem to be of a personal and subjective nature. At other times, though, the explanations and judgments of a moral nature which embellish the narration are presented in a very objective and impersonal way: the Narrator as *persona* vanishes, and we are left with a disembodied and omniscient voice uttering fundamental truths (ll. 1145–52; 1573–92).

It is important to note that—whether in his narrative and descriptive passages or in his commentary—it is to *us* that the Narrator is speaking. The frequency of references to the reader (or readers: "vos") is strikingly high—even in the context of medieval literature where this was a fairly common procedure. For example, N addresses us seven times in less than eighty verses. (vv. 785–862):

> mes *sachiez* que mout m'agrea
> dont Cortoise me prea
> et me dit que je querolasse,   (ll. 789–91; my emphasis)

> but *know* that it pleased me greatly
> that Courtesy asked me
> and told me that I should join the round dance,

> des genz qui ilec queroloient,
> si *vos* dirai queus il estoient.   (ll. 797–98; my emphasis)

> of the people who were dancing
> I will tell *you* who they were.

> ja mes entre gent ne viendroiz
> ou *vos* veez nul plus bel homme.   (ll. 800–801; my emphasis)

> never will *you* come among people
> where *you* will see any handsomer man.

And so on.

Though these phrases are full of rhetorical formulas, still they indicate our importance in this literary project, and suggest the type of relationship the Narrator is trying to establish with us. Clearly, he wants us to "see" his "vision"—to see what he claims to have "seen"—and to share in its beauty and its emotional impact. To achieve this, he constantly tries to draw us into his story. The questions N puts to us are only partly rhetorical: we are called upon to become *involved* in what we are reading—involved to an extent which Chrétien de Troyes, always smiling and faintly ironical, would never dream of asking of us.[19] The Narrator seems to want us to be caught up by and in his story.

We will return to differences between the *Roman de la Rose* and oral "literature" later on: many aspects of narrative style, not to speak of content, are markedly different. At this point, though, let me just point out that in the *Roman de la Rose*, as in the *chanson de geste*, the Narrator tries to minimize the emotional distance (and therefore the irony) between the public and the main characters in his story, and to enlist the public's full and intense participation in the action.

The innumerable first-person pronouns in the *Roman de la Rose* thus converge into four distinct identities, covering a period of five or more years, the dream having taken place about five years before the moment when N begins to speak (v. 46). It might, of course, be said that in any autobiographical work, indeed any work revolving about a hero who exists over a period of time, there are a number—indeed an infinite number—of different identities corresponding to the different moments of the story. In a sense, this is true. What is most curious here, though, is that these different *I*'s are discontinuous, discrete, and cut off from one another. This technique is similar to the flashbacks utilized in contemporary films and novels. And such a technique, as employed in both modern narrative art and the *Roman de la Rose*, would seem to reflect a certain view of human personality and experience: rather than extending along a simple, linear time axis, life is continuously re-viewed and relived, in a time dimension which is both discontinuous and nearly circular. (This is very similar to Abelard's presentation of himself in watertight sections—and as he narrates his past, he relives it and reidentifies with it.) What sets apart the use of a discontinuous hero-identity in the *Roman de la Rose* (and this discontinuity is counterbalanced by the psychologically "fragmentary" portrait of the heroine) is the fact that all the *I*'s are structured around a single event, or nucleus of events: the dream. All four intervals of time are curiously embedded in and intertwined with one another. HD's life becomes a part of D's; HD's experience reflects and echos that of RH.

What characterizes the relationship between the different *I*'s? As an example, if one examines the passages in which HD yearns to enter the garden (ll. 473–94) or watches the garden's inhabitants dancing (ll. 1177–98), it is obvious that the Narrator is in complete agreement with HD's values. His remarks show quite clearly that N finds this *hortus deliciarum* every bit as beautiful and its way of life every bit as appealing as does HD. A number of verses stress this harmony of viewpoint:

> car tel joie ne tel deduit
> ne vit mes hom, si com je cuit. (ll. 473–74)

> for such joy, such pleasure
> no man ever saw, so I believe.

With regard to the birdsongs:

> Mout estoit bele l'acordance
> de lor piteus chanz a oïr;
> toz li moz s'en doit esjoïr. (ll. 482–84)

> Very beautiful to hear was the harmony
> of their pitious songs;
> everyone should enjoy it.

In describing the people present:

> Franches genz et bien enseignies
> et gent de bel afaitement
> estoient tuit comunement. (ll. 1280–81)

> Noble and well brought-up people
> and people of beautiful manners
> were they all.

Finally, describing this sweet lovers' life, he states:

> Dex! com menoient bone vie!
> Fox est qui n'a de tel envie! (ll. 1293–94)

> God! What a good life they led!
> Anyone who doesn't want to live like that is crazy!

And, as we have already seen, D too is filled with admiration for the spectacle: "moult fu biaus" (was very beautiful); "mout ne plot" (it pleased me greatly). So is RH. All the other voices of the hero thus contribute implicitly their expression of enthrallment with the wonders described.

Such harmony creates the effect of a chorale—much as did the birdsongs whose "harmony" *(accordance)* was so "beautiful" (v.

482). At times, this autobiographical poem, like a "congruent meeting of different voices"[20] takes on a truly polyphonic quality. Four voices, each singing its part, answer and echo one another:

Beau!
 Beau!
  Beau!
   Beau!

This phenomenon contributes immeasurably to the emotional and esthetic density—and intensity—of the work.

It is taken for granted that the reader too will sing his part in this chorale; his

Beau!

is implicitly understood, his complicity assumed. The text is unfailingly optimistic in its didactic pretentions: it nevers occurs to the Narrator that the reader might be hostile or refractory to his message. The innumerable "vos savez bien" (well you know; ll. 404, 1265, 3396, 3428) the "sachiez" (know; ll. 221, 251, 260, 323, 334, 422, 429, and so forth)—all without benefit of argumentation—presuppose a reader open and receptive to N's words, a reader in agreement with his values and his attitudes. N's only fear, insofar as we are concerned, seems to be that we might feel he has exaggerated the beauty of the place, the people, the things he describes (ll. 1051–55).

The Narrator's placid conviction that his readers will be favorably disposed suggests that this is a work speaking to and about a particular social class—both the class and the work being closed in upon themselves, their own values, their own worldview, their own "code."

It is not only in a metaphorical sense that N and HD see eye to eye. Even the narrative structure emphasizes their harmony. When the subject of the verb is *I*, it is usually possible to distinguish the different *I*'s. In many of the descriptive passages, however, it is impossible to isolate the different points of view. It is obvious that HD is the subject of the following verbs: "En droit de moi, m'en esjoï/ si durement, quant je l'oï" (As for me, I rejoiced/ so strongly, when I heard; ll. 485–86), and "Quant j'oi veües les semblances/ de

ceux qui menoient les dances,/ j'oi lors talant que le vergier/ alasse
veoir et cerchier" (When I saw the appearance/ of those who led
the dance/ then I had the desire/ to go see and look around the
garden; ll. 1284–87). But the Narrator does not say "*I thought that*
the birds sang like angels," but rather "They sang as though they
were angels" (ll. 661–62). He says "one could compare their song to
that of the sirens of the sea" (ll. 669–70) rather than "*It seemed to
me then* that one could compare their song . . . ," and so on. That
is, in the descriptions, the different perspectives merge and, indeed,
through their absolute character, attain the level of objective truth.[21]

Is this a refusal, on the Narrator's part, to mark a clear distinction
between HD's viewpoint and his own? A break in the autobiographical facade? Or simply a nondistinction among the various perspectives? At any rate, the phenomenon is typically medieval and is
presumably attributable in part to a belief in an objective truth.
But it is worth remembering that even some modern writings offer
striking similarities. In Gide's *Si le grain ne meurt*, for example, the
descriptions are equally devoid of irony, of distance between points
of view ("then" versus "now") regarding places and persons. And
the warmth of this text—like that of the *Roman de la Rose*—is
perhaps due, to a considerable extent, to this marriage of the past
and present.[22]

This impression of unity of worldview between HD and N is
reinforced by the fairly frequent use of the present tense in certain
descriptions. The fountain of Narcissus, for example, *is* (ll. 1521–
34). The strictly narrative aspect continues in the preterite, while
in the descriptions the present makes its appearance. And the rose
chosen by HD *is* magnificent (ll. 1657–66).

Does N's approval of HD's values extend also to his acts? Every so
often, a distance in their perspectives becomes apparent. After all,
N knows what is going to happen; he knows how painful this
pursuit is going to become. His time horizon is vaster. When N
describes how HD goes off alone in the garden and how the God of
Love follows him, bow in hand (l. 1312), he exclaims:

Or me gart Dex de mortel plaie,
se tant avient qu'il a moi traie!
Je, cui de ce ne fu noient,
m'alai adez esbanoiant

par le vergier tot a delivre,
et cil pensa tost de moi sivre. (ll. 1313–18)

May God preserve me from mortal wound
if it should happen that he shoots at me!
I, who knew nothing of this,
went around amusing myself
through the garden freely,
and he had the idea of following me.

It is the Narrator who is afraid here, he who feels the suspense; HD fears nothing. N experiences a stronger, more intense emotion in recalling the event, than HD in living it. Instead of leaving N with a more or less ironic detachment as regards the past, the intervening lapse of time has deepened his involvement, heightened rather than lessened the intensity of his experience! Elsewhere the Narrator recounts:

Adés me plot a demorer
a la fontaine remirer
et as cristaus, qui me mostroient
mil choses que entor estoient.
Mes de fort eure m'i miré.
Las! tant en ai puis soupiré!
Cil miroërs m'a deceü:
se j'eüsse avant conneü
quex ert sa force et sa vertuz,
ne m'i fusse ja embatuz,
que maintenant ou laz cheï
que maint home a pris et traï. (ll. 1601–12)

Then it pleased me to stay
to look at the fountain
and at the cristals, which showed me
a thousand things that were around there.
But to my own sorrow have I looked in.
Alas! I have sighed so much since!
That mirror has deceived me:
if I had known beforehand
about its force and power,
I would not have rushed in,
for now I have fallen into the net
that has caught and betrayed many a man.

But N seems to recognize that the young man he once was had *not* known in advance about the power of love. And N's awareness of the suffering and disappointment brought by love is by no means, it seems to me, tantamount to a condemnation of HD.

In order fully to understand N's attitude toward HD, it is important to realize that this "love story," even as N tells it, seems not as yet to have reached its conclusion. In the introduction, he announced:

> ce est li *Romanz de la Rose,*
> ou l'art d'Amors est tote enclose.
> La matire est et bone et neuve,
> or doint Dex qu'en gré le receve
> cele por qui je l'ai empris:
> c'est cele qui tant a de pris
> et tant est digne d'estre amee
> qu'el doit estre Rose clamee. (ll. 37–44)

> this is the *Romance of the Rose,*
> where the art of Love is all enclosed.
> The subject matter is good and new,
> now may God grant that she deign to receive it
> she for whom I have undertaken it:
> it is she who has such great value,
> and is so worthy of being loved
> that she must be called "Rose."

In lines 3487–92, he declares:

> Tote l'estoire veil parsuivre,
> ja ne m'est parece d'escrivre,
> par quoi je cuit qu'il abelise
> a la bele, que Dex guerisse,
> qui le guerredon m'en rendra
> mieuz que nule, quant el voudra.

> I want to follow the whole story through,
> it is never wearisome for me to write,
> so I think that it will please
> the beauty, whom God save,
> who will reward me
> better than anyone, when she wishes.

N is therefore writing for a "beauty" *(bele)*, who would seem to be one and the same as the heroine of his story. At any rate, it seems hard to imagine, as some critics would have us believe, that this "beauty," this "rose," is the Virgin Mary or Dame Raison.[23] Nowhere in the text is there the slightest suggestion that HD's human and sensual love has been transcended by RH or N into a religious or philosophical devotion. Whoever the lady (our "rose" or another), N, as a man, is still involved in the experience of loving. His wounds have not healed. Quite the contrary, the narrative is presented as an offering made in the hope of winning over the reluctant lady.

As I have already pointed out, the narrative part of the text is based on the simple past or preterite (with, of course, the imperfect, the pluperfect, and the conditional as supporting tenses). In line 787, however, the Narrator speaks of HD in these terms: "A la querole me suis pris" (I have joined the round dance). Although isolated in a context dominated by the preterite, this instance of the use of the compound past or *passé composé*—the first such case in a narrative passage—is highly significant, in my opinion, for it offers the first hint of what will later reveal itself as a new attitude, on N's part, toward his material. Little by little, as the narrative progresses, the *passé composé* and then the present will almost completely replace the preterite as the basic tenses of the text. To start with, there is a single, isolated line using the *passé composé*, like the one just quoted. A few hundred lines later, perhaps, another: the God of Love calls "Sweet Glance" (Dolz Regart) and "li dex d'Amors m'a seu" (the god of Love has followed me; l. 1418) and so on. Starting with the passage in which HD peers into the fountain of love, this tendency gains momentum:

> Mes de fort eure m'i miré.
> Las! tant en ai puis soupiré!
> Cil miroërs m'a deceü . . . (ll. 1605–7)

> But to my own sorrow have I looked it.
> Alas! I have sighed so much since!
> That mirror has deceived me . . .

In this particular case, the *passés composés* express the continuity between the past and the Narrator's present. But a bit further on, things become much more complicated. In particular, in lines 1679 through 1718, there is a mixture of all the past tenses and the present. Along with the preterite, one finds: "il a tantost pris une floiche" (right away he has taken an arrow; l. 1687); "il tret a moi" (he shoots at me; l. 1691); "arieres suis tantost versez" (right away I have fallen backwards; l. 1698); "Li cuers me faut, li cuers me ment" (My heart fails me, my heart gives way; l. 1999); "Mes la saiete qui me point/ ne tret onques sanc de moi point" (But the arrow that pierces me/ never draws any blood from me; ll. 1704–5); "la saiete barbelee . . . remest encore dedans" (the barbed arrow . . . still remains within; l. 1717), and so forth.

By the end of the work here is the "verbal" state of affairs:

Mais je, qui *sui* dehors le mur,
sui livrez a duel et a point.
Qui savroit quel vie je *moine*,
il l'en devroit grant pitié prendre.
Amors me *set* ore bien vendre
les biens que il m'avoit pretez.
Jes cuidoie avoir achetez;
or les me *vent* tot de rechief,
que je *sui* a plus grant meschief
por la joie que j'ai *perdue*
que s'onques ne l'eüse eue. (ll. 3920–30; my emphasis)

But I, who *am* outside the wall,
am given over to sorrow and pain.
Anyone who knew what a life I *lead*
should feel great pity for it.
Love *knows* how to sell to me dearly
the goods that he had lent me.
I thought I had bought them;
but he *sells* them to me all over again,
I *am* in greater misery
for the joy that I *have lost*
than if I had never had it.

And the poem breaks off after the following lines:

Hé! Bel Acueil, ce *sai* de voir
qu'il vos *beent* a decevoir,
et, se *devient*, si *ont* il *fet*.
Je ne *sai* or coment il *vet*,
mes durement *suis* esmaiez
que entroblié ne m'*aiez*,
si en *ai* duel et desconfort.

Ja mes n'iert rien qui me confort
se je pert vostre bienveillance
car je n'ai mes aillors fiance. (ll. 4019–28; my emphasis)

Ah! Fair Welcome, this I know for sure:
they are trying to deceive you,
and if it *happens*, they *have done* it.
I *do not know* how things *are*.
but I *am* very much afraid
that you *have forgotten* me,
and I *feel* grief and unhappiness.
There will never be anything else that comforts me
if I lose your benevolence,
for I have no trust in anything else.

The preterite has almost entirely disappeared; even the *passé composé* (along with the other past tenses) now refers almost exclusively to HD's past in the dream.

Little by little, then, the emotional distance separating HD and N —a distance which permitted and, indeed, necessitated the use of the preterite—is annulled by a shift to the *passé composé* and the present, those tenses which express, respectively, closeness and continuity with the past, and present reality itself. And this impression that the chronological center of gravity has shifted from the past to the present is heightened by the marked dominance of quotations (direct discourse) over narration as such:[24] the romance takes on the quality of a dramatic dialogue; and in the theater, precisely, there is *only* present.

Thus it is that the voice to which we are listening—the voice relating what happened in the dream, becomes increasingly that of HD himself, no longer that of N, who, at the outset, spoke *for* HD. Or rather, their voices—without losing certain chronological overtones—merge into a single voice.

In other words, the tension between discourse and narrative resolves itself, in this work, into discourse—and, oddly enough, that of the past self.

This use of the *passé composé* and present in the chronological organization of the narrative must, of course, be compared with what exists in other narrative works of the eleventh through the thirteenth centuries. D. R. Sutherland and Tatiana Fotitch, in particular, have studied this question, the former from a general stand-point, the latter through a careful analysis of the use of tenses in the works of Chrétien de Troyes.[25] One point that emerges from these studies is the flexibility of Old French. Eleventh- and twelfth-century authors used several tenses alternatively in narrative passages. As Sutherland explains:

> Much of the vigour and directness of Old French narrative can be at-tributed to this variety in the use of tense; it serves not only to break the monotony of a recital of successive gestures, but also to give the audience a feeling of intimate connection with the action.[26]

This mixture of preterite and present seems to have constituted a technique used deliberately as a means of dramatization rather than for logical considerations, a technique obviously linked to oral tradition. Its main advantage lay in the fact that it allowed an author constantly to change his viewpoint.[27] It might be said that the medieval writer used tenses much as the contemporary film-maker uses camera lenses: with the preterite he maintained a certain distance, presented the past mainly as a spectacle, defined the chronological relationship between events; the *passé composé* allowed him to maintain a relationship between past and present,[28] to get a close-up of any given scene or event; the present added immediacy and intensity, giving the listeners the impression that they were personally taking part in the action.[29] The author (or *jongleur*) was of course free to use the resources afforded by this stylistic flexibility as he wished.

At the time the first part of the *Roman de la Rose* was written, however—c. 1240—the situation was already quite different: solitary reading was beginning to take the place of oral delivery; the dramatic (and flexible) use of tense was being replaced by a more regular and logical system.[30] The *Roman de la Rose* was certainly meant to be read: the story which the Narrator "rhymes" *(rime)*, "relates and tells" *(conte et dit)* is written: "ja ne m'est parece d'escrivre" (it is never wearisome for me to write; l. 3488). By and large, this work is not esthetically conservative; quite the contrary, the Narrator intends it to be innovative: "La matire est et bone et nueve" (The subject matter is good and new; l. 39). Comparison of the use of tenses here with that characteristic of the preceding period reveals several major differences. The *passé composé* and the present are not employed here simply to vary the point of view from which the story is presented. Neither are they used *systematically*, in the sense of having an unvarying, albeit intermittent, utilization throughout the work. Instead, they are used *progressively*: they gradually gain ground until they take over the text. If in the *chanson de geste*, as in the novels of Chrétien, the effect of shifts in tense is to change *our* perspective of the scene described, the most striking thing about the *Roman de la Rose* is that it is the *Narrator* who seems to see things differently. Thus employed, the present tense is not just a rhetorical or stylistic device, but rather, at least in appearance, the expression of an emotional attitude. (And here we find ourselves in that curious intermediary zone between narrative technique and the substance of narration itself.) An artistic illusion? How much of all this is purely rhetorical? Let us just say that this quadruple *I* remains, in the last analysis, a purely grammatical entity: verbal and pronominal. The anonymous, symbolic hero-narrator is always both present *and* absent. And whatever its grounding in autobiographical fact, the text is nothing more, from a thematic standpoint, than a splendid reworking of courtly topoi: courtly commonplaces. But this reworking—or *revivification*—is *so* lifelike, *so* moving that as sophisticated a reader as Poirion has taken the narrative seriously as autobiography:

> Guillaume seems to have been, himself, the victim of this somber magic, the magic of the Fountain. He died before he was able to finish the story, or rather, it is his own story that he has told, and he was not able to avoid the fate of Narcissus whose image haunted him. We see in this romance nothing more than a literary game. But who knows if the myth of Narcissus was not evoked precisely because it was, for the author, the truth of his existence?[31]

One last question—a major one—remains to be raised, if not answered. Is there, in this romance, a fifth voice, a fifth point of view, that of the "implicit author," to use Booth's expression?[32] And, as a corollary question, is the Narrator "trustworthy"? The separation between Narrator and author would reveal itself as follows: whereas N stresses the *authenticity* of his story, the author would have invented—"found" and fashioned—it for esthetic and moral purposes. Any irony to be found in the text would have to come from the author, for the Narrator, as I hope to have shown, adopts the attitudes and desires of HD (and RH). What of the Author, then? Does he approve or condemn HD—and RH or even N? Any such irony would be all the more devastating because the internal structure of the work is so intensely harmonious!

The critics who have read the *Roman de la Rose* in an ironic vein do not seem to have done so because the author makes his presence felt, since the latter, hidden behind the Narrator, is *extremely* unobtrusive. Their interpretation is apparently motivated rather by the fact that many of the aspects of love, as described in the work, are highly disturbing, so disturbing as to seem unacceptable. To mention a few: HD is let into the garden by Oiseuse (Idleness), a sinful conflation of the vices Sloth and Lust? Poverty and Old Age are excluded from the garden; Wealth and Hypocrisy are described as being essential to the lover; the fountain of love is known as the Fountain of Narcissus; the God of Love's commandments are imitated from (a parody of?) the Ten Commandments; HD brushes Reason aside, and so on. These details are indeed disturbing. It is debatable, however, whether they warrant interpretation such as the following, advanced by John V. Fleming in his *The Roman de la Rose*:

> The *Roman de la Rose* is ironic. It is the chronicle of a hero who is neither wise nor admirable, a young man who, overcome with carnal infatuation (Lechery, as the Middle english translation puts it), rejects Reason and embraces false courtesy, hypocrisy, and wicked counsel to achieve the sordid "heroism" of a seduction. His close friends and helpers include the most notorious old whore in medieval literature and a hypocritical friar of diabolically evil character. His sworn "enemy" (his word) is Reason, whom Guillaume de Lorris had called the "daughter of God" and who is obviously the close cousin of Lady Philosophy in the *Consolation of Philosophy*. The course of action which he follows in the poem is the typical path of sin as described by innumerable medieval psychologists. As Charles Dahlberg has shown, what happens in the *hortus deliciarum* of the Roman is essentially what happened in the Garden of Eden: Reason is overthrown by Passion, which has enslaved Amant.[33]

But, as Fleming himself is the first to point out,[34] such irony as there is here is *not* localized in the text, but stems rather from the latter's relationship with the historical context in its theological, literary, and iconographical aspects. One wonders, though, whether the moral and artistic context was as simple and as monolithic as Fleming would have us believe. The history of philosophy and literature—even within a given period—is surely that of a dialogue rather than a monologue. And the doctrine of "fin amors" was particularly apt to stir up controversy! Be this as it may, the reconstruction of an "intellectual climate" which would define, from without, the "meaning" of a work of art is an extremely delicate undertaking, one whose results cannot help but remain debatable.

Thus far I have refrained from analysing the *content* of the dream. But now let us have a look at a few of its more puzzling features. First of all, Oiseuse, who lets HD into the garden. I am far from convinced that Oiseuse is supposed to be thought of as sinful. We must remember that this work was not intended for a public of monks, but rather, in all probability, for noble, well-to-do, persons of leisure, a public which cultivated all of life's pleasure, including (and perhaps above all) love. In the eyes of such a public, could the leisurely life—in itself—have been thought of as "vicious," "sinful"? It seems most unlikely!

Insofar as the "Fountain of Narcissus" is concerned, there is nothing to indicate that Guillaume interpreted this Ovidian personage as a symbol of what is known today as "narcissism." Here is the ending of the story of Narcissus, as carved in the fountain:

> Car quant il vit qu'il ne porroit
> accomplir ce qu'il desiroit
> et qu'il estoit si pris par fort
> qu'il ne porroit avoir confort
> en nule fin ne en nul sens,
> il perdi d'ire tot le sens
> et fu morz en poi de termine.
> Ensi si out de la meschine
> qu'il avoit devant escondite
> son guerredon et sa merite.
> Dames, cest essample aprenez,
> qui vers vos amis mesprenez;
> car se vos les lessiez morir,
> Dex le vos savra bien merir. (ll. 1495–1508)

> For when he saw that he could not
> accomplish what he desired
> and that he was so strongly caught

that he could have no comfort
ever, in any sense,
he lost his mind from fury
and died shortly thereafter.
Thus he had, from the girl
he had previously refused,
his reward and his just deserts.
Ladies, take this as a lesson,
you who treat your lovers badly;
for if you let them die,
God will know how to make you pay.

The tragedy of Narcissus, according to Guillaume—the cause of his despair and death—is not his self-infatuation, but rather his inability to *possess* himself, to consummate his love. This love, made "tragic" by the fact that it is, quite literally, impossible, is Narcissus's punishment for having spurned the advances of Echo.

And finally, the fact that HD gives Reason the brush-off: to say that "passionate" love is "unreasoning" is a tautology, not a condemnation. At the very most, it is a recognition—such as one also finds in the works of Béroul, Thomas, Marie de France, Chrétien, and in *Aucassin et Nicolette*—of one of the negative aspects of love. All these authors are very much aware of the madness, the selfishness (on the part of the individual and of the couple)—indeed the idolatry, the irreligion, the perversity—that are part and parcel of love. But this did not prevent them from siding to varying degrees with their love-stricken heros and heroines. Like Guillaume de Lorris, they seem to have recognized the beauty and the power of Love.

Let's not yield to the typically modern temptation to see irony everywhere—and to judge the quality of a literary work on this basis.[35] And let's conclude, quite simply, that within a genre as readily and as naturally ironical as autobiography, Guillaume de Lorris's *Roman de la Rose* constitutes a strange and a profoundly medieval case. Despite the multiplicity of *I*'s, and the varying points of view, this work, far from being torn apart by irony, remains intensely harmonious and unified. Analytical in its allegory and in its representation of the world, the *Roman de la Rose* tends unfailingly, in its overall message, toward a profoundly moving synthesis.

NOTES

1. "Le discours exclura l'aoriste, mais le récit historique, qui l'emploie constamment, n'en retiendra que les formes de 3e personne," *Problèmes de linquistique générale* (Paris: Gallimard, 1966), 244; my translation.
2. See, e.g., Robert Scholes and Robert Kellogg, *The Nature of Narrative* (Oxford: Oxford University Press, 1966), 240.
3. Stephen A. Shapiro, "The Dark Continent of Literature," *Comparative Literature Studies* 5, no. 4 (December 1968): 437.
4. Augustine's *Confessions* was, of course, its illustrious, and unique, predecessor.
5. Shapiro, 423–25.
6. *Inventio* is that part of rhetoric that deals with the "finding" of the subject matter, and of things to say about it; *dispositio* deals with the organization and order of presentation of what is said.
7. Quotations are from the Félix Lecoy edition in the classiques français du moyen âge edition (Paris: Champion, 1965). The English translations are mine. I apologize for their occasional flat-footedness, but my primary desire here is to stay close to the French. For general reading purposes, I recommend Harry W. Robbins's translation, *The Romance of the Rose* (New York: Dutton, 1962), available in paperback.
8. Scholes and Kellogg, 84.
9. Paul Strohm has isolated quite distinctly these two identities, and his remarks are highly interesting:

   Since the Lover of the dream is an imaginative projection of the Narrator, readers have tended to identify the two points of view. This identification oversimplifies the relation of Guillaume the Narrator and Guillaume the Lover. Although the Narrator often adopts the point of view of the Lover, many of his comments are based on a wider perspective of the events of the dream than the Lover can possibly have. The most obvious assertion of this wider perspective is purely visual; the reader sometimes looks at the Lover through the Narrator's eyes.

   ("Guillaume as Narrator and Lover in the *Roman de la Rose*," *Romanic Review* 59, no. 1 (1968): 3–9; citation p. 4.)
10. That is, dealing with ongoing or repeated acts.
11. C. S. Lewis, in his *The Allegory of Love* (Oxford: Oxford University Press, 1936), p. 118 of the 1958 printing, stated that: "The whole poem is in the first person and we look through the lover's eyes, not at him." We hope to prove (as Strohm had already begun to do) that even though the hero is not presented, visually or psychologically, from a completely outside point of view, his viewpoint does not merge so simply with that of the narrator.
12. I will also refer to this tense as the preterite.
13. Cf. A. J. Greimas, *Dictionnaire de l'ancien français* (Paris: Larousse, 1968), 348; R. Grandsaignes d'Hauterive, *Dictionnaire d'ancien français* (Paris: Larousse, 1947), 369.
14. Even in Old French—as flexible and as complex as was the use of tenses in this period. We shall deal with this problem later on.
15. This name is, admittedly, debatable. It is, at least, convenient.
16. Mes ja mes n'oroiz mielz descrivre

> la verité de la matere
> quant j'avré apost le mistere.
> (ll. 2071–74)

17. ". . . dont les conéquences durent encore": Lucien Foulet, *Petite syntaxe de l'ancien français* (Paris: Champion, 1968), 228; my translation.
18. This technique which is constantly calling our attention to the time in which the narrative itself is embedded—and our literary "experience"—is similar to that used in the *chanson de queste*.
19. Cf. Peter Haidu, *Aesthetic Distance in Chrétien de Troyes: Irony and comedy in Cligés and Perceval* Geneva: Droz, 1968), in particular, p. 263.
20. ". . . réunion congrue de voix différentes"—according to the definition in the ninth-century *Musica Enchiriadis:* "Harmonia est diversarum vocum apta coadunatio." Quoted by Jacques Chailley, *Histoire musicale du moyen âge* (Paris: Publications Universitaires de France, 1969), 69–70.
21. It might perhaps be objected that such sentences are implicit indirect quotes from HD's inner monologue. Who could maintain, though, that the following two sentences have the same stylistic impact: "She was beautiful" and "He found her beautiful"?
22. In the case of Gide, this "marriage" of present and past is typical only of the descriptions, not of the narrative passages.
23. For the Virgin Mary, see John Fleming, *The Roman de la Rose* (Princeton: Princeton University Press, 1969), 101; for Dame Raison, Lewis, 122.
24. Vv. 0–1000—51: 0–500—0
        500–1000—51
    1000–2000—108
    2000–3000—815
    3000–4028—445
25. D. R. Sutherland, "On the Use of Tenses in Old and Middle French," in *Studies in French Language and Medieval Literature Presented to Professor Mildred K. Pope,* by pupils, colleagues and friends, (Manchester: Manchester University Press, 1939), 329–37; Tatiana Fotitch, *The Narrative Tenses in Chrétien de Troyes* (Washington, D.C.: Catholic University of America, 1950).
26. Sutherland, 330.
27. Ibid., 330–31.
28. Ibid., 331; Fotitch, 27, especially 65–70.
29. See Fotitch, 6–27.
30. Sutherland, 221–332; Chrétien's use of tenses is distinctly more "logical" and more systematic than that of the author-performers of the early *chansons de geste.* And, of course, his works are no longer oral in the sense of being "sung" or even "recited from memory."
31. Guillaume semble bien avoir été lui-même victime de cette sombre magie, la magie de la Fontaine. Il est mort avant d'avoir pu finir son récit, ou plutôt, c'est sa propre expérience qu'il a racontée, et il n'a pu éviter le destin de Narcisse dont l'image le hantait. Nous ne voyons plus dans ce roman que jeu littéraire. Mais qui sait si le mythe n'était pas évoqué justement parce qu'il était, pour l'auteur, la vérité de son existence?

Daniel Poirion, "Narcisse et Pygmalion dans le *Roman de la Rose,* in *Essays in Honor of Louis Francis Solano,* ed. Raymond J. Cormier and Urban T. Holmes (Chapel Hill, N.C.: University of North Carolina Press, 1970), 153–65; the passage quoted is on p. 162; my translation. It might be added that such an interpretation presupposes that the identity of the Narrator coincides exactly with that of Guillaume de Lorris . . .

32. Wayne C. Booth, *The Rhetoric of Fiction* (Chicago: University of Chicago Press, 1961), 71.

33. Fleming, 50. Fleming considers the two parts of the *Roman de la Rose* as forming a coherent whole.

34. Ibid., 109–10. His point remains the same in *Reason and the Lover* (Princeton: Princeton University Press, 1984), reviewed by me in *Modern Language Quarterly*, July 1985.

35. See Booth, 367–74, for a very interesting discussion of this problem. As one of my colleagues put it recently: "Soon they are going to tell us that the *Divina Comedia* is essentially ironic, because 'surely Dante doesn't expect us to take seriously that old windbag, Beatrice?'!"

CHAPTER 3

Inside/Outside: Guillaume's *Roman de la Rose* and Medieval Selfhood

Voyages, wanderings, quests, pilgrimages—spatial displacements—
provide both subject matter and structural elements in many a
medieval narrative. The space involved generally has a strong symbolic component. But one of the most curious uses of spatial imagery—especially of dichotomies between inside and outside, opened
and closed—is to express structures of the self. In these pages I will
return to Guillaume de Lorris's *Roman de la Rose*—a work that is
nothing less than obsessed by these dichotomies—in order to look
at the various aspects and levels of the text that are structured by
these oppositions. Not only do such antitheses occur constantly;
more importantly, they give to the work a central structural element. And there is a great deal at stake in the way in which these
antitheses are set up and invested with content and meaning, as
well as in the way they correspond to the subject/object dichotomy,
so central to modern narrative analysis (among other things). At
stake is the very notion of the subject, and of interiority, desire, and
the relation to others.

In the *Roman de la Rose*, space is never merely literal or physical,
but is immediately symbolic and significant, by the very fact that
this is an allegorical narrative, the story of the hero's passage in a
dream through a sort of *pays du tendre*.

The hero, having risen (in the dream) from his bed, leaves the town, and following a clear stream comes upon a garden "tot clos de haut mur bataillié" (all enclosed with a high, battlemented wall).[1] On the outside are painted images of those who may not enter. The narrator tells us:

Quant j'oï les oisiaus chanter,
former me pris a dementer
par quel art ne par quel engin
je porroie entrer el jardin.
Mes je ne poi onques trover
leu par ou je peűse entrer,
si sachiez que je ne savoie
s'il i avoit pertuis ne voie
ne leu par ou l'en i entrast;
ne hom nez qui le me mostrast
n'iert ilec, que j'estoie seus.
Destroiz fui et mout engoiseus,
tant qu'au derrean me sovint
c'onques en nul sens ce n'avint
qu'en si biau vergier n'eűst huit
ou eschiele ou quelque pertuis.
Lors m'en alai grant aleűre,
acernant la compasseűre
et la cloison dou mur querré
tant c'un huisset mout bien serré
trovai, petitet et estroit.
Par autre leu nus n'i entroit.
A l'uis comançai a ferir
qu'autre entrée n'i soi querir.
Assez i feri et bouté,
et par maintes foiz escouté
se j'oroie venir nule ame.
Le guichoit, qui estoit de charme,
adonc m'ovri une pucele, . . . (ll. 495–523)

When I heard the birds sing
I began to torment myself to find
by what art or use
I could enter the garden.
But I could never find
an opening by which I could enter,
know that I did not know
if there were a gate or a passageway

or a place where one could enter;
no man who could show me one
was there, for I was alone.
I was distraught and full of anguish,
until finally I remembered
that it never happened
that in such a beautiful garden there was not a door
or a ladder or some opening.
Then I went off quickly
examining the circumference of the garden
and I looked over the points of closure of the wall
so long that finally a very narrow little gate
I found, one that was small and tight.
By no other passageway could anyone get in.
I began to beat at the door,
for I did not know how to find any other entry-way.
I beat and pounded a great deal,
and several times listened to see
if I could hear anyone coming.
The wicket, which was made of hornbeam wood
Was then opened for me by a young lady . . .

I will try to refrain from quoting so extensively in general, but it
is important to recognize just how dense this language of enclosure
is in the *Rose*, and just how anxious the hero is to enter this and
other infinitely appealing places. The frequency of words referring
to small apertures is, in particular, very striking, even in light of
medieval writers' predilection for repetition and tautology. In the
space of twenty-five lines—from 499 to 523—there are thirteen
such references:

> *leu* (meaning here not "place" but "opening")—3
> *huis/ uis/ huisset* (door, little door)—3
> *pertuis* (hole, passage-way)—2
> *voie* (path)—1
> *eschiele* (ladder)—1
> *quichoit* (little door, wicket)—1

This entire passage consists of nothing but a virtually obsessive
repetition of words of entry. And in its insistence on inclusion as
the hero's major concern, the passage prefigures the entire *Rose*.
From now on in this work all spaces encountered by the hero will
be enclosures, and his reaction to them will prove to be a constant:
a desire to *enter*; he never wants *out*.

Here is a schematic summary of his entries into closed spaces in the first 2,000 lines:

The hero is admitted into the "garden" ("vergier") by Idleness (Oiseuse).

He enters the "small retreat" ("réduit") where Pleasure (Déduit) and his company are enjoying themselves, by following a "little path" ("une petite sente"; ll. 713–16).

Once in the retreat, he is invited by Courtesy to join the caroling with the other dancers.

He then goes to a "secluded spot" ("destor") where, "within a marble stone" ("Dedenz une piere de mabre") he sees the Fountain of Narcissus (ll. 1424–40).

"In" ("dedenz") the fountain he sees reflected a rose garden, it too "in a plot enclosed by a hedge" ("en un destor d'une haie bien clos"; ll. 1513; 1615–16).

Inside the rose garden, he sees a particularly appealing rose that he wants to pluck. First serious obstacle to his desire—the rose has a wall of thorns and spines to protect her.

In short: in/in/in/in/in—then an obstacle.

If I lay such heavy stress on these entries into enclosures, it is not to make the obvious point that a hero has to get (in) someplace before he can do something, but, rather, to make it clear that this one does nothing *but* enter. This is not so much a story of heroic actions as of the protagonist's inclusion into and (soon) exclusion from desirable places. In fact, this novel is almost entirely composed of: (1) acts of entering, being refused entry; finding obstacles to entry, and being expelled, (2) expressions of the hero's dismay at being outside, or of his joy at being inside, and (3) conversations of various kinds—frequently dealing with the hero's request that he be allowed in someplace.

Aside from going in and being forced out, this hero never *does* anything except kiss the rose—once. Or perhaps I should say that in Guillaume's work the heroic quest is divested of all its elements save one: an essential aspiration toward some crucial point or goal: the "end" of desire. In any case the events of this story consist primarily of things done *to* the hero—acts that he undergoes and to which he reacts—rather than actions that *he* performs.

But two facts concern us here: once the hero is fully in love, he is ever more anxious to enter the enclosures that present themselves to him; and as the story progresses the in/in/in/in pattern that we saw earlier is replaced by an in/out/in/out (or in/obstacle/in/obstacle) alternation: *In:* Fair Welcome invites the Hero into the rose garden, past the prickly hedge. *Out:* "Danger" throws him out. *In:* Once again "within the close" after flattering Danger. *Out:* He had the temerity to kiss the rosebud and is forced to leave the rose garden.

The lover is now back in the main part of the garden. But this garden, which was so recently the *inside* within which the lover desired passionately to be, and which he saw as the locus of all bliss, as "an earthly paradise" (634), is now the *outside*, is "hell" (3775). Paradise now is the rose bed. In other words, there is now a new "inside," for this concept is not permanently fixed but relative: in this work the inside is there where one wants to be at any given moment. Not only can one be expelled from a place of bliss (our hero never gets to be there for very long), but there is another reason why he is never at rest: as soon as the hero gets inside something, he discovers that he is, at the same time, outside something new; that is, he discovers that he wants to be *further* in. First it was the garden, then a series of retreats and secluded spots within the garden; then the rose garden, and then the rose inside its private hedge of thorns. And now Fear, Danger, and so forth, raise a fortress to protect the Rose and Fair Welcome from the lover, to close him out. Jealousy declares that she wants to build a garrison in order to protect Chastity, and "to build a new wall to enclose the rosebushes and the roses; I will no longer leave them displayed" ("por ce feré de noveil mur/ cloire les rosiers et les roses;/ nes lerai plus issi descloses"; ll. 3591–93). As the story ends—abruptly, and we are told, unintentionally[2]—the lover weeps outside the *new* wall: "But I who am outside the wall, am given over to grief and pain" ("Mais je, qui sui dehors le mur,/ sui livrez a duel et a poine"; ll. 3920–21). Once again, he weeps at the pain of his exclusion from paradise.

Thus far we have been focusing on the hero as the subject of this dream, as the subject of these verbs of entry (and attempted penetration); but he is also himself a penetrable object or space. Even as the hero seeks to enter more deeply into love's garden, Love is stalking him. Love shoots him with an arrow—the first of five—named Beauty. Following the standard medieval trajectory, the arrow goes through the lover's eye into his heart. After fainting initially ("Li cuers me faut, li cuers me ment"; My heart fails, my heart lets me down; l. 1699), the lover regains consciousness and is able to pull out the shaft of the arrow. The tip, however, cannot be removed and is still stuck in his heart (". . . ele n'en pot estre esrachiee, ançois remest encor dedens;" ll. 1716–17). The lover's heart is thus itself an enclosure that is suddenly attacked and penetrated by a new and devastating—almost fatal—experience: love. There is then a curious symmetry between his penetration of the garden, and love's penetration of him.

Now, in a very interesting scene, the lover becomes the vassal of Love. In a curiously eroticized version of the traditional feudal gesture, he kisses Love:

> Atant devins ses hom mains jointes,
> et sachiez que mout me fis cointes
> dont sa bouche baisa la moie:
> ce fu ce dont j'oi greignor joie. (ll. 1953–56)

> Then I became his man, with hands joined together;
> know that it was very delightful to me
> that his mouth kissed mine:
> that is what gave me the greatest joy.

Love then asks his new vassal for hostages (as is customary), and this is the lover's reply:

> —Sire, fis je, or m'entendez:
> ne sai por quoi vos demandez
> plege de moi ne seürté.
> Ja savez vos de verité
> que mon cuer m'avez si toloit
> et si pris que, s'il bien vouloit,
> ne puet il fere rien por moi,
> se ce n'estoit par vostre estroi.
> Le cuers est vostres, non pas miens,
> car il covient, soit maus soit biens,
> que il face vostre pleisir,
> nus ne vos en puet desaisir.
> Tele garde i avez vos mise
> qui le garde bien a devise;
> et, par tot ce, se rien doutez,
> fetes i clef, si l'emportez,
> et la clef soit en leu d'outages.

—Par mon chief, ce n'est mie outrages,
respont Amors, je m'i acors.
Il est assez sire dou cors
qui a le cuer en sa comande:
outrages est, qui plus demande."
Lors a de s'aumouniere treite
une petite clef bien feite,
qui fu de fin or esmeré:
"A ceste, dit il, fermeré
ton cuer, ne quier autre apoal.
Soz ceste clef sont mi joal,
si te di verité sus m'ame
que ele est de mon escrin dame,
et si a mout grant poesté."
Lors la me toucha au costé
et ferma mon cuer si souef
qu'a grant poine senti la clef. (ll. 1975–2008)

"Sire," I said, "Listen to me:
I do not know why you ask of me
a pledge or security.
You know in truth
that you have so taken my heart from me
and so captured it, that even if it wished
it couldn't do anything for me,
unless it had your permission.
The heart is yours, not mine
for it has agreed, for good or ill,
to do your pleasure,
no one can take it from you.
You have put so careful a warden over it
that it is well guarded;
and for this reason, if you have any fear,
make a key, and take the heart away,
and let the key stand as a hostage."
"By my head, that isn't an outrageous idea,"
replies Love. "I agree.
He is master of the body
Who has the heart under its command:
it would be an outrage to ask for more."
Then he [has] pulled from his alms-purse
a little well-made key,
which was made of pure fine gold:

"With this," he said, "I will close up
your heart, I seek no other pledge.
Under this key are my jewels,
I tell you the truth, on my soul,
this key is the mistress of my coffer
and has very great power."
then he touched me on the side
and closed my heart so gently
that I barely felt the key.

What interests us in this scene is the notion of what is inside. The lover's heart is, anatomically and psychologically, in him. Strictly speaking, Love has not "stolen it away," but the lover's heart has become inaccessible to him: it has been taken over—locked up— by Love and is no longer his. His heart, though not actually removed from his breast, is henceforth under lock and key in Love's treasury: one of his "jewels."

Now and henceforth love is "enclosed" within the lover's heart. As he says to Fair Welcome: "j'ai dedenz le cuer enclouse une mout pesant maladie" (I have, enclosed within my heart, a very heavy malady; ll. 2870–73). This love cannot escape; it is trapped inside. The lover cannot cure himself or be cured from this illness. His heart, being locked up, is protected from any new intrusion and from any possible antidote: thus when Reason tries (what else?) to reason with the lover, to talk him out of loving the rosebud, and to make him love *her*, her little sermon is angrily rejected.

The lover is told by Love that he must not speak or "uncover" his heart openly, but only to one person, and to someone discreet, who will in turn keep hidden what he has learned. The lover follows Love's guidance, seeks out "Friend" and to him alone does he disclose his grief: all that was "nailed shut within" (encloé) his heart. Or rather to Friend and to us: for since, according to the narrator, he and the hero are one and the same, his story is itself a disclosure —an allegorically discreet opening up of the secrets of his heart to his sympathetic listeners.

Thus the language of space—of penetrated enclosures and of disclosure—provides, even at the simplest level of the plot, a major element in this work. This dichotomy is a structural element in the work, in that the opposition between its two terms provides a form that can be repeated in many ways and used to express many different things. We have just seen this dichotomy applied to the lover's anatomical and psychological insides. His heart can be penetrated by arrows sent in from the outside; it can be invaded and conquered. Earlier we saw the dichotomy applied to the spaces within the garden. A third domain for which the language of enclosure and of space is significant is the concept of knowledge, of truth. The crystals in the Fountain of Narcissus are described thus:

> Si est cil cristaus merveilleus,
> une tel force a que li leus,
> arbres et flors, et quant qu'aorne
> le vergier, i pert tot a orne.
> Et por la chose feire entendre
> un essample vos voil aprendre:
> aussi con li mireors montre
> les choses qui sont a l'encontre
> et i voit l'en sans coverture
> et lor color et lor figure
> tot autre si vos dis poir voir
> que li cristaus sanz decevoir
> tot l'estre dou vergier encuse
> a celui qui en l'eve muse;
> car torjors, quel que part qu' il soit,
> l'une moitié dou vergier voit;
> et c'il se torne, maintenant
> porra veoir le remenant;
> si n'i a si petite chose,
> Tant soit reposte de enclouse,
> dont demontrance ne soit feite
> com s'ele ert ou cristal portrete. (ll. 1547–68)

> This crystal is so marvelous
> and it has so much power that the place,
> trees and flowers, and everything that adorns
> the garden, appears, in it, right in its proper place.
> And to make the thing more clearly understood,
> I want to give you an example:
> just as a mirror shows
> the things that are opposite it;
> and one sees in a mirror, unveiled [uncovered],
> their color and appearance,
> in the same way, I tell you truly,
> the crystal, without any deceit,

shows forth the entire being of the garden
to anyone who looks in the water;
for always, wherever he may be in the garden
he can see one half of it;
and if he turns, now
he will be able to see the rest;
there isn't in it anything, however small,
however hidden or enclosed it may be,
that isn't brought out in the open [demonstrated]
just as if it were portrayed on the crystal.

The crystal is thus a mirror: everything that faces it is seen "un-
covered" ("sans coverture"); the entire garden is "shown" ("en-
cusé") in it. Everything, no matter how "hidden" or "enclosed," is
"demonstrated" and "portrayed" upon the crystal rock. The exact
meaning of the controversial crystal need not concern us here; what
is of interest is that the language used to describe what it, as a
mirror, does is that of revelation or disclosure. Mirrors uncover
things that before were hidden, unseen, or unappreciated for what
they really were. Until now, the lover had not perceived how "lovable" were the objects surrounding him. Such a discovery effects a
radical transfiguration in him, beholding such a spectacle; indeed
he will never be the same again:

Qui en ce miroẽr se mire
ne puet avoir garant ne mire
que il tel chose as ieuz ne voit
qui d' amors l'a mis tost en voie. . . .
Ci sort as genz noveile rage
ici se changent li corage,
ci n'a mestier sens ne mesure,
ci est d'amer volenté pure,
ci ne se set conseiller nus. (ll. 1573–85)

He who looks in this mirror
can never have any guarantee, any doctor,
against seeing something with his eyes,
that puts his right away on love's path. . . .
Here a new madness befalls people,
here hearts are changed,
here sense and moderation hold no sway,
here is the pure desire to love
here no one can take counsel.

But dreams, and this story itself, are also presented as mirrors that disclose a hidden meaning. The work begins with a discussion of the nature of dreams:

Aucunes genz dient qu'en songes
n'a se fables non et mençonges;
mes l'en puet tex songes songier
qui ne sont mie mençongier,
ainz sont après bien aparant,
si en puis bien traire a garant
un auctor qui ot non Macrobes,
qui ne tint pas songes a lobes,
ançois escrit l'avision
qui avint au roi Scypion.
Qui c'onques cuit ne qui que die
qu'il est folor et musardie
de croire que songe aviegne,
qui se voudra, par fol m'en tiegne,
quar endroit moi ai ge fiance
que songes est senfiance
des biens as genz et des anniz,
que li plusor songent de nuiz
maintes choses covertement
que l'en voit puis apertement. (ll. 1–20)

Some people say that in dreams
there is nothing but fables and lies;
but one can dream dreams
that are not lies at all,
but that afterwards come true [are apparent]
and to guarantee the truth of my words,
I can call an author [authority] named Macrobius,
who did not hold dreams to be just jokes,
but wrote about the dream vision
that happened to King Scipio.
He who believes or says
that it is foolish or stupid
to believe that a dream can happen,
if he wants to, he can think I am a fool,
for as for me I believe
that a dream has meaning
about the good and evil that happen to people,
and that many people dream at night
all sorts of things in a covert way
that afterwards are seen openly.

And, according to the narrator, the dream *he* had was no "joke." It had hidden meaning, in that it referred, in a veiled fashion, to things that were true, would happen in reality. After the dream, in real life, he too saw the things "openly" (apertement) that had had seen "closed" (covertement) in his dream.

> et vi un songe en mon dormant
> qui mout fu biaus et mout me plot;
> mes en ce songes onques rien n'ot
> qui treto avenu ne soit
> si con li songes recensoit. (ll. 26–30)

> and I saw a dream while I was sleeping
> that was very beautiful and pleased me greatly;
> but in this dream there was nothing
> that didn't happen soon
> just as the dream described it.

What we are reading, then, is the *closed* version of the narrator's love experience. After presenting his descriptions of the Fountain of Narcissus, he says:

> Mes je mes m'oroiz mielz descrivre
> la verité de la matere,
> quant j'avré apost le mistere. (ll. 1598–1600)

> But never will you have heard better explained
> the truth of the matter,
> than when I have opened up the mystery.

He is going to "open up," "expose," the mysteries of this place to us. And the narrator assures us that, at the end of the dream (and text):

> La verité, qui est coverte,
> vos sera lores toute overte
> quant espondre m'oroiz le songe,
> car il n'i a mot de mençonge. (ll. 2071–74)

> The truth, which is covered,
> will then be all opened to you,
> when you have heard me expound the dream,
> for there is not a false word in it.

The story we are reading (like the dream itself) is a "mystery" (mistere), a "hidden truth" (vérité . . . coverte) which Guillaume promises to "expound" and "open" for us. That he never got around to completing this exegesis is irrelevant here; what is important is the fact that Guillaume presents his text as a closed one, one needing and deserving to be opened up.

The reader's experience of the events recounted in this work—like that of the hero—also has an important spatial dimension. He too is to find here his initiation into the art of love. After the God of Love has delivered his Ten (give or take one) Commandments to the lover, the narrator asserts:

Li dieux a'Amors lors m'encharja,
tot issi com vos oroiz ja,
mot a mot ses commandemenz.
Bien les devise cist romanz;
qui amer veut, or i entende,
que li romanz des or amende,
Des or le fet bon escouter,
s'il est qui le sache conter,
car la fin dou songe est mout bele
et la matiere en est novele.
Qui dou songe la fin ora,
je vos di bien que il porra
des jeux d'Amors assez aprendre,
puis que il veille tant atendre
que je die et que j'encomance
dou songe la senefiance.   (ll. 2055–70)

The god of Love then gave me his charge,
just as you will hear now,
word for word his commandments.
This romance lays them out well;
he who wants to love, let him listen well,
for the story is about to get better.
From now on it's good to listen,
and the the story-teller knows his business,
for the end of the dream is very beautiful
and the subject matter is new.
He who hears the end of the dream,
I tell you truly that he will be able
to learn a lot about the game of love,
if he is willing to wait

for me to begin telling
the significance of the dream.

The narrator assumes a reader who "wants to love" *("qui amer veut")*. And as he is addressing us (as *"vos"* [you]) all through the course of the work, he continually makes us aware of the passage of time in our experience of this narrative by reminding us of what we have already heard and learned, and by suggesting what is yet to come. This is of course a common medieval technique. In Chrétien de Troyes, it shows his connection to the oral tradition; but by the time Guillaume is using it, this device is largely anachronistic, and is used intentionally: to express something. The narrator has structured his presentation so that our experience of the events parallels that of the hero. One important detail of this parallel is the narrator's insistence that we also must wait until the "dream's end" in order to understand its meaning. That is, when the hero has finally understood the meaning of what has happened to him, then the *Roman de la Rose*, "in which the art of love is all enclosed," will be opened to us as well (or we will now be in it).

The commentary or "expounding" that the narrator promises is surely to be taken less as a true allegorical exegesis than as a sort of poetic unveiling, a device by which the nature of our experience of this work is brought into full harmony with the narrative structure of the story and with the message contained within that story. That is one of the most original features of Guillaume's use of the allegorical mode, traditionally applied to sacred texts. He has made this symbolic language, with its dichotomy between open and closed speech, function in a truly poetic—and not simply didactic—way: it reenforces the essential theme of the work, and the reader's experience echoes that of the lover.

Spatial structures in the *Roman de la Rose* are thus applied to several different domains of narrative and poetic reality, and there is a real coherence in their use. Nothing here is, of itself, open: everything—at least everything of value—is and should remain closed off. Indeed things here are of value partly for the very reason that they *are* closed:

• The garden from which so many are clearly excluded (for example, the poor, the old, and so forth)

- The rosebushes surrounded by a hedge "si comme il durent" (just as they should be) (2764)
- The rosebud, of which/whom the narrator says:

La rose auques s'eslargissoit
par amont, si m'abellissoit
ce qu'el n'iere pas si overte
que la graine fust descovierte;
ençois estoit encor enclose
entre les fueilles de la rose
qui amont droites se levoient
et la place dedenz emploient,
si ne pooit paroir la graine
por la rose qui estoit pleine. (ll. 3343–52)

The rose was getting a little larger
on the top, but it pleased me
that it [she] wasn't so far open
that the seeds showed;
rather it was still closed up
within the leaves of the rose
which stood straight up
and enfolded the place within,
so that the seeds were not visible
though the rose was full of them.

The lover has chosen a bud that was closed, and he is happy that although it has grown and is flourishing, it is not too "open" (overte), but rather is still enclosed within the walls of its leaves.
- The lover's heart, which Love locks up and takes as his hostage. The emprisoned heart is a symbol of the lover's fidelity to Love. This "locking up" of the lover's heart is a concrete representation of the value placed upon fidelity (and chastity) in this period: fidelity means that your heart and mind are open only to him who has the key, and are locked up to all others.
- The garden's true beauty, the dream, the book's meaning: they too are all closed.

What is represented here—at every level of experience—is the passionate process of initiation into mystery. I will return later to the concept of initiation that is implicit here, and to the erotic quality of the mysteries involved. But for the moment let us merely note that although there is in this work a great deal of *entering*, through some sort of opening, there is not really any opening *outward*, any opening *up:* walls are never razed, doors are never to be left open. There is only the penetration, by the elect, into enclosed spaces, which are then sealed off again. It is Jean de Meung who opens this work out onto the world: the walled garden imagery largely disappears, the tower is torn down. In more fundamental ways as well Jean breaks out of the narrow confines of courtly literature.

And let us note here that, although there is much *entry*, there is very little true *arrival;* one never has the feeling that one has gotten in far *enough.*

In this text we have, then, a first-person, or "autobiographical" narrative, in which the inside/outside dichotomy plays a major role. It is the nature of the relationship between this first person—the "I" of the text—and this dichotomy that will now concern us. Jacques Ehrmann, in his "Le Dedans et le dehors," asserted that the terms of the inside/outside opposition could provide a major axis to which other important dichotomies, such as that of subject/object, could be linked.[3] He then offered a definition of the traditional *récit,* or first-person narrative:

> The traditional narrative *[récit]* being the story of an interiority, or the story being the narrative of an interiority, it is they [the narrative, the story] that give body to the subjectivity, and allow the "I" or the "we" to be pronounced. To speak in the first person thus presupposes that the subject perceives himself as the origin and end of the story and also, of course, of the language that allows him to tell it. Such limits separate him radically from that which is not he, that is, from that which is other, different . . . outside, and which he necessarily treats as object. (P. 35)

He goes on to say:

> One is always reminded of what appears to be the fundamental element of the narrative, namely, "the expression of a subject," which, by the simple fact that he relates, "brings back" and "ex-perience," brings an outside (object) back to an inside (subject); the outside providing, precisely, the subject of the tale. (P. 37)

Ehrmann's definition of the *récit* makes several major assumptions, and is in fact a complex hypothesis. It asserts that the "I" of the narrative corresponds to the notion of a "subject"—the subject being conceived not merely grammatically but also semantically: thus the "I" is the primary mover of the verb of the text. Moreover, this "I" is the actor not only within the story (as hero), but also in the very telling of the story (as narrator); the story is, thus, *doubly* "his." In other words, the "Subject" as Ehrmann defines him here combines the Greimasian notion of the Subject with the Jakobsonian *Destinateur* or Sender of a message. Finally, Ehrmann relates this "I"—this Subject—to the notion, or structure, of "inside," whereas that with which (or those with whom) this "I" comes into contact, upon which he acts, are the "other(s)" and the "outside." (I should add that Ehrmann's hypothesis is all the more complex in that it is ironic: he distances himself from the system that he is describing: the "traditional *récit*." There is nothing normative about his definition: he is not saying that this is the way things *should* be.)

In general I believe that this representation of the "traditional (modern) tale" is accurate; I will postulate, here, its validity. In any case, I take up this model not merely because I think it is true of the sort of *récit* in question, but because I think that, in a strange sense, it is truer still of those metatexts that are the modern theories of narrative themselves. That is, I consider that the dichotomies that Ehrmann sees as lying at the heart of the modern tale also lie —and still more deeply—at the heart of most modern theories of narrative in general. Ehrmann has expressed (often in ironic terms) the essence of what a wide variety of modern narratologists, from Propp to Greimas, Campbell to Frye, have declared—seriously, unironically—and generally assumed, about literature, and about the self, or soul, for what we are seeing articulated through many of these theories is not merely a reflection of the reality of texts, or a theory of literature, but a particular view of human psychology; in fact, an ideology. All of these theorists demonstrate an extreme interest in heroic literature—to the point where they have held out heroic stories and myths as providing the basic model for all storytelling (all *récits*). And when these theories speak of the hero (or subject), they are all concerned with his "departure" and "return" as well as with his "*ex*-periences"—with what he does "out there." This departure and return are often interpreted—here I am thinking of Campbell and of psychologists like Jung—psychically and culturally as well as literally, literarily. Now I am not denying that some literary heroes do go out and then come back; but I believe that the extreme emphasis on these goings and comings is a modern phenomenon, one which corresponds very significantly to the rise in interest in the "ego" and the "self."[4] The hero is ego incarnate; we have superself and superman. The soul is now a Subject, and the Subject (whether male or female) is a *Mensch*. This view of human psychology and destiny—of man and his end—which can be found in much modern narrative, and which is shared by many contemporary narratologists and psychologists (especially the "ego psychologists") may or may not be true;[5] that does not concern us for the moment. What does concern us is, first, the fact that this image of the self, of the individual psyche, that they share allows, indeed encourages, a theoretical correlation between the literary "I," the "subject," and the "inside." Second, it is crucial to recognize (and I will attempt to demonstrate) that medieval writers, theologians, historians, and so forth would not in general have shared either this view or the consequent correlation.

I am well aware that in recent years, and especially in France, the entire notion of the subject has been under discussion—indeed under heavy fire from various quarters. As Peter Caws has put it: "There have been repeated attempts in this century to exorcise literature, and some of them have involved attempts to exorcise the subject as well."[6] At any rate, if many European psycholoanalysts are acting as though the subject has been satisfactorily blown to bits, most narratologists just have not *noticed*. And this is my reproach: not that they disagree with the recent efforts to atomize the subject—they have every right to disagree—but that they themselves have remained oblivious to serious reflection about the nature of this mysterious entity, and that their theories and models have therefore remained all too often naive and superficial where the subject was concerned.

Ehrmann clearly associated the dichotomies of inside/outside and subject/object—indeed first-person narrative itself—with modernity. But the *Roman de la Rose* is a medieval first-person narrative where the inside/outside dichotomy plays a major role. We thus have here an ideal opportunity to examine the way in which a medieval text of major importance structures the inside/outside, subject/object oppositions. In this work does the inside correspond to the "I," and, if not, to what *does* it correspond? What, then, is "I"?

I will take the correspondence between "I" and inside to imply two concepts which are different but nonetheless related. First, the "I" has "insides"—psychological interiority of some kind. Now one of the strangest features of the *Rose* is that although the word "I" is extremely frequent[7] and although this is the story of an inner transformation (of how the hero fell in love, and so forth), it seems impossible to speak of any psychological interiority or inwardness here. Psychologically the hero is a void. He is as opaque as any "he" of medieval romance. We occasionally know *what* he thinks—but never *why*. For example, here is the passage where the lover arrives at the Fountain of Narcissus. He reads the inscription on the fountain, telling the sad story. The narrator tells us:

> je me suis trez un poi ensus,
> que dedenz n'ousai esgarder,
> ainz comançai a coarder,
> que de Narcisus me sovint
> cui malement en mesavint.
> Mes me pensai que a seūr,
> sanz peor de mauvé eūr,
> a la fontaine aler pooie;
> por folie m'en esloignoie. (ll. 1512–20)

> I drew [have drawn] back a bit
> because I did not dare to look inside,
> but began to be afraid,
> when I remembered Narcissus,
> to whom such misadventures happened.
> But I thought to myself that safely
> and without fear of misfortune,
> I could look at the fountain;
> I was foolish to keep away.

I for one would very much like to know the thought process by which he arrived at that conclusion that it was safe to look in the fountain, and just why he saw himself as different from Narcissus. But we find in this passage, and in the work as a whole, no sense of the thought process as anything other than a linear succession of simple "I thought's." There is no sense of a mind coming to grips with, reacting to external stimuli; no mental life. And there is no sense of what we commonly call inner "breadth" or "depth" here: of an interior space with several forces or voices within. There is no psychological plurality, no idea—as one finds in Montaigne[8]—that one might "keep oneself company." I elaborated in chapter 2 the complexities of the "I" that is articulated in this text. But whatever else may be said about them, each of these various selves is *isolated* from the others; they are the selves of different moments in time, of different modes of relation to the events recounted in the story. So they provide no feeling of inner conversation or debate; no plurality. Each "I" is alone. There is a sense in which the hero (as distinct from the narrator, who does talk a lot about telling his tale) seems almost semihuman. But it would be more accurate to say that this work, like so many others, is concerned with man as a creature endowed with will and desire more than with reason, with a mind. (I am reminded of the complaint that one of my students made a few years ago: "Beroul's Tristan and Iseut aren't very smart.")

Insofar as we do receive an image of what it is like—what it *feels* like—to love, we get this image in a very peculiar way: the God of Love announces, in the future tense, what the lover *"will do,"* these "thou shalts" sounding very much like commandments and not much like description. Moreover, they describe less what the lover will feel than what he will *do* and how he will *look;* they give not the inward state, in its inwardness, but its outward manifestations: he will weep, moan, grow thin and pale, go off by himself, stand as still as an "image," and so forth. (See lines 2263–86.) Love concludes by saying:

> et soupirras de cuer parfont;
> car bien saches qu'ensi le font
> cil qui ont les maus essaiez
> dont tu es or si esmaiez. (ll. 2283–86)

> and you will sigh from the bottom of your heart;
> for know that everybody does it—
> all those who experience the ills
> that now cause you such distress.

All this is part of serving Love.

There *is* a kind of inwardness—an experience on the part of the hero of his "insides"—but one hesitates to call it psychological, because it occurs below the neck: in the heart. The heart here has a triple meaning: it is the symbol of vitality (when it stops, one faints or dies); it is the seat of affectivity; and it is also an organ, a physical thing. But whatever it is, it is not psychological but physiological; it is as a sort of heartburn, or heartache that the lover experiences (what we might think of as) the mental anguish of being in love. It is his *heart* that, from that moment on, *hurts*. So uncerebral, so unmental a representation of interiority is—or, until very recently,[9] would have seemed—strange to us. Most of psychology, even of "modern" psychology, has been mentalistic: that is, it has been almost exclusively concerned with faculties or instincts conceived of as being in the *mind* —and the concept of mind has been primarily restricted to what we now know to be the left hemisphere of the brain: the verbal, analytical faculties.[10] In other words, psychological "science" has been interested in that part of the "psyche" which operates like it: logically, scientifically. Be all that as it may, in this work, insofar as there is any interiority to speak of, it is located in the body, in the *guts*, rather than in the mind, in processes of thought. And this inner world of affect is presented as inaccessible to verbal analysis: it is one of the few things in the work not to be treated with personification and prosopopoeia. (It is worth noting here that the heart, as the seat of affect, is seen as something precious: it is Love's "gem.")

It might be argued that this absence of any sense of mental interiority or inwardness results precisely from the fact that allegory has turned the hero inside out, that the characters he meets up with "outside" of himself (and who are all in fact better "characterized"—described, individualized—than he!) are really to be understood as his own insides, his own faculties. Now insofar as it is true that allegory tends to turn things inside out, to externalize internal forces, this is itself significant—as well as being typical of much of medieval psychological representation. It is significant because it bears on the very notion of a clear distinction between "I" and "you," between inside (my insides) and the outside (the world out there). The hero meets up with characters who may well, but also who may well *not*, represent parts of his own psychology, and with other characters who may or may not be parts of the lady's psychology. Let us take Reason, for example: are we to understand the lover's exhortation by this lofty dame as an inner monologue, an abortive struggle between his good sense and his new-found passion? Or rather, did he (when all this took place "in reality") get a lecture from his mother or his father, or some kindly chaplain? We have no way of telling, from the text itself, whether this reasonable voice was his or someone else's. The same goes for the allegories that are commonly grouped around the rosebud and seen as "hers." Is Danger the maiden's father or husband, or a churlish side of her own character?[11]

The point is not only that we do not know but that it does not matter, because psychology, the faculties, are not conceived of as individual at all, as being "mine" or "yours," or even really as being "in" me or you, but in supraindividual terms.

This does not mean that "I" cannot articulate his suffering or pleasure or desire in the first-person singular. The "I" is the very focus of all sensation and sentiment here. It is rather that the moment "I" wishes to define or analyze the nature of his experience, he must present it in transindividual and external terms, and not as "his."

The medieval period seems to have had little sense of one self as being different from another. Individuation was a *spiritual* principle not a *psychological* one; that is, it was based on the *soul* (only individual souls could be saved), not on what we call the *personality*. This is, I believe, a distinction of major importance. Moreover, several major symbolic systems deemphasized the separateness of individuals: thus, the doctrine of the church (and of the family) as a body, of which individuals were only members. Both astrology and the psychology of the "humours" stressed the reciprocities of microcosm and macrocosm and ignored conceptually any barriers between an inside and an outside. As to the domain of verbal eloquence: subject matter was to be found in the "places"—and these were *common* places.[12]

The first factor in an I/inside correlation is then the concept that one *has* psychological "insides," or interiority. The second factor is the idea that the self *is*, or constitutes, the "inside." While these two factors are separable, they are also related. To think of oneself as *being* the inside, one must *have* some inside within which to *be:*

namely some "inner self" or wholeness within which one can collect oneself, from which one can emerge in action, and to which one can return. One provides (or one's culture, as a macrocosm for the self, provides) one's own psychic home.[13]

At any rate, in this text, the self is not identified as being (the) inside. On the contrary, this "I" is quite reliably represented as being outside. The inside is defined with respect to and is centered on, not him, but the place where he wants to be at any given moment. Inside refers here to the goal or *end* of *desire*, not to the subject of the desire: the *desirer*. We will come back shortly to some of the erotic implications of this work, but let's just note for the moment that the inside cannot be taken to refer simply to the rosebud. The inside refers less often to a *person* or *object* than to a *place* of bliss, from which the hero is generally and increasingly excluded. Moreover, it is a movable concept, in that it refers to several different places through the course of the work.

There are, indeed, many barriers, many walls in this work. They have to do not with *knowledge* of the other—for the psyche (his, hers, anyone's) is laid perfectly open to the hero to know. The barriers here have to do not with knowledge but with possession and presence—and with the continual dissatisfaction of desire. They have to do not with some modern notion of the impossibility of authentic relationships but with the structure of desire.

To put all this a little differently: the barriers to acquaintanceship, to a recognition of the factors at work in (one's own and others') psychology are extraordinarily permeable here. Others (and their "inner world") are no more or less outside than the "I" itself. The hero is always allowed to *see*, to *know*, but not to *have*, what he wants, not to *be* where he wants to be. Thus we have here, not a problem of mind, of conscience, but of affect, of *desire*.

Desire, then, in this work, implies a profound sense of impoverishment; to rephrase Rimbaud, it is not merely that "la vraie vie (m') est absente" but rather "je suis absent de la vraie vie:"[14] it is not life but *I* who am absent. To love is to be outside. Love is experienced as an ever-painful and unsatisfied yearning for some ever-absent pleasure, which is the ultimate locus of value and interest. Yet this yearning is of value: the lover's faith heart is love's "jewel"; moreover the lover will find frequent consolations in his torment:

sweet thought, sweet speech, sweet sight, hope, and the kiss that he manages to bestow on the rosebud, that it consoles him to recall.

Now what are we to make of this image of love? This work has been condemned by many—beginning with Jean de Meung himself and ending with modern more-or-less Freudians—as presenting an unnatural, perhaps a homosexual[15] notion of love. It has been said that this text glorifies frustration, that love here is narcissistic (whatever that word is taken to mean).

To account for this representation of love we must now take up briefly the role of religious allegories and metaphors in this work. The *Rose* is deeply religious—but not, I believe, in the way that D. W. Robertson and his disciples mean; this is not, in any simple sense, a "Christian book."[16] Rather, it is religious in the language it uses to talk about love,[17] and in its structures: the way in which it conceives of the nature of the love experience. The most important fact here is that the lover serves not a love object, not a lady, but a Lord—the God of Love. And his relationship to this Lord is peculiarly intense: as in the scene which I analyzed earlier where the lover kisses Amors and becomes his "man." That kiss on the mouth and the pleasure that the lover derives from it are rather disconcerting to modern readers, who are naturally inclined to think in terms of homosexuality. But as one familiarizes oneself with works of twelfth-century mysticism, one discovers that the image of the self or soul as the Bride of Christ, often desiring to kiss her God on the lips, is not at all an uncommon one.[18] I think that part of our surprise at such passages results from the fact that today the center of consciousness—insofar as there is thought to be such a center— is the self or ego, which are seen as *masculine* (indeed as *male*). But in the Middle Ages the soul is that center, and it is commonly understood as *feminine*—and not just grammatically (anima/âme): "she" is passive, receptive, waiting upon God's pleasure, waiting for God's embrace or even for the "kiss of his mouth." "She" does His will—for it is in that sense that she is "willing." And, as the soul is commonly seen as the center of the self, intensely spiritual men— men very much involved in the love of God—might naturally speak of themselves as feminine.[19]

Though the lover's desire is occasioned by his attraction to the rosebud, his yearning is not confined to this object; and indeed the lover's relationship to any ostensible "object" becomes increasingly problematic as the story progresses. For it is not just the rose—that one erotic thing—that the lover wants, but also Fair Welcome. They are both locked up, and the lover wants them both. Increasingly, no one object or act would be adequate to satisfy the lover. In short, I would argue that his yearning is partly modeled on the mystical concept of a diffuse and infinite, an essentially spiritual, yearning. He wants paradise—but does not really know how to conceive of having it, of being in it.

One of the most curious features of this profoundly erotic text is that ultimately there is no true carnality in it: the lover is a *man* who falls in love with a *flower*. Now you can pluck a flower[20] and you can deflower a maiden, but it is very difficult to deflower a flower. What *is* is a deflowered flower? How is one to make love to a metaphor? (Of course, Jean de Meung, in one of the great scenes of medieval burlesque, manages, at the end of his work, to have his persona do just about that . . . but it is not easy!) Guillaume's is a peculiarly chaste book, because it is not about sex, or the sexes, at all: it is about *desire*, about being *outside*.

I believe, then, that Guillaume has attempted, in this work, to apply a religious, a Christian, structure of desire—as in infinite yearning—to a finite and human attraction. That he has done this should really not surprise us: the twelfth and thirteenth centuries were, as is well recognized today, fascinated by the phenomenon of love, both human and divine. The number of theological and literary texts of the period that are devoted to the nature of love is nothing less than staggering.[21] Numerous attempts were made in this period to account for love theoretically. But it happens that most learning in this period was religious in its orientation, that most theories and most logic were then strongly theo-logical. So it is to be expected that there should have been, and quite obvious that there was, mutual influence between secular and religious notions of love. We see in particular the use of erotic metaphors to speak of religious ardor, and of religious metaphors to speak of human loves.

It should also not surprise us that this is a strange book. It is not easy to represent an infinite desire for what is given as a finite object (a flower, symbolizing a woman). St. Bernard would have agreed with modern psychologically oriented readers in find the book rather perverse—though for different reasons.[22]

Not all medieval texts are as radical as this one in their application of religious structures and vocabulary to the theme of human and earthly love,[23] but in any case love in the medieval period is very commonly conceived of as impoverishment, dependency, as an ongoing state of loss of autonomy and self-sufficiency. Insofar as one loves, one is not the Subject (in the senses in which Greimas or Ehrmann presents it), but an Object; not a master but a servant; not a conqueror but a victim; not a man but a woman; not the inside but the outside. The concept of love as an overpowering force, as a god, as the true Subject in love stories, is by no means unique to the *Roman de la Rose*—far from it!—and is to be found well before and well after this work. What *is* striking here is that allegories (both characters such as love, and things such as his arrows) that play only a limited and local role in previous medieval narratives (for example the novels of Chrétien) here completely dominate the text and provide, not merely figures of embellishment or occasional analysis, but the plot itself.

In the traditional modern tale, according to Ehrmann—and in the narratologists' model—the Subject goes "out there," acts, and then "brings back" the "outside," at least by returning and telling the story. But in this work such terms must, all along the line, be reversed. Not only does the lover not constitute the "inside": he is ever outside, trying to get in. Moreover, far from wanting to "bring back that outside," this lover asks nothing better than to remain *in* Love's garden, to serve Love and to be near the rose. And since this garden reflects a state of mind, the lover/narrator (unlike Gulliver in Lilliput, for example) need not leave it in order to bring it to us. In fact, rather than bringing it to us, the narrator's efforts go to leading us to it. The reader is called upon to enter the garden to attend to the book's message in order to become, like the lover, Love's vassal. And even here, the reader is not to *penetrate*, but to be *let* in. Insofar as there is a knowledge or art of love imparted by this work, it does not (as in the case of Ovid's *Art of Love*) exist as much for the benefit of the reader as he for its service. It is clear that in this work to *know love* means to submit *to love*; only lovers know love. To be initiated into love is to be in love.

One final reversal of the traditional *récit* as defined by Ehrmann: he speaks of the narrator as guiding, moving his tale. This story contains not one but two conversions or transformations: that contained within the work (the story line itself) and another one that unfolds in the very telling. Early in the story the narrator uses the *passé simple*[24] and maintains a clear distinction between his present self, his literary task—and the hero, that past self, that grammatical other. But, little by little, he introduces the *passé composé*, and ultimately he slips into the present. In other words, as he tells his story, he is caught up *in it*, brought back *into it*. Even in the telling of his story, he is not master of his verb or of Love's garden, but Love's servant.

But all these reversals imply a peculiar understanding of the nature of initiation in this work. There are in fact two different ways of conceiving of initiation, one of which has been rather neglected by modern literary theorists and anthropologists alike. The difference between them turns on the question: *who/what* is primarily being taken *into whom/what?* The man into the mystery, or the mystery into the man? Who has digested whom, who now contains whom? Who has power over whom? A secular (or anthropocentric) society, critic, or text can be defined as one that primarily presents the man as coming to mastery over the mystery—as taking *it* in, as coming to control over *it*. A religious or theocentric one sees the man as being subsumed *into* the sacred, as being taken *into* it, as becoming not its master but its servant. In this case, the man is understood as being—at least in some sense, to some degree—fulfilled by being taken *into* the mystery. At least he is "in" love.

Let me give another example of a medieval representation of the inside/outside dichotomy and of the language on initiation, an example at once very different from and very similar to that provided by the *Rose*. In the thirteenth-century *Queste du saint Graal* many of the knights of Arthur's court believe, as the quest begins, that what they have been offered is just another adventure, the chance to go out and hunt for a holy object, which the most successful will then bring back to their personal glory and to the honor of the Round Table. But those who think this way have completely failed to understand what the quest is all about. In fact (as the narrator presents it), the knights have been summoned to a new initiation, called—at least those few who are worthy—to enter *into* the sacred. And it is the *failures* who come back to tell their story: the most perfect never return; they tell no stories; they are no longer of the Round Table, but with God.[25]

The dichotomy between inside and outside is as central to Guillaume's *Rose* and to various other medieval works as it is to many modern texts. But the terms of this opposition can be posed in very different ways. In this work, the inside does not correspond to "I" or "we" or "here"—nor does outside refer to the contrary. The inside is not conceived egocentrically, nor even really psychologically.[26] The inside is here primarily a locus not of affect or sensation or thought, not of personality, but of *value*. And the individual is not seen as an adequate source of value; he is not adequate to constitute an inside. Not that the individual is conceived as being of *no* value; on the contrary, many medieval texts are concerned with the destiny—whether spiritual, amorous, or social—of individuals. And there are many medieval heroes, many highly praised protagonists. One could even argue that the very notion of the value of the individual (of *any* individual) is Judeo-Christian in origin, since from the beginning it was understood that only individuals, only single souls, could be saved. But the self or individual is not of *adequate* value to be represented as the inside; it is not complete; it is always, in some sense, deficient—which is perhaps merely another way of saying that it is sinful. And it is of value only with respect to some extrinsic value (or Evaluator), which is itself represented as the inside.

In the representation of reality in literature throughout the Middle Ages, there is a strong tendency for man to be presented as the object of God's, Love's, Fortune's verbs. Man is not the "mover," but the "moved"—will he, or nill he. Yet, at least in literature that is religious in spirit or that is inspired by courtly or feudal ideals, there is also a conviction that one must *willingly* "lose oneself to find oneself"; that the meaning, value, and salvation of human life come from the surrender of pride, of the will, of the self to a higher order, an embracing harmony. The individual self is simply not seen as complete, as autonomous, as constituting a satisfactory whole. It has no fullness, but needs to be fulfilled within some greater whole.[27] The medieval preoccupation with service is but one expression of this sense that the protagonist—however heroic—is not an adequate Subject, or inside. Medieval heroes submit—to varying degrees, to be sure (and some of those epic heroes least of all!)[28]—to Love, to God, or to some other ideal.[29] And writers too accept to speak within the confines of literary tradition, of which they—often anonymous—accept to be merely a part.

One frequently finds in the Middle Ages (and in the Bible) references to the self (or soul, or heart) as a container, as a house for example, or a dwelling place, a temple. Occasionally it is active, as a host who invites something or someone in. And one finds references to the self (often the heart) as a guest or dweller within something or someone else. The self can thus *contain* (be filled by) something, or it can be *contained by* something. What one does *not* find, I submit, is the notion that one can be "in oneself"; one cannot *fill* oneself.[30] It is in the late Middle Ages that a new concept of the self begins to be articulated, in the poetry of Charles d'Orléans,[31] for example, and then more insistently in Montigne's *Essais;* this is the idea of an interior space inhabited by and controlled by itself, or by an "ego." But this *idea* is an *ideal* as well—or perhaps even primarily—and that is what makes its expression in Montaigne "modern." That is, insofar as there was in the Middle Ages any clear notion of a self-possessed self, this thrust toward automony tended to be identified with the sin of pride, and to be condemned. In Montaigne, such a concept of the self is not merely articulated, but its functioning presented as *desirable.*[32] This is surely a great shift.

NOTES

1. As in the previous chapter, French quotations are taken from the Lecoy edition of *Le Roman de la Rose,* vol 1; English translations are mine, with closeness to the original being the primary aim.

2. According to Jean de Meung, Guillaume died before completing his work. Or is this a story that *could* not be finished, for internal reasons?

3. *Poétique,* Jacques Ehrmann, "Le Dedans et le dehors," 9 (1972): 31; my translation.

4. This phenomenon in intellectual history has been on the rise roughly from the sixteenth century until very recently, but is perhaps slightly on the wane. I do not, incidentally, take "self" and "ego" to be synonymous, but both function as part of the same general language of aggressive and autonomous individuality.

5. I am not denying that there is a foundation in reality to the notion of the "ego" as articulated by modern psychology. But what concerns me here is the very interest in and glorification of this psychic entity.

6. Peter Caws, *Semiotexte* 1, No. 3 (1975) ("Ego Traps"): 44.

7. The word *je* occurs about 250 times referring to the hero. In this period, the use of the first-person pronoun with a verb was not necessary.

8. See, for example, "Of Solitude": "We must reserve a back shop all our own, entirely free, in which to establish our real liberty and our principal retreat and solitude. Here our ordinary conversation must be between us and ourselves. . . . We have a soul that can be turned upon itself; it can keep itself company" (*Essays*, trans. Donald M. Frame [New York: St. Martin's Press, 1963], 123); and passim.

9. Modern French psychoanalytical and anthropological theory is a good deal less "mentalistic" than psychology has been traditionally.

10. The left hemisphere is concerned with temporal, sequential organization, and handles logical processes, as well as speech—in its sequential components. The right hemisphere deals with spatial organization, with events perceived atemporally; and is involved with emotion. See my Conclusions.

11. It is worth noting that our confusion between inside and outside is markedly more acute in this work than in Prudentius's *Psychomachia*, since in the latter we are dealing *only* with one person's psychology—though he represents us all: Everyman. So we can readily translate phenomena seen "outside" as referring to the soul's "inside": its own internal struggle. I do not therefore take it to be *necessary* that allegory blur the inside/outside distinction. This distinction can also be blurred *without* there being any recourse to allegory: in the romances of Chrétien one occasionally wonders—when an adversary appears who seems to embody a particular temptation for the hero—"Is he fighting someone else, or part of himself?"

12. On the "commonplaces," see, for example, Richard A. Lanham, *A Handlist of Rhetorical Terms: A Guide for Students of English Literature* (Berkeley, Calif.: University of California Press, 1969), 110–111.

13. Of course the question may well be asked: "If the self is such a happy home, why bother to go out at all?" Why indeed . . . In any case, heroic models imply that the hero only had to go out *once*. By contrast, an Augustine, a Bernard, a Pascal, would speak of the intrinsic "restlessness" of the human heart; and, in different terms, a Freud, a Lacan, a Bataille would say much the same thing.

14. Literally: "Real life is absent (from me)" vs. "I am absent from real life."

15. Essentially for the following reasons: Fair Welcome and Love are masculine; and there is never any question of fruition (i.e., progeny) here, as there is in Jean's work.

16. His thesis is that it is ironic; that it satirizes cupidity and exalts charity. See, for example, D. W. Robertson, Jr., "The Doctrine of Charity in Medieval Literary Gardens," *Speculum* 26 (1951):24–49, p. 46 in particular.

17. Among the major religious terms and ideas are these: a God of Love, commandment; garden, paradise, hell; deadly sins (Envy, etc.—along with Old Age, etc.!) shown as obstacles to love; sanctuary; martyr.

18. In William of St. Thierry and St. Bernard in particular: see note 21. The source of this metaphor is clearly the biblical *Song of Songs*.

19. This is not always the case. It is most common in works where the writer wishes

to stress the divine rather than the human, initiative: God as the source—the "Father"—of all human creativity and fertility; God as the lover. When the human initiative is stressed, along with the "ardor" and eagerness of the soul's or heart's desire of God, then it is not uncommon to find a more masculine representation.

20. Our lover does in fact try to pluck that rosebud, early in the game, eliciting a horrified response from Fair Welcome (11. 2891–2903).

21. As for literary works, it would be easier to list those that do not treat of love than those that do. Here are some of the important theological writers who dealt with love as a major concern. These writers were all active in the middle and late twelfth century—and I should add that I consider the first *Rose* to be a book that in many ways looks backward rather than forward in its understanding of love and in its relation to religious questions: Bernard of Clairvaux; William of St. Thierry; Hugh of St. Victor; Richard of St. Victor. Incidentally, William's work entitled *On the Nature and Dignity of Love* begins "The art of arts is the art of love."

22. See St. Bernard's *On the Love of God*, trans. Sister Penelope, (London: Mowbrays, 1950): 48.

23. In some works—as often postmedieval as medieval—the love-object becomes itself the god(dess): that which is adored; the creature that one loves instead of the Creator, etc.

24. See chapter 2 for a discussion of this tense.

25. Galahad has been carried off by angels; Perceval became a hermit just outside the quasi-celestial city of Sarraz and then died; only Bohort—the least perfect of the spiritual threesome—finally returns to Camelot. All of King Arthur's other knights—those who survived—had returned long before in varying states of mortification.

26. They were not defined racially: the "bad" men (and women) of the epics—that is, the infidels—become "good" as soon as they convert; evil was thus religious or ideological, and not a racial, outside. Moreover, even this concept of a religious outside was rather shaky: as Benjamin N. Nelson makes clear in his *The Idea of Usury, from Tribal Brotherhood to Universal Otherhood* (Princeton: Princeton University Press, 1949), the "we" of Christendom was understood to include, ultimately, and mystically, everyone. The Christian ideal was of a "universal brotherhood'; as usury could be practiced only against those who were not brothers, it could not be practiced by Christians at all.

27. The major debate seems to have turned on the question: in *what* can one, should one, attempt to find fulfillment? What should one serve? For example, was the couple a satisfactory unit, or did it too have to be integrated into a still broader social or religious context?

28. A Raoul de Cambrai springs immediately to mind!

29. For an interesting example of this phenomenon, see Erwin Panofsky's discussion of Abbot Suger's egocentrism and of the way in which this "selfishness" is put at the service of Saint Denis, in *Meaning in the Visual Arts* (New York: Doubleday, 1955).

30. A striking case of a religious concept of the soul within itself—or the self within the soul—is to be found in St. Teresa of Avila's *The Interior Castle*. This castle, which is the soul, and which is marvelous, miraculous ("made of a single diamond or of very clear crystal, in which there are many rooms"); E. Allison

Peers, trans [Garden City, N.Y.: Doubleday/Image, 1961] 28), takes all its beauty from the fact that it is ultimately God's, and was made in His image. There are in the soul "many rooms, just as in Heaven there are many mansions," etc. In other words, to be in your soul is to be in God or to have God in you.

31. He speaks of himself as having rooms, with windows—eyes—that his "I" can open and close at will. Within those rooms—within himself—are various allegorical characters (some of which are apparently original, such as Nonchaloir and Souci); these figures, occasionally marked with a possessive, argue and converse.

32. Montaigne is, in fact, less descriptive than prescriptive: "let us . . . ," "we must . . . ," etc. (See "Of Solitude.")

CHAPTER 4

Story, Chronicle, History:
La Fille du comte de Pontieu

La Fille du comte de Pontieu is hardly one of the most famous of medieval titles. But though it has not been especially popular with modern scholars, this legend—embodied in several texts—was popular throughout the Middle Ages. The text I should like to discuss dates from the mid-thirteenth century.[1] (Also extant are a late thirteenth-century amplified reworking, inserted into a longer text, and a fifteenth-century version.) I have no particular desire to argue that this work is an undersung masterpiece—though in point of fact, I find it is powerful and intriguing, and full of surprises; it certainly is not boring even if it is not exactly beautiful. But I have chosen it primarily because it forces us, in a striking way, to ask some basic questions about medieval narrative literature—and about the ways in which modern narratology has both served us and obfuscated matters for us as concerns our understanding of medieval characters—subjects, selves—and their relation to the narrative structures (the plots, for example) in which they find themselves.

The choice of this text was also dictated—and, I confess, not without a bit of malice—by a desire to break out of those *loci* constituted by a very small number of medieval works to which medievalists have generally been forced to confine themselves if they wished to carry on a dialogue about literature, and literarity, with "normal" people, that is, modernists. On this shortlist are the *Chanson de Roland*, one or two of Chrétien de Troyes's romances, the Bédier rewrite of the Tristan story, the *Roman de la Rose*—and that is about it, for the French side of things.

This prose *récit*—I use the word advisedly!—is 620 lines[2] long. Here is the summary provided by the modern editor Brunel; in brackets, I will add details not mentioned by Brunel, but which seem to me important:

> Thibaut, son of the Lady of Domart, had married the daughter of the Count of Pontieu. Distressed to have no child, Thibaut undertakes with his wife a pilgrimage to Santiago da Compostella. Along the way, the travelers are set upon by brigands who take advantage of [read: rape] Thibaut's wife and then abandon their victims. Far from freeing her husband whose hands and feet are tied, the Count of Pontieu's daughter takes a sword and tries to kill him. She manages only to undo the ropes that bound him, and the sole regret that she expresses is that she has been unable to achieve her goal. [Thibaut, leaving his wife in a convent, completes the pilgrimage alone; he then comes back to take her home with him to Pontieu.] The Count, indignant at the behavior of his daughter, on her return has her put into a barrel that he sets out to sea. Saved by Flemish merchants, she is offered to the Sultan of Aumarie who marries her. But the Count of Pontieu, [his son] and Thibaut, overcome with remorse, go off to fight the Infidels, and are thrown by a storm onto the Island of Aumarie. Chosen, first one then the other, to serve as targets for the archers, they are saved by the Sultaness who recognizes them. She has them tell her their story, and when they get to the point where the daughter of the Count of Pontieu wanted to kill her husband, she interrupts them: "I well know why she acted thus. It was because of the great shame that she had suffered before her husband's eyes." "Was it her fault?" interrupts Thibaut. "I would never have treated her badly because of it." "That isn't what she thought *then*," she replies. She reveals her identity to them, and managing to leave Aumarie by a ruse, she returns to her country with her husband and father [taking with her a son she has had by the sultan]. From a daughter [also by the sultan] whom she left behind in the East, is descended Saladin, the sultan who took Jerusalem back from the Christians. [Later on, she and Thibaut have two sons.] (P. vii)

Brunel makes the following comments about this story: "Written no doubt in the last years of the reign of Philip Augustus, this must be considered the earliest short story *[nouvelle]* in French prose. It already has the clear character of this literary genre. The rapid narrative develops a single action whose interest continues to increase until the conclusion [dénouement] which is rendered in rapid strokes. Then, the desired effect having been obtained, the reader is left with his impression; the ending is simply sketched in to complete the contour." (p. iii)

First problem: far from developing "a single action" (une action unique) this work is, I believe, very peculiarly conceived and constructed, and its narrative unity is problematic indeed. Perhaps this "peculiarity"—this problem—can best be defined, at least initially, by a Greimasian look at the narrative structure.

We have (at first glance) a rather nice manque or "lack" here. In fact we have three of them: first, the lack of a child; second, the lack of understanding about why the "daughter of the Count of Pontieu"—"fille du comte de Pontieu" (=F)—tried to kill her husband. These two manques, or lacks, do not exist at the same level, nor are they of the same order: the first exists at the level of plot, the second at the level of narration itself. Third is the guilt-ridden uncertainty on the part of her family as to her fate. These lacks are liquidated (although, as we will see later, in rather strange terms). Tiebaus (=T) finds out why F tried to kill him. And at the end, after the return of the Pontieu[3] group to France, he gets two sons. (This last detail is omitted by Brunel. I will suggest later a possible reason why he may have forgotten—or chosen to ignore—this apparently crucial narrative fact.) And we have several trials (épreuves) in between: journeys, battles, and so forth.

But—in Greimasian terms—who is the Subject here? Every major character in this work has serious, yet somehow inadequate, pretensions to being the "Subject"—and until we have a Subject, we cannot begin to identify the rest of the actantial personnel. These multiple claims present serious problems to our analysis, and even our reading, of the text. Who is this story "about"?

THIBAUT (TIEBAUS). It is he who, desirous of a child (heir) initiates the pilgrimage. And, obviously, he wants to know why F tried to kill him. And T undergoes two épreuves. The first, it must be said, is rather a disaster: he manages to kill three of the brigands who attack him and his wife, but the other five overpower him and rape her. (We are told that his senc was pesant that day. A hero with "tired blood!" Not unheard of, but certainly rare in medieval heroic narrative.) The other trial, which is rather artificially arranged for him by his wife (now the sultana), is to help the sultan defeat his enemies—and of course, primarily, regain his "honor," his self-esteem. This time (presumably his old self) T is very successful, and routs all the sultan's adversaries. But if the *manques* and *liquidations* and two *épreuves* are Tiebaus's, most of the trials in this story go to his wife.

THE DAUGHTER (LA FILLE).[4] Most of the story is, for all practical purposes, "about" her and her experiences (mostly tribulations): *her* rape; *her* attempt to kill her husband; *her* father's attempt to murder her; *her* "rescue" by the merchants; *her* marriage to the sultan and two children by him; *her* rescuing from death of her father, (first) husband, and brother; *her* engineering of their return home. The word "her" has, granted, many different relationships to the nouns (and the verbs which they imply) here but, at any rate, this story—as the title suggests—really seems to be about "la fille du comte de Pontieu." Yet, to paraphrase Freud, "What does (this) woman *want?*"

THE COUNT. It is the count (= C) who *asks* his daughter why she tried to kill her husband (T we only *assume* to have wanted to know); he who tried to kill—execute—her; and it is he who initiated the second (penitential) pilgrimage, or crusade; he whom F first saves from death; he who tells her her "own" story. But here too, what, exactly, does he want? What is his object?

THE SULTAN. He (= S) certainly intends to be (a) Subject. And his object is clear: F herself.

In short, this is, in a sense, T's story *and* F's story *and* C's story *and* S's story.

Before we strain ourselves any further to isolate *the* true Subject, perhaps we should stop and ask ourselves whether this story *has*, in fact *a* Subject, in any single, simple sense. But, before pursuing this discussion, I should like to make a digression, which will help us to pose the "subject problem" in all its medieval starkness: William Ryding, in an extremely interesting and provocative study entitled *Structure in Medieval Narrative*,[5] has pointed out that medieval "narratives," are often not very unified—at least in the modern sense of that word—and that they often contain not one "story"[6] but in fact several "stories." Sometimes the work is essentially bipartite,[7] structured by a shame/rehabilitation reversal: examples would be Chrétien de Troyes's *Erec et Enide* and *Yvain*. Sometimes they contain several stories intertwined or interlaced,[8] often in complex ways, such as the *Lancelot en prose*, the *Queste du saint Graal*, or Ariosto's *Orlando furioso*. And Ryding speaks of the tendency—especially from the thirteenth century on—for works to bifurcate (though this word is not his) into several different stories, the work's unity being provided by various kinds of parallelisms, and thematic concerns.

Ryding's points are well taken. But one weakness in his thesis is that he never defines just what he means by "narrative" or by "story,"[9] and his use of these terms remains unclear. I propose the following clarification: a literary "work" is a kind of "space" which may contain *several* "stories." It may also contain types of "narrative" *(récit) other* than stories (see below). Moreover, these narratives may be, in the work, subordinated to purposes that are not necessarily or primarily narrative.[10] Ryding does not go far *enough*. It is not only that medieval "narratives" tend to bifurcate—indeed trifurcate . . . '*n*-furcate"—into thirty stories or more,[11] medieval "*stories*"—or *récits*—*themselves* have this sort of centrifugal quality. The center (as represented in Greimasian terms by the Subject) does not *hold*—especially during and after the thirteenth century. And this can happen even to short works—such as this one of 620 lines—as well as to romances of 30,000 lines!

Now the work at hand is full of and, in a sense, unified by, repetitions, and various kinds of redundancy. For example, binarities:

- There are two pilgrimages: the one made by T and F; the one made by T, C, and the count's son.
- There are two "battles": T's unsuccessful one with the brigands; his successful one against the sultan's enemies.
- There are two men who love and want to marry F: T and the sultan.
- F has two children by the sultan: a boy and a girl; and two by T: two boys.
- F is twice at the mercy of libidinous or lecherous men: the brigands; the sultan.
- T is twice captive: to the brigands; to the sultan.
- There are two maidens loved by their fathers' *serviteurs:* la Fille and her daughter, called "la Belle Cetive" (*chetive [captive, wretch]*).

As to other repetitions:

- There are several illnesses: T has "heavy blood" the day he meets the brigands; F is ill when removed from the barrel; T, C, and the count's son are all ill in the sultan's prison; F pretends to be pregnant and ill in order to obtain her departure, with her family, from Aumarie; the count's son dies.
- There are numerous sea voyages: F in the barrel, the pilgrimage-crusade, the joint return home.

And so forth.

When one casts a Todorovian glance[12] at this text, among the first things to become apparent is that we have here a small number of basic activities (or verbs) which occur over and over again, and which are modulated—or "transformed"—according to a small number of syntactical (and semantic) principles. These primary verbs can be, rather roughly, defined as those involving:

- Travel: physical displacement, by land or sea.
- Love, and eroticism, in their various modes (for example, erotic desire, tenderness, or affection, and so forth).
- Physical power: primarily over others (for example, the power to emprison and to free, to kill and to save, to destroy life and to reproduce or nurture it).[13]

The transformations occur through combinations of such categories:

- Active versus passive
- Transitive versus intransitive
- Positive versus negative

and, less purely grammatical:

- Voluntary versus involuntary[14]
- Successful versus unsuccessful.[15]

I have just been analyzing two different types of unity which characterize this work: that provided by repetition and contrast (mostly binary), and that provided by the very slimness of the array of possibilities—the repetitiveness—of human action. Neither of these constitutes what one would normally call "narrative" unity. The first could be called "figural": it consists of the transposition into narrative technique of rhetorical figures such as antithesis, comparison, and so forth. These figures provide a sort of narrative *elocutio*, and, as if by a curious corollary, the style—or surface *elocutio*—of the text is figureless,[16] "colorless," almost drab. The second is essentially a semantic or thematic redundancy.

To put it differently: the writer of this text was more concerned with the unity of his *work* than with that of his *récit* (or story); more with the static positioning of motifs, with the balancing and gradation of episodes, than with the logic of their *déroulement*— their "unfolding"—or with their finality and ultimate narrative cohesion.

And yet there is some way in which the center *does* hold, narratively speaking. There may be a proliferation of would-be Subjects, but they are not independent of each other. Their stories are related. The closer one looks at this text the clearer it becomes that this *récit* is not about one person, or even one couple[17]—or about individual people at all. It is about a family, the motivating spirit of a family, and including not only the present but the past and the future: the "house of Pontieu."

We will return shortly to a consideration of the theoretical implications of such an actantial structure. But first, a few remarks.

Such a hypothesis—that the family is, more than any individual protagonist, the Subject here—would certainly correspond to an interesting phenomenon that occurred in the late twelfth and thirteenth centuries.[18] In this period, the epic poems of the eleventh and early twelfth centuries, with their great individual heroes,[19] became the nuclei for massive epic cycles, based on the notion of family. To oversimplify somewhat: the great heroes are given *enfances* (childhood stories) and a father; then, perhaps, a grandfather, then a nephew or a son and grandsons; then cousins, and uncles, and so forth. They are increasingly surrounded, literarily, by other members (and feudal *serviteurs*) of their clan. And their women begin to play important roles too: there are some very impressive heroines in these epics. (The Arthurian *romans* too are organized into great cycles.)[20] To put it differently: in a great many works, the single heroic event is no longer enough; it is now set in the context of a life. And the single Subject is, indeed, no longer enough. He must be part of a group—a family or dynasty—and his heroic action is now only one manifestation of his family's heroic tradition. He is bringing his stone to the edifice of dynastic honor.

But, more important, this hypothesis corresponds to what one finds in our text: the introduction to this work is rather long, surprisingly (for so short a text) full of details about the family situation of the various characters: that the count had two children, that his wife had died when their daughter was only three, that Thibaut was the son of the dame de Domart who is the count's sister, that he had long served the count faithfully before asking to marry F, and so forth. And the story ends with several more pages of commentary on the family's subsequent fortunes (pp. 41–44). In short, this story is rather like a page out of the annals of the *maison de Pontieu*. It is the story—or history—of one generation. (It is perhaps worth mentioning here that the Pontieu family was a powerful family in the medieval period, and that they seem to have been important literary patrons.)

I am arguing that the Subject is the family or dynasty of Pontieu. Its Object is its own glory and greatness (and the service of God). Now is such a reading—such a distribution of functions—compatible with Greimas's theories? This question is hard to answer partly because there are many aspects of his system—of the rules of its operation, and of its fundamental implications—that Greimas never spells out. Just who is, who can be, the Subject of a work? Greimas always seems to see the Subject in a single person, or in a group that functions collectively as a single person, or by "investissement thématique"[21] in a force or concept presented as a personification. Thus, for example, in his diagram of the Marxist view of history, he presents mankind as a mass, as *Homme*, and casts it as the Subject.[22] There may be, in his view, two Subjects—S_1 versus S_2[23]—but they are each conceived individually, even if they have the same Object; each has his *own* Object.

But what of a case like ours? Here we have neither the simplicity of a single medieval Subject nor even of a pair of antagonistic Subjects, nor yet the tidiness of a Marxist view that would make of men a great single entity, mankind. Rather we have a clutch of rather independent characters, only more or less unified by the fact and the sense that they belong to something greater than themselves, by the fact that they share a common Object. To put the problem a little differently: it is not that Greimas could not conceive of "family" as the Subject; and one could argue that the mere detail that this Subject is not lexically present, not "attested," presents no problem. The problem is this: once we have accepted an abstraction, the Pontieu dynasty, as the Subject, in traditional Greimasian terms, what are we to do with the characters who *are* attested—who are in fact alive and kicking—in this work? What are they? What is their function? We are forced to supply a term such as "sub-Subjects" to cope with them, these representatives or embodiments of the family. They could occasionally be called its *Adjuvants;* but they are often, despite their best intentions, its *Opposants.* At any rate, they are the only concrete Subjects—and they are concrete indeed. But they do not have private, individualized Objects. Their purpose is not, to put it in modern jargon, "self-fulfillment," but the fulfillment of their family. Insofar as we can see their inner life, insofar as they articulate desires, they seek to perpetuate and glorify their family in the eyes of the world and of God, to make it great and good.[24] (It goes surely without saying that if our couple wants a child, it is not because they love babies. They need—their dynasty needs—an heir.)[25]

These various "members" of the family have varied and distinct roles, or functions. The medieval period could not have conceived that different individuals might participate equally, that is, identically, in any "body," or institution. The count is the "head" of the family: it is he who judges, who provides the conscience. Thibaut[26] is its "arm"; and he must father the next generation. As to the *Fille:* she is there to bear the dynasty's future; she is, if you will, its "womb," and its female *sexe,* its feminine and maternal principle. It is this function that would account for her somewhat paradoxical combination of inertness and energy.[27] She is an active agent of passivity; it is her nature to be actively feminine, receptive, mothering—to her family's glory. She is defined as (reduced to) a sort of "animate womb," and *sexe.*

To put all this another way: I contend that none of these characters is conceived as being fully *autonomous.* Each of them is, essentially, a member, and a servant, of the family.

And each of these members, while it can bring glory and honor to the family through its specialized function, can also, through the same "organs," as it were, bring sin and dishonor. Thibaut's arm is, at first, too weak to defend his wife. Her degradation and humiliation through rape reflect on the family, just as her sterility denied it a future.[28] The count's sense of justice was faulty. If each of these members first brings disgrace (though known only to them and to God)[29] on the family, afterward each of them redeems his initial failure. The count repents and initiates the crusade, then becomes a Templar. F becomes the wife of the great sultan, and has four children—thereby glorifying her *sexe* (which had been sullied by the brigands) and bearing heirs for the future. (It is, incidentally, clear that a woman is completly defined here by her relation to men: whose daughter she is, whom she sleeps with or is raped by or is married to, and whom she is the mother or ancestor of. A man is defined here by what land he holds, and whose heir he is.) She saves her family and nurses them back to health—thus reaffirming her bonds of family loyalty and love, and her nurturing nature. Thibaut gets a chance to show that his arm is strong, and to father two sons.

In a sense the writer himself is yet another sub-Subject[30] attempting, through his story, to glorify the *maison de Pontieu*. Moreover, the little that we can surmise[31] about the circumstances of the composition tends to justify this assessment of our anonymous writer's purpose in writing.

We will return shortly to the question of God's relation to the *maison de Pontieu*, for while he too seems to wish its glory, the narrator does not present him as purely its *Adjuvant* or sub-Subject. We will also find shortly that we must take up the Subject problem again, at a higher level. But, for the moment, one final comment. The phenomenon that we have been discussing is quite a common one in medieval narrative works. Often there is no adequate, autonomous Subject.[32] Several protagonists may be "subject, with respect to x." But the true Subject may well be a sort of vast entity—vast, but unpersonified, even unnamed—or a class to which the various sub-Subjects all belong. In this work I have suggested—inferred— the "body" image as the integrative principle (that is, the family as a body, with members). This is certainly a familiar medieval metaphor for collectivities and institutions—the Church, as the body of Christ,[33] providing the most striking, and the original, example.

Other works present other configurations: the analysis and embodiment of (abstract) Subject into sub-Subjects can proceed on more clearly moral or ideational lines.[34]

As I mentioned above, if I speak of the family or dynasty as (at one level at least) the true Subject of this *récit*, it is by inference that I am speaking. That is, we do not meet this Subject in the text, nor do the characters ever speak about, for example, being members of their family. What I am arguing is that it is the spirit of the family that gives its greatest degree of cohesion to these various episodes, to the presence and actions of the various characters. What the characters all have "in common" is their family bond. And the maintenance and glorification of their family seems to be the unspoken goal—Object—of most of the characters' behavior.

(As will soon become clear, I by no means claim that the cohesiveness of this *récit* is total. Moreover, there are medieval *récits* where not only can the individual protagonists not be said to constitute a viable Subject, but where there seems to be no organism, no entity which they embody, and which can provide the—hypothetically—necessary Subject. This is, for example, the case in many *fabliaux*.)

Even if we have resolved one aspect of the Subject problem, we are still left with some problems (among them, the sultan) on our hands. This *récit*, like many medieval *récits*, seems oddly uncohesive in structure, oddly disjointed. To give, for the moment, but one example: What is the relation—other than chronological, sequential—between F's trials, and either the beginning or the end of the text, the essential lack and its liquidation. Are her trials *épreuves*, in the strict sense of the word: "tests," things that "prove" her? And if so, just what *do* they prove? These adventures seem to exist largely as independent[35] episodes, and to have very little narrative functionality at all. That is, in no clear way do they speed us toward solution of the initial problem: the childlessness of the couple.

As I said, it is now clear[36] that this lack of cohesion is a very common situation in medieval works. How could medieval writers and their public have tolerated such strange, disjointed, often long and often "pointless" and even chaotic *récits*—such "unsatisfactory" (from Greimas's point of view) *récits*? Were the writers (and their readers) all "neurotic"?[37] Are these *récits* just "bad" *récits?* But such a term is meaningless; a bad *récit* is no less a *récit* for being bad. The point is, we must look more closely at our terminology. It is not only the English word "story"—and the French *histoire, a fortiori*—that can lead us astray. Even the word *récit,* in itself very neutral and theoretically satisfactory, has been used, by numerous theorists—and prominent among them, Greimas—as if it *meant* "story." But medieval *récits* are often not *récits* in the sense in which Greimas (et al.) have, implicitly, defined the term.

The Middle Ages knew,[38] and practiced widely, several rather peculiar blendings of two very different modes of narrative, modes which at most periods either remain separate or are blended in different fashions: what I shall call "story" and "chronicle."

I doubt that it is necessary to belabor the distinction between story and chronicle, which is not a new one.[39] But we must analyze further the standard opposition in order to facilitate our discussion and analysis of the text—and problems—at hand.

Chronicle is essentially linear:[40] a listing of events happening to a person or a group or, often, many people (though generally with some common denominator). If $A,B,C, \ldots N$ are taken to represent characters; and $a,b,c, \ldots n$, "functions"; and $1,2,3, \ldots x$, "time 1," "time 2," and so on; then chronicle can be represented as follows:

$$x(A)_1, p(T_2, f(R)_3, \ldots n(N)_x.$$

Or if it deals with only one character it might be:

$$c(A)_1, s(A)_2, o(A)_3, \ldots n(A)_x$$

In other words, it is a random, open-ended series. It may contain any number of "transformations"[41] but no one of them is privileged.[42] And the series can go on forever, or until the people or institutions of which it speaks cease, simply, to exist, or until the period in question ends. Its structure is based on a process of sequential "addition," or "accretion."

As to "story": such disparate theorists as Propp, Frye, Joseph Campbell, Greimas, and Todorov[43] all stress the essential "circularity" of story (or myth, or folktale, or *récit*)[44] as well as its "unity of action." "Story" involves a problem and its solution, the opening the closing of a parenthesis, a departure and a return, a *manque* to be *liquidé*, a process begun and completed—in short, something being brought "full circle."

The definition of "story"—or *récit* when it is used to *mean* story —as an "utterance in which a transformation occurs" increasingly appears inadequate to me. It is crucial—for there to be "story"— that the transformation be *awaited:* awaited if only by the narrator and *us!* And it is crucial that it be *"the"* transformation; not just *any* transformation will do. That is, what good would it do for the hero to "finally" get a gold ring or reach the top of the mountain— if what he wanted was a baby son! Or for Proust's "Marcel" finally to become a *barber* (whereas he *wanted,* of course, to become a *writer*). It is crucial that a spring have been set—at some level— which that change released. Story is informed by a desire, a will, an end, a *telos;* it is not random sequence. The beginning implies the end, and vice versa. If Genette is right in saying[45] that the simplest *récit* is "Marcel becomes a writer," the simplest "story" is "Marcel *finally* becomes a writer." Indeed, the definition of story might well be: "an utterance in which an *awaited* (or desired) transformation occurs"; whereas *"récit"* would be, simply, "an utterance containing at least one verb (or implied verb)."[46]

It is not simply that in story causality predominates, whereas in chronicle, temporality obtains. In story—in its ideal form—events are functionally connected to the problem that the story posits. Story might be represented thus: M *(manque)* and L (its liquidation) provide the problem "around which the story revolves"; x is that with respect to which the lack is perceived; S is the central protagonist (in Greimas's terms, the Subject); $e_1, e_2, e_3, \ldots$ n are

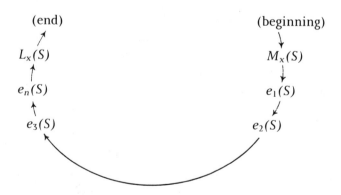

the various events or *épreuves* whose fulfillment leads to the solution of the problem.

The formal or structural relations and possible interactions between chronicle and story are complex indeed. It would probably be most accurate to think of these two "ideal" modes as constituting the two opposite poles of a complex several-stranded continuum.

Pure chronicle—that is, purely linear, sequential, chronologically structured narrative—is rare indeed: it can even be said to be an abomination to the human spirit, so profound is our need to project onto chronicity (or to find embedded therein) story-type structures. Most "history"—that is, factual (or supposedly so) narrative written by historians—is, *formally* speaking, a sort of "storyized chronicle."[47] it is partially structured according to patterns of problem solving, developmental process (rise and fall, and so forth), cause and effect, and of course the great modern structuring myth, "progress." Certain temporal chunks do become, in their hands, both (in principle at least) "true" and "stories." Nevertheless, most modern historians present the whole of history as open-ended: its beginning and end are to be defined with *points de suspension: ". . . ."* Thus their stories remain localized to particular periods or to particular sequences of events; and their histories could often be represented thus:

The little circles representing storylike episodes are strung onto the linearity or sequentiality of time.

We have "chroniclized story," for example:

- Whenever, in a work which is ostensibly a story—that is, when an "initial problem" is posited—the structure of a "life," in all its sequentiality and randomness, takes over;
- Whenever episodes are of interest in themselves, merely because they occurred, and not because of their cause/effect relationship to each other; not because of their relevance to the initial lack and its liquidation;
- Whenever the Subject does not clearly control his destiny, or, perhaps, even have a clear purpose at all.

And so on. There are several different ways in which story can be chroniclized. Most commonly, in the Middle Ages, it is as if the "rubber band" of story—that tension, that tautness that gives it its energy, its cohesion, its circularity—collapsed or came unsprung. *Récits* (stories?) ramble on interminably. Protagonists (Subjects?) get constantly diverted, deflected from their path, their goal (Object). And we are constantly meeting new would-be subjects on our path. One occasionally has the impression that a *récit* will conclude only as the last trumpet sounds; the narrative thread seems lost. (Interesting examples of the cross between story and chronicle are several epics discussed by Aristotle—*Poetics*, chapter xxiii—and which he considers, for this reason, to be *bad* epics. There are, in fact, many medieval *récits* which clearly do not want to end, to conclude, but to spin on forever in little (relatively) self-contained episodes. To paraphrase Donne (on love), the writers seem to have forgotten "the right true end" of story: its consummation. What seems to appeal to them is not preparing the "transformation," which will solve the problem and end the story, but, rather, playing interminably with the kinds of adventures—little episodes—that the characters' ongoing personalities and problems invite. They are interested not in transformation, in change, but in stability. This is particularly clear in the case of the Tristan material and the *Roman de Renart*. To take the former: the many writers who work with the Tristan legend clearly do not want *ever* to solve the lovers' "problem." They want Tristan and Iseut to go on forever loving and repenting and meeting secretly and separating and loving . . . The appeal is, precisely though paradoxically, in the stability of the instability of that triangle, Tristan + Iseut + Marc. It occurs to no one, writers and lovers alike, to do away with the husband and thereby permit the story to conclude.[48]

It might be objected that what these medieval narrators do is what any narrator does: after all, in the *Odyssey*, Ulysses does not go straight home. But the point that I am trying to make here is that if (certain) medieval narrators were to get hold of Ulysses, he would *never* get home!

Such a narrative blend is by no means the monopoly either of the Middle Ages or of France. It is to be found, for example, in the so-called Byzantine romances (which apparently influenced the medieval French romance), in seventeenth-century French novels, and in the serial romance *(roman feuilleton)*, as well as in autobiography and the autobigraphical novel. In many cases this blend appears to constitute an attempted mimesis of the effects of destiny[49] on human life.

This cross between chronicle and story is, at any rate, particularly common in the Middle Ages. Why? To some extent, this phenomenon should come as no surprise if Zumthor is right in arguing[50] that the medieval *roman* emerged largely from "historiography" (or chronicle). But it is not only *romans*—"*romans d'aventure,*"[51] "biographical romances,"[52] and so forth—that display this marked affinity for chronological or sequential principles of organization. Even short narrative works[53] can show this tendency to "flatten out," to lose their circular quality, to be essentially episodes strung together.

We are dealing here not simply with a question of *genre*—the emergence of the roman from historiography—nor purely with the mimesis of destiny, but with (among other things) the medieval understanding of the relations between truth and narrative, reality and art.

In modern letters, chronicle-type narrative tends to be associated with historical (that is, true) subject matter, and story-type narrative with fiction. The latter has consistently had greater artistic pretentions—so much so that biography and history and have often been excluded by literary theorists from "literature."[54] The historiographer's artistic control over his material—the data of history—is considered more limited than that of the "original" author who fabricates (more or less *ex nihilo*) his own material, gives it cohesion and wholeness, and freely shapes his events into a story.

But the Middle Ages viewed these matters quite differently, and the dichotomies which we take for granted were not reliably perceived as dichotomies by them. First, what is peculiar about the medieval—or (Judeo-)Christian—way of viewing the phenomena of history is that they were considered not to consist of mere sequence, of shapelessly temporal raw data, but they constituted *a priori* a story: God's story. Time[55] was the sequential revelation to man of God acting purposefully in history (though God also transcended time: we will return to this idea). Time was an open parenthesis, human history a lack awaiting liquidation. Time began with the Creation and would end with the Four Last Things, which would not just end it, but complete it, perfect it. History was a story, and even the life of each individual man was not just a random string of temporal events but was itself a story; or at the very least, it had an order and a meaning, and it fit into the story of mankind in some significant way. One did not, as in modern times, have to invent one's own life story—to make it up—but rather to find out what it already *was*.

If history was a story, the problem was that only God—its author—really knew, in detail, what the story was; man could only conjecture. Indeed history often *looked* random and pointless. One is reminded of the expression: "cela va comme il plaît au bon Dieu" (things are going along as it pleases the good Lord). This French saying cuts both ways: it expresses both the impression that things are rather a mess, and the conviction (or perhaps more accurately, the bemused remnants of one) that God is in control.

At any rate, to the medieval way of seeing things, one did not need human artistic intervention in order to have a story. God was the fundamental artist whom all other artists merely imitated.[56] The dividing line between reality and art was very different for the Middle Ages than for the modern period.

On the one hand then we have the medieval conviction that every sequence of events which occurs is a "story," that all events have causality, meaning, finality; that every living creature has a function, though often known only to God. The profound effect of such a notion on the ways in which people composed and read narrative can, I believe, hardly be overestimated.

But this phenomenon—the pervasive medieval assurance that every *récit* is, somehow, a story—is itself the compounding, at a higher level, of a more basic problem: the haziness of the distinction between truth and untruth in medieval letters. Underlying this distinction is obviously the conviction that one can—at least roughly—determine what is historically true and what is merely the figment of human imagination. Now the medieval period was interested in this distinction; the word *vrai* (true) does often occur in medieval narrative (as well as in more strictly didactic works). But it is used in two different and revealing ways. *Vrai* is used, in a way familiar to us, to express the degree of fidelity of a message to its historical referent—as for example commonly in the claims of hagiographers that what they are telling is the truth.[57] (The writer asserts that he was an eyewitness, or that he has read or heard eyewitness accounts.) But *vrai* is also frequently used in a more peculiar way. Often it can only be said to refer to the faithfulness of the text to *another* text, or to a literary tradition. Clearly the referent here is no longer an event, but the literary account(s) of an event. And it is not only texts which we would call historical (or pseudohistorical) that protest as to their faithfulness; many works that seem to us patently fictional make the same claim.[58] They can do so of course for a simple reason: medieval narrators often did not make up their stories—their plots—and did not claim that they had. Their plots—"historical" and "fictional"—were largely traditional. Their stories were not, in fact, "theirs," except by the art with which they were told; and their stories were not reliably "stories." Vinaver neatly defines a phenomenon common in medieval *récits* when he says of romances that they broaden into even wider and centerless "panoramas"; when he speaks of the "feeling that there is no single beginning, no single end, that each initial adventure can be extended into the past and each final adventure into the future by a further lengthening of the narrative threads."[59]

To put all this another way: this blurring of the notion of the true, or this shift in what it refers to, is central to our point. For a narrator to conceive of truth in terms of being true to literary tradition—true to other stories, to *texts*, rather than to *facts*—means that he exists in relation to his data in much the same way the historiographer does to his, the raw material of history. I often suspect that the writer of a medieval narrative text, although deeply moved by the events he is recounting or characters he is describing, and concerned to make me also find them beautiful and compelling is, in fact, mystified by them; as mystified as I am. The fact that he is relating events—telling a "story"(?)—does not mean that he understands it all. He may well not understand—for example—the function of a given character. (In history, how are we to know what someone's function is?) But the fact that he does not understand something does not mean that in his eyes it means nothing. It may well have a meaning and a narrative structure that he feels escape him.[60]

This is precisely the situation in the text at hand: we have a story that has a persistent tendency to slip toward chronicle; that is like a page from the *Annales de la maison de Pontieu* as if written by their family chronicler. It tends to become a series of rather disconnected events or episodes. And yet the narrator appears convinced that it does mean something, that each of these episodes is relevant to the characters' itinerary through life, to their problem and its final solution. In particular, he flirts with allegory. For example, T and F enter the forest in which they are going to be attacked, and she, raped:

> . . . et mesire Tiebaus vint a la forest et trova la deus voies, et ne seut lequele aler, et demanda le dame: "Laquele irons nous?" Et elle dist: "Sire, se Diu plaist, la bone." En la forest avoit larons, qui mibatoient la fause voie pour faire les pelerins desvoier. Mesire Tiebaus descendi et esgarda la voie et trova la fause voie plus antee et plus large que la boine, et dist: "Dame, alons, de par Diu, cesti." . . . (7)

> . . . and Mylord Thibaut came to the forest and found the two paths, and did not know which one to take, and asked the lady: "Which one shall we take?" And she said: "Sire, if it please God, the good one." In the forest there were robbers, who widened [?] the false way in order to lead pilgrims astray. Mylord Thibaut got down and looked at the road and found the false way larger and wider than the good one, and said to the "Lady, let us, by God, go this way."

The narrator is toying here with the idea that T's error is a kind of sin; the echoing of the *New Testament* is unmistakable. Instead of choosing the "right way"—that leads to . . . St. Jacques!—he chose the "wide road, the false way," the hellish one. The robbers even hint at being "deadly sins," leading pilgrims off the track. In other words, N wants this mistake to be meaningful, as well as narratively functional. He does succeed in making it at least suggestive, but the story does not maintain this allegorical character.

It is probably true that no self-respecting medieval narrator would have passed up a chance to suggest the moral implications of "choosing the wrong path." (We cannot say whether our narrator added this detail himself, or whether it was in his sources.) In any case I am happy to concede that this is a cliché: it is indeed, a typically medieval way of making inexplicable actions seem resonant with meaning.

There is an even more important way in which our story shows the influence of chronicle. The text, which is full of binarities (parallelisms, and so forth), is but loosely controlled and focused by the essential binarity (lack/liquidation) of story. I remember my experience as a reader, reading this work for the first time. It starts out as a "story," in a perfectly canonical way. We have our noble young married couple, who want a child, and who start off to visit St. James, that *Adjuvant* to fertility. And then the heroine gets raped! And then she tries to kill her husband, and then her father tries to kill her, and so on . . . The story is never the same again. Thibaut does, dutifully, complete the pilgrimage alone (leaving F in a nearby nunnery) but now it seems rather pointless; it serves no visible purpose. It is as if there had been a violent disruption, not only in the lives of the characters, but also in our lives as story-readers; a radical intrusion into the world of "story" of a different kind of narration. The Subjects (that is, the couple who initially appeared to constitute the joint Subject) suddenly lose control of their story and are subjected to the apparently random violence of human life, to the often pointless brutality of other people's wills. We no longer know who the Subject is . . .

The entire middle section reads like a series of episodes, only loosely subordinated to the story that we thought we were being told.[61] Or rather, there *is* a tension here between story structure, which is hierarchical, and chronicle structure, which is sequential and juxtapositional. One amusing example of this would be the Aumarie section where "sultan sees girl, sultan wants girl, sultan gets girl—and later loses girl." This part can be read in two quite different ways, depending on whether we think of ourselves as dealing with essentially independent episodes, or truly with a story. On the one hand, the sultan is very much the Subject of his little episode, his mini-story—with of course a rival: $S_2 = T$. But on the other hand, he is also to be understood as subordinated, subjected, to the purposes of the story as a whole. In this light, he exists only in order to glorify the *maison de Pontieu*—to give them the "courtois Salehadin" (44) as an ancestor! Rather than being his own

Subject, he is merely an Adjuvant to the Pontieu family in its acquisition of glory. His narrative status can shift back and forth, depending on whether we are thinking of this work more as a chronicle (as a free succession of episodes) or as a single story.

Moreover the essential binarity—the initial problem and its solution—is problematic here. The lack is clear: no heir. But its liquidation is not so apparent; or rather, one is not sure *when* it occurs. How are we to read the two children born to F while she is the sultan's wife? One certainly cannot dismiss them: the daughter will be the grandmother of Saladin, and the narrator speaks of her at some length. (Indeed he spins off a final little episode dealing with her wooing by a Saracen.) As to F's son by the sultan: she takes him back to France with her and has him baptized Guillaume. He will marry the "molt bele fille" of Raoul de Praiax, will indeed become "sires de Praiax." But then F has two *more* children—sons —born from her marriage to T. Which child or pair of children liquidates the lack? This is unclear—and no doubt explains why Brunel forgets to mention the second pair in his *résumé*. All these children may be here because they really existed—or because N thought they had. But if so, that is merely a reminder that history makes sloppy stories.

Finally, as I mentioned above, what do the characters' various adventures (other than the initial and abortive pilgrimage to St. Jacques) have to do with the basic problem or its solution? How can their behavior be said to bring about—engender—the ultimate fertility?

Be all that as it may, the narrator does introduce his *récit* as a story, and he concludes it as one—for it does conclude, it does not just stop short. The lack is remedied. But most of the time this *récit* is more like an episodic semihistorical chronicle of varied adventures. And all the superficial repetitions (the echos, symmetries, and so forth) which suggest *retour* just give the illusion that the various episodes are connected in some profound causality, give the illusion of circularity, give the illusion of story. They provide a sort of surface *trompe l'oeil* of story.

It is crucial to note that Greimas's actantial structure works adequately only on story, and not on chronicle—insofar as this latter presents events (history) as structureless, haphazard. The actant notion is based on what one might call the "carrot approach" to motivation: the *Destinateur* places a carrot (or Object) in front of the Subject (or tells him that it is there) and off he goes . . . But, as any donkey knows, motivation can also be provided by a stick! The protagonist, like most mortals, most of the time, may ask little more of life than his daily bread—and *pas d'histoire(s)!* He may *move* only to *re*move himself from harm's way, to avoid being kicked in the pants by "Destiny." In other words, the motivating force is not necessarily internalized by the (apparent) Subject. Greimas's categories cannot be satisfactorily applied to the raw data of history. Who is the Subject of history, and of historical text? Who is indeed the Subject in the lives of most human beings?

But, of course, to the Christian Middle Ages, God was not only the author but also the Subject of history, and of men's lives. That is, he was fulfilling mysterious purposes—*His* purposes—*through* them. And God is a character here. He does play a central and explicit—if mysterious—role in this text. Behind and underlying and somehow explaining the "transformation" (the shift from childlessness to fertility) is God. If in the beginning they do not have a child, it is because God wills it thus:

> Et a grant deduit vesquirent bien cinc ans ensamble, mais *ne plut a Diu* qu'il eusent nul oir. (3; my emphasis)

> And in great pleasure they lived a full five years together, but *it did not please God* that they have an heir. (My emphasis)

If, at the end, they have two sons, again it is God's will:

> Molt fu li pais en grant joie et mesires Tiebaus eut *par le volenté de Dieu* deux fiex de sa fame. (42; my emphasis)

> The country was in great joy and Mylord Thibaut had *by the will of God* two sons by his wife. (My emphasis)

God also has an important and indeed explanatory (if not in any comprehensible sense causal) role in several other episodes. Or at least his name is evoked in a disturbing—and conventionally medieval—way. When asked by T which way they should take, F replies "Sire, se Diu plaist, la bone" (7); (Lord, if it pleases God, the good one). Did it "please God" that they take the wrong path? What

I am suggesting here is that we take seriously the medieval cliché: if God is consistently invoked in medieval narrative it is often to justify the mysteries of the plot. But do we always know when reference to God in medieval texts is merely a habit of speech, and when God truly fills some function? I am being only partly facetious when I say that many medieval narrative works—especially long ones—seem to be held together by, and *only* by, recourse to divine will.

During the combat between T and the robbers:

> *Ensi pleut a Diu* que des uit ocit les trois, et li cinc l'avronnerent et ocisent sen palefroi, et il cai sans avoir bleceure qui li grevast. (9; my emphasis)

> *Thus it pleased God* that of the eight he killed three, and the other five surrounded him and killed his palfrey, and he fell, without having any serious wound. (My emphasis)

Much later, when the sultan calls upon (or rather allows) T to help him defeat his enemies, we are told:

> *Par le volenté de Dieu* et en l'aie d'autrui, tant fist mesire Tiebaus qu'en pau de tans mist les anemis le soudant au desous. (36; my emphasis)

> *By the will of God* and with the help of others, Mylord Thibaut did so well that in a short time he routed the enemies of the sultan. (My emphasis)

One final, and crucial, example: near the end of the story we are told that the Pontieu group all went to Rome and visited the pope:

> Chascuns se confessa a lui, et quant il eut chou oï, si fist molt grant joie *des oeuvres et du miracle que Diex moustroit a sen tans.* (40; my emphasis)

> Each one confessed to him, and when he had heard it all, he rejoiced at *the works and the miracle that God showed to his time.* (My emphasis)

In other words, this text is, at some level, explicitly God's story, God's work; this mysterious plot, these events are God's miracles. God is not only its author, but its true Subject. It is He whose will —whose desire, whose Object—determines the action. And cannot this be said of all narrative literature, at some basic level? The genesis of the *récit*—the story of how the story came to be written, of what the narrator wanted—is often actantially significant. Insofar as the narrator is the author, it is *his* will which overlies and guides the plot. What *he* wants, happens. (One is very aware of this in a work such as Flaubert's *Bouvard et Pécuchet*.) We do not really know, in this text and in many other medieval texts, what God wants, what He is trying to tell.

We find in this work—as in many others—a tension between the Christian idea that God is changeless and the fact that human beings experience change. (God even seems here to have changed his mind.) I should like to explore briefly here this idea, implicit in medieval notions of history, that not only does God not change, but that history and change itself are really a sort of illusion; that what seem time and change to us are, in God's eyes, an eternal moment. Such a conviction had profound consequences on medieval notions of narrativity. To get at this issue we might compare the kinds of structures that we have in this work with those characteristic of another kind of medieval narrativity: that to be found in medieval pictorial or sculptural art; for example, in tympana, those extraordinary bas-relief sculptures that stand over the portals of cathedrals. Granted, there are many obvious differences between this short prose narrative work and a tympanum. But nonetheless this work is "narrative" in rather the same way as a tympanum. If both "tell a story," "depict events," they do it in curiously timeless terms. This story, like a tympanum, is structured less by narrative techniques—by transformation, unfolding, process—than by *figures*, in all the visuality and static character of that term.[62] (The figures are those that I mentioned above: repetitions, parallelisms, symmetries, and so forth.) Such figures diminish the sequentiality of the work; they collect images into a sort of contemporaneity. Medieval narrative —this one and many others—is often surprisingly like a picture, in that the episodes are masses, visualizable motif clusters—grouped, balanced, and contrasted in various ways. The unity of this work is more that of the complex image than that of the *récit*.[63]

In short, it is not merely that many medieval "stories" are disconcertingly un-*storylike*; many (this one included) are still more disconcertingly un-*narrative*. Or, to put it more prudently: we are invited, by these "narrative" texts, to transcend their sequentialy, to see them not only—or not so much—as a temporal unfolding, or *déroulement;* but also—more—as a great single spectacle.

If the story on a medieval tympanum can be defined as "chronicity (or diachrony) displayed synchronically"—history as it appears to God, as God knows it, sees it—then medieval *récits* often seem to be a sort of "narratively expanded synchrony." In spite of the fundamental linearity of the text, we are called upon to keep every element or detail *present* as we are looking at the others. But we are allowed to forget how (the process by which) we get from one element to another.

In the case of the medieval *récit,* as in that of the tympanum, we can be said to have the intrusion of the idea of the divine perspective—for which change does not occur—into the human experience of change.

Are we are dealing, in this type of "narrative," with a highly cognitive and philosophical understanding of art and its purposes? Are the perceptual (and sensorial) pleasures of story to be superseded by more intellectual satisfactions? If this should be so, we would be moving from imagination (through which the various moments of the story would be perceived) to the common sense (which would collect these moments into a whole), and ultimately to intellectual processes—intellect being, in at least part of the Christian tradition, the highest of the faculties. But in fact, I think that such an explanation may be inappropriately intellectualistic: it requires that we assume for this work (and for the tympanum) an audience of a very high calibre, which seems unlikely: whatever its pretentions, *La Fille du comte de Pontieu* is surely not intended for the intellectual elite of France, any more than is the sculpture on the facades of French cathedrals.

But it is true, the unity of the complex medieval narrative (of which we have been speaking), or of a tympanum, is the unity of a static composition of immobilized images and gestures; it is the unity of *pattern,* not of *process.* To some degree this is, I believe, attributable to the medieval view of time as an illusion—but it is also surely related to the importance of memory, and memorability, in medieval narrative. Medieval narrators (like other medieval artists) attempt to fix their stories firmly in the memory of their public, and this surely accounts for much of medieval narrative practice.

NOTES

1. I shall be using the edition of Clovis Brunel, *La Fille du comte de Pontieu, Nouvelle du XIIIe s.* Paris: Champion [classiques français du Moyen Age], 1926). Translations are mine, with closeness to the original being the goal.
2. About twenty pages; it runs to forty-four pages in Brunel's edition, but over half of each page is taken up with the late thirteenth-century version of the story.
3. I will spell the name of the geographical place Ponthieu as the text does—"Pontieu"—in order to avoid constantly switching back and forth.
4. Like her father, the count, and her brother, the count's son, she has no other name. She is referred to simply as "la fille," or sometimes "la dame," or "ele."
5. William Ryding, *Structure in Medieval Narrative* (The Hague: Mouton, 1971). At roughly the same time Eugene Vinaver published his *The Rise of Romance* (Oxford: Oxford University Press, 1971), which makes many points rather similar to Ryding's. Although I will address myself, here, primarily to the issues as Ryding poses them, I will take up Vinaver's approach, and many of his valuable remarks, at various points below.
6. Ryding, chapter 3 ("The Question of Unity") in particular.
7. See Ryding, 25–27, 117–35, etc.
8. Ryding, 16–17, 24–25, 139–54.
9. It is not clear what Vinaver means by this term either, or by "theme."
10. This phenomenon is extremely common: the narrative element in many "narrative" works is, often, in some very important way, secondary. Many of these works are primarily didactic (or at least *say* they are: the *fabliaux*), or broadly moral or religious (saints' lives; see also above, chapter 1). Or the narrator, through his story, may be seeking primarily to *move* his listener (or reader), to produce some affective impact. Vinaver (p. 139) gives (to different effect) an interesting quote from Steinbeck: the old pioneer (in *Leader of the People*) says: "I tell those old stories, but they're not what I want to tell. I only know how I want people to feel when I tell them." This very commonly, I believe, is the attitude of medieval storytellers.
11. See Ryding, 153–55.
12. Tzetan Todorov, *Grammaire du Décaméron* (The Hague: Mouton, 1969).
13. One could make of this schematization the same objection that Bremond makes of Todorov's list of verbs in the *Decameron:* that the verbs mentioned here exist at different "levels" (*Poétique* 6 [1971]: 204–7). This is true. Moreover, I can imagine several other and rather different ways of structuring the material in question, for example, along the lines of oppositions between the *sèmes* (or minimum units of meaning) of *absence/présence, vie/mort, clôture/ouverture, puissance/impuissance,* etc. I am aware that to go seriously into this problem could lead us very far afield; and, here, I am trying to make a simple point: that this text is heavily concerned with a limited set of basic kinds of activities.
14. There is some overlap here with the "exercise of power" category.

15. Some examples:

    Travel (transitive or intransitive)

    intransitive and voluntary: departure(s) on pilgrimage
    transitive (passive) and voluntary: F taken by merchants to Aumarie
    transitive (passive) and involuntary: F sent to sea in barrel.

    Love (always transitive)

    active and voluntary: F's marriage to T
    passive and voluntary: F's marriage to S
    passive and involuntary: F's rape by brigands.

    Power (always transitive)

    active, voluntary, and unsuccessful: attempt by F to kill T.
    active, voluntary, and successful: attempt by F to save T, C, and brother
    involuntary: F's delivery to death of a prisoner whom she does *not* recognize (28).

    Obviously, not all the categories apply all the time. At any rate, the writer does work out a good many of the possible permutations.

16. There are virtually no figures; the work has in fact very limited literary (i.e., rhetorical) pretentions. Its very shortness—its lack of *amplificatio*—is but one sign of this lack of artistic ambitiousness. There is one trope here, and it is very much a conventional one: The count, to reward Thibaut for his service, asks him: "Tiebaut, qel joel de ma terre ameries vous le mix?—Sire," fait Thiebaus, "je suis uns povre bacelers, mais de tous less joiaus de vostre terre je n'ameroie tant nul con damoiselle vostre fille" (2): ("Thibaut, what jewel from my land would you like the best?" "Sire," replies Thibaut, "I am a poor bachelor, but of all the jewels of your land there is none that I would love more than my lady your daughter.") In any case, we are very much in the realm of "*histoire*," in the Benvenistian sense.

17. One couple: I was initially tempted to see "F & T" as the joint Subject, on the model of "Romeo and Juliet", or, to pick an example closer to home, "Aucassin et Nicolette". But this couple hardly functions as a unit, nor do their interests overlap much—indeed, of course, she tries to kill him. They are separated spiritually as well as physically much of the time; in fact, in an important sense their marriage had been terminated by the count's attempted murder of his daughter, with T's complicity. And yet T and F are not *rivals* either—S_1 vs. S_2— along the lines that Greimas suggested in "Un problème de sémiotigne narrative: Les objets de valeur," *Langages* 31 (1973): 13–35.

18. On this development, see for example Paul Zumthor, *Histoire littéraire de la France médiévale* (Paris: Presses Universitaires de France, 1954), 209–10, 250–51.

19. Though it is certainly true that family was always an important theme in the *chansons de qeste*.

20. These cycles are based not strictly on the family but on Arthur and his court— which is, of course, a sort of brotherhood, with Arthur as the father—and a severe incest problem!

21. Greimas, A. J. *Sémantique structurale* (Paris: Larousse, 1966), 180–88.

22. Ibid., 181. Incidentally, Greimas's application of his model to an ideology—and not merely to texts—points up a difficulty, a hesitation, at the very heart of his system, as noted previously. Is he talking about literature, about narrative works? And if not, just what *is* he talking about?

23. Greimas, "Un problème de sémiotique narrative," 23–32.
24. The two are not completely compatible: it is not always easy, particularly in the Middle Ages, both to "amer le siecle" (1) and "servir Diu" (3). And at the end of the work, the characters feel a distinct need to "get right with God again." As we will see later, they all make a joint pilgrimage to Rome to visit the pope.
25. This text speaks often of heirs (oirs). Whether or not a male character has an heir is clearly a crucial bit of information.
26. C is T's maternal uncle (and we know how thick a bloodline that is in medieval literature; see Charlemagne and Roland, Marc and Tristan); and the count's own son will die at the end, making of T and F's children the heirs to Pontieu.
27. She is the weeping victim of rape; she (presumably) offers no resistance to her father's attempt to kill her. She is active in that she wants to be able to choose her mate(s): she chooses to marry T (her father asks her if she would like to and she says yes); she chooses to marry S rather than risk another rape ("Ele vit bien que mix li valoit faire par amours que par force" (20); (She well saw that it was better to do it for love than by force); she chooses to return to her first husband. She is active too in that she tried, clumsily, to kill the witness to her "shame." Finally, she is active, and even enterprising, in the way in which she saves the lives of her emprisoned family and manages to arrange their escape from Au-marie.
28. To usurp an inappropriate function also seems an error here—as in F's ineffectual attempt to kill her husband.
29. The distinction between "shame" and "guilt" in such a work and such a culture would appear rather futile: it does not matter if no one else sees your "shame," if God sees it.
30. I am aware that I am shifting levels when I speak of the narrator as an "actant." I will return shortly to this problem.
31. See Brunel, ix. It seems quite probable that this work, like several others from this period, was written for Marie, countess of Pontieu, 1221–51.
32. Moreover, even if there is a single and fixed Subject, he may not have a single and fixed Object: this is the case of Erec in Erec et Enide, for example.
33. Scriptural basis for this metaphor is provided by 1 Corinthians 12:12–31, among others.
34. This would, I think, be true of various of the Grail texts, where the different protagonists could be said to represent or embody different virtues and vices, or often, different degrees of virtue, within humanity.
35. Independent, that is, narratively, but not necessarily figuratively or symbolically.
36. See, for example, Paul Zumthor, Essai de poétique médiévale (Paris: Seuil, 1972).
37. Such is (implicitly) Greimas's interpretation of several of the initial stories produced by a child undergoing psychotherapy: Sémantique structurale, "Le Modèle transformationnel et le psychodrame," 213–21. There is, in Greimas's view, something "wrong" with the child's first attempts at narrative; only as he works through his "problems" does he produce "satisfactory" narrative; and indeed only his entire corpus can be said to constitute—through "transformation"—a récit (in Greimasian terms; a "story").
38. See Zumthor, Histoire littéraire 170–73, for example.
39. Indeed, it is already to be found in Aristotle's Poetics, chapter xxiii.
40. Though, in its extreme form, it is more a dotted line—a succession of separate

phenomena—than a true *continuity*, or line. The journal, the annal are, obviously, constructed of temporal atoms (days, years) conceived of as units and strung together.

41. In fact, every verb constitutes or creates a "transformation" (excluding *perhaps*, "to be" and "to have" insofar as they record stasis, not change).

42. In this sense, chronicle is nonhierarchical; each episode is on an "equal" footing with the others; none is *more* important, *more* significant. Chronicle, in this sense, is structurally paratactic.

43. Bremond is ambiguous on this issue; he speaks of "unity of action"; but it is unclear how this concept relates to the notion of the *récit*.

44. *Récit*, when used to mean "story," that is. Theorists would appear to have extended, unjustifiably, the structures characteristic of the *conte* (as identified by Propp, et al.) to the *récit* in general.

45. Gérard Genette, *Figures III* (Paris: Seuil, 1972), 75.

46. A case of an utterance with an implied verb might be: "Woe!"="I suffer." We must note, however, that at this extreme limit, *récit* and lyric are virtually indistinguishable.

47. I am not speaking here to the issue of the factual accuracy or inaccuracy of either of the two—or to the type of *discours*—but only to the degree and kinds of pattern and structure that characterize them.

48. At any rate, they do not want to—need to—conclude enough to *make* the problem solvable. If it is "impossible" for a nephew to do away with his maternal uncle cum lord—why can a writer not *change* the story and remove that blood relationship? Why indeed . . .

49. That is, as a random, mindless force; or destiny—which it is hard to distinguish from providence, or God. More on this question later.

50. He states that the *roman* "semble bien provenir de la convergence de deux traditions: celle des chansons de geste et celle . . . des historiographes" (*Essai*, 346).

51. The term "*aventure*"—taken by the Middle Ages, though apparently erroneously, to be derived from the Latin *aventura*, "the things which are going to happen" to a protagonist—suggests the unpredictability (and lack of causal linkage) of the episodes of such works. Ibid., 361–62.

52. A term used by Ryding (p. 14) and which he says originates with Giraldi (1549), according to whom "many actions of one man consitute biographical romance." (G. B. Giraldi Cintio, *Scritti Estetici: De'romanzi delle comedie e delle tragedie*, ed G. Antimaco (Milan, 1864). 1: 24–52), reference in Ryding.

53. Though, clearly, short narrative prose works are more vulnerable than verse narrative.

54. For example: René Wellek and Austin Warren, *Theory of Literature* (New York: Harcourt Brace, 1942), "The Nature of Literature," 22ff.

55. See, of course, Georges Poulet, *Studies in Human Time*, Elliott Coleman, trans. (Baltimore: Johns Hopkins University Press, 1956), "Introduction." The points that I will be making will, however, be rather different, as I am particularly interested in the three-tiered medieval conception of time.

56. See Graham Castor, *Pleiade Poetics* (Cambridge: Cambridge University Press, 1964).

57. That was virtually the only way that—in their eyes—hagiographers could ascertain the truth of the accounts of miracles. Since God's power was limitless, no

miracle was too extreme to be *a priori* incredible. Such a notion complicated considerably the medieval notion of verisimilitude!

58. *La Mort le roi Artur*, for example, often begins new sections with words such as: "En ceste partie dit li contes que."

59. Vinaver, 76.

60. Vinaver argues convincingly (pp. 37f.) that the very essence of the *roman*—its fundamental enterprise—was to make intelligible, to demystify, old stories (or *contes*); to supply them with "*sens*." But the meaning that he speaks of is often a symbolical or allegorical meaning more than a narrative meaning (or cohesiveness, or functionality). That is, the narrator of a *roman* does not make the *récit* (or story) "hang together" any better; the story line, the "letter" of the narration remains often obscure, in terms of the narrative connectedness of events. What the narrator adds is meaning—at *another*—symbolic—level. Vinaver himself points out that there is often rather a conflict, or a tension, between the old *conte*—still crudely present in the *roman*—and the new, *romanesque* (as it were) meaning which the novelist has added: see Vinaver, the *conjointure*, 39–44).

61. They are subordinated only in the sense that they constitute the openings of *new* parentheses—the posing of *new* problems—*within* the old: "Why did she do it (i.e., try to kill T)?" Then "What has become of F (i.e., is she dead)?"

62. Like the term "colors of rhetoric" *(colores rethorici)*. Both imply something on the surface.

63. It has been stated, of works such as the *Vie de saint Alexis*, or the *Chanson de Roland*, that the various narrative moments are like a series of static visual (or visualizable) images: "Alexis under the stairs," etc. I am making a somewhat similar point, except that we are confronted here, not merely with a *sequence* of images, but with what is, at some very important level, *one* image. That is, to give an example: this is rather like those pictorial representations of the "story" of Adam and Eve where *all* the moments of their drama are included within the *same* picture.

CHAPTER 5

La Vie de saint Alexis: Narrative Analysis and the Quest for the Sacred Subject

Desire clearly plays a central role in much of medieval literature and theology. The relationship, through desire or urgent need, between someone (a literary character, the self, or the soul) and someone or something else (its *finis*) is, as we have already seen, a central preoccupation, as is the role of others to the fulfillment of that desire. (The medieval theme of the quest is but one expression of this teleological tendency in narrative.) It is therefore of considerable importance in the analysis of medieval plots to determine the nature and structures of this desire. In other words, we must ask: what moves the characters and the story—and toward what? Who wants what? In these pages I will look at a particular set of desires and sort of narrative work: those characterizing the saint and his literary "life."

The terms that we choose to affix to the desirer and the desired are always somewhat arbitrary. But, as in chapter 4, I will again here have recourse to the terms used by Greimas in his actantial system: Subject, Object, and so forth. In the course of my analysis of the *Alexis*[1] (as in my discussion of the *Fille du comte de Pontieu*) I will demonstrate some of the weaknesses of Greimas's model, but

I will also point up ways in which such concepts and terminology can nonetheless be useful to us in the formulation of a hagiographical heuristic.

Our recognition that desire is crucial in many medieval texts and that the terms Subject and Object can be used does not really clarify how these entities function in narrative. When we say that the Subject desires the Object, what do we really mean by this? What exactly *does* he (or she) desire with respect to that Object? Although most contemporary narratologists—Greimas in particular— never define clearly what they mean by the term "desire,"[2] they have generally used it as if it referred to the Subject's wish or need for something clear and specific that he does not *have*, that he discovers he *wants*, and—this detail is also crucial—that he can get, that can be *got*. He wants this Object—for example, the throne or some love object—as something "to have, control, possess." Or the object may be something not yet done that the Subject wishes to do—or, more accurately, to have done. The knight is, generally, not so eager to kill the dragon as to have killed the dragon; he is not a sadist but a would-be hero; he wants the dragon dead, the problem solved, the glory won. It is clear that the satisfaction of such desires as these can provide narrative closure.

This sort of model of desire provides an orgasmic sort of release and satisfaction, and narrative closure. But, of course, desire—both in art and in life—is not always so simple or so readily satisfied. Is it always clear who or what the Object of the desire is? Is it even certain that all desire has an Object? Certainly medieval religious narrative, and hagiography in particular, though deeply suffused with what must be called, and often was called, "desire," presents peculiar features. It requires us to examine further what the desire can mean, how it can function in narrative, and what kinds of structures, as well as what kinds of content, it can imply.

To what theorist should we turn for a more adequate analysis of the complex nature and literary functioning of desire, one in particular that will serve us in our examination of the *Alexis* and of hagiography as a whole? To one of the psychocritics? After all, they are nothing if not obsessed with desire and with the idea of the Subject (whose very existence they debate). But while these modern *auctores* may present a tempting—certainly a fashionable—

choice to any modern critic, I should like to propose a "theoretician of desire" of a rather different stripe: Saint Bernard of Clairvaux. It is not merely *pour épater le moderniste* that I select him, but for a more significant reason: the psychocritics are, almost without exception, completely secular thinkers who have worked on modern, secular texts; indeed, they are often, explicitly or implicitly, hostile to religious ideas ("Comment peut-on être chrétien?"). It would surely come as no surprise if their models of desire turned out to be culture-bound. At any rate, there is no question in my mind that Saint Bernard's analysis (which is, in the bargain, profound and compelling) can help us more than a modern, secular model to understand how a deeply religious medieval work conceives the structure of desire and of the Subject-Object relationship. I therefore yield to Bernard for a Christian analysis and discussion of desire. I should like to quote at length from his little book, *De Diligendo Deo (On the Love of God)*,[3] but here I can only summarize a few of his ideas. In his definition of the nature of the love between the Christian Subject and his divine Object, Bernard makes three points that are of special interest to us:

1. The true Christian is in a paradoxical relation to God, for his desire for this Object is complex and contradictory in nature and effect. His Object is both absent and present; hidden, to be enjoyed fully only in the future, in paradise, yet constantly possessed, through prayer or meditation. The soul both "yearns for" and "sweetly rests in" God. The Christian "lover" is dissatisfied, in that he "seeks" and "languishes for God's presence"; but he also "takes delight" constantly in the thought of Him.

2. The full satisfaction that the Christian will ultimately enjoy—his Object—is no different from what he already enjoys: it will just be a perfected experience of the same joy that he already has. In one sense, the Christian has his Object at any given moment. This is why Bernard says that there are profound "self-sufficiency" and "self-containment" in loving God: in loving God, one "has" God. Unlike the would-be dragon killer, whose Object is to have killed the dragon the Christian desires, not to have loved God, but to love God; and this he can do at every moment. The only "reward" for loving God is to be allowed to love God more, ultimately perhaps "to see Him face to face." But, in another sense, the Christian will never get his Object. A throne may be possessable; a woman, only in certain senses; but God Himself, obviously, is simply not obtainable, accomplishable: one cannot "get" God.

3. But what exactly does the Christian desire with respect to God? The relation of the Christian Subject to his divine Object is most commonly conceived—explicitly by theologians like Bernard, implicitly by narrators—as presupposing the insertion of another verb, an infinitive, between desire and God. The Christian, and in particular the saint, wants to know God, ultimately to see God (to see the "face of the God of Jacob"), but for the time being, on earth, to worship and to serve God. And, of course, in serving God, the Christian already has what he wants.

Now there are certainly many literary figures identified as Christians who do not conform at all to Bernard's definition of a Christian: they want, not God, but money, or erotic pleasure, or power. One could say of them that their Christianness is purely incidental: the stories in which they appear are interested in them not as Christians but simply as human beings. And others, both real and literary—even insofar as they are Christian—desire primarily to be saved or, more precisely, not to be damned. Salvation is, in this sense, their Object; the Devil (as he was commonly called) their "Enemy." As we shall see, there are such Christians in the *Alexis*. Their relation to God is defined by fear.

But Bernard is talking about what the Christian should be, should want, should aspire toward; he is talking about saints, about the kind of characters who fill the *vitae* and *acta sanctorum*. And this sort of Christian obliges us to redefine our notion of desire, and of narrative time; the sketchiness of Greimas's definitions just will not do. Since every moment is full of God's presence, we clearly will not have that dissatisfaction with, or devaluation of, the present which is characteristic of texts where everything tends toward a future fulfillment, leaving (correlatively) the present empty. This sort of narrative time, which many modern narratologists have established as normal and indeed as normative, implies a relation between Subject and Object that is not by any means the only conceivable one. This relation is essentially profane, being based on what we might call, in theological terms, *concupiscentia:* "eager and passionate desire." But it is *caritas* that is seen as defining the Christian's ideal relation to his Object (indeed to any object) and *caritas* provides little concept of closure, since one is never through doing God's will. Or rather, there is a concept of closure in *caritas*, but it is a peculiar one, perhaps best understood through Bernard's re-

marks on the nature of the closure provided by acts of concupiscence (lust, avarice, and so forth). He disparages the satisfaction of
such acts, by reminding us that it is only temporary, even illusory:

> There is no limit to such restlessness, because in all these things the
> absolute can never be attained. And yet why should we wonder at man's
> discontent with that which is less and worse, since he can find his peace
> in nothing save only in the highest and the best? (P. 48)

In other words, concupiscence thinks its desire is finite, that some
object will slake its thirst. But the point made by Bernard is that
human desire is infinite, while human objects—however long the
list—are only finite. Bernard does say that "peace" is to be "found"
in the "highest and the best," in the Infinite that is God. But he
makes it very clear that the Christian does not seek that peace; it is
given by God, it is the Christian's reward and rest, but it is not his
goal or Object, which is to love and serve God. It is also important
to note that, according to Bernard, the peace, the satisfaction, that
the Christian finds in God, the Infinite, is itself infinite, inexhausti-
ble, unending—and hence different from that conceived by Greimas.

In short, the desire of the saints is different not only in content
but in structure from that proposed in the Greimasian model. Saints,
as Bernard defines them, and Christians, insofar as they are Christian, are extremely resistant to having a "story" at all, to desiring,
or being part of, any significant narrative "transformation." This is
of considerable significance, since numerous modern theorists have
regarded transformation as the essential feature of narrative. And
saints are resistant to having "problems" that in the work can be
"solved." A Christian holy man, for example, who contentedly
loves God all his life, who is absolutely incapable of being distracted
from God, his Object, can provide no transformation. He already
lives "happily ever after": at peace. It is clear that many hagiographical texts, though dominated by an intense Subject-Object
relation, lend themselves poorly to this contemporary notion of
narrative transformation. In discussing what happens in a saint's
life, we would do better to talk about a gradual process of transcendence than about a transformation; we can speak less of a modification, from something to something else, than of an increase,

through degrees, from partial to complete, not yet perfect to perfected.

But if it is true that in many medieval texts transcendence rather than transformation provides the narrative dynamic, medieval narrators themselves often seem to have found transcendence narratively unsatisfying; it was apparently a sort of narrative (or narrator's) *pis-aller*. Why else are there so many more accounts of the deaths of martyrs (at least something happens to them!) than of the narratively more monotonous lives of the confessors? Martyrs may be said to provide transformation material more easily than confessors; but the transformation that they undergo—death—they commonly regard as insignificant or blandly ignore (much to the irritation of their executioners), like Saint Cecilia, who, the stories say, sang as she was being tortured to death.

I suspect that the narrative transformation is a deeply ingrained —natural, if you will—characteristic of narrative and that it is abandoned only under considerable ideological (in the *Alexis*, theological) stress. Medieval hagiographers often seem to sense the narrative inadequacy, despite the moral superiority, of their saintly protagonists. (I will point out later some of the ways in which medieval narrators resolve this problem.) This would come as no surprise to a theologian: he would merely note that our literature is as fallen—as natural—as the human beings who produce it.

Let us now, in the context of the preceding discussion, turn to the *Alexis*. First, for those whose recollection of this text is musty, here is a brief plot summary:

A certain lord of Rome, Eufemieens by name, has been married for many years but has not been blessed with children. He and his wife pray to God with such earnestness that his wife conceives. A son is born and is called Alexis. When the boy is full-grown, his father, resigned to having no more progeny, determines to marry Alexis off at once so that he may see his lineage survive. The wedding is brought about, but Alexis's thoughts have been turning toward higher things. He leaves his wife on the wedding night and sails away to Alsis, a distant city. He lives there as a beggar for seventeen years. God then causes an image of the Virgin to speak, proclaiming Alexis a man of God. To avoid the honor that has come to him, Alexis once more takes ship, this time for Tarson, but the winds are contrary and he is carried back to Rome. Knowing that his father will not recognize him, he asks for a pallet under his father's stairs and the leavings from his table. For another seventeen years he dwells in this fashion, reviled and abused by the servants of the household and oblivious to the laments of his family. When he is about to die, he asks for ink and parchment and writes an account of his life. A voice once again speaks, by God's command, warning the city of destruction unless the holy man is found. The emperor and the pope seek him out. The letter found on the body of Alexis is read aloud. Alexis's body performs many miracles and is buried with great honors.[4]

We need to examine carefully Alexis's role in the text and his relation to God, who is, of course, Alexis's Object.

Alexis does have to overcome obstacles between himself and God: he has to reject, first, the world, his bride, his family and, later, fame as a holy man. But once Alexis is sitting among the poor in Alsis, and again when he is sitting under the stairs at his father's house, there is no suggestion that he is anything but perfectly happy, no suggestion that he wants anything more than what he has. He is presented as content. He has what he wants—and what he wants is to serve God. The text speaks often of his service (for example, 11. 85, 170–73, 276–77), and makes it clear that Alexis's Object is to serve God—and that is his only Object. Alexis asks, indeed he wants, no other recompense. He persists in serving God, well after God is ready to let him enter paradise as the reward for his already excellent service (11. 171–73). God asks far less in the way of service than Alexis wants to give. In short, one cannot say that "Alexis wants paradise"—and as for "Alexis wants to be honored as a saint," God forbid!

But when we say that Alexis is the Subject and that his only Object is to serve God, it is surely evident that he whom one serves, he whose will one does, he of whom one is the *Adjuvant* (to use Greimas's term) must be a Subject himself. He who is served precedes, at least in Christian terms, him who serves.

Indeed, God is presented as a Subject in this text. It is God who dominates and determines the action in this world. It is God who gives this son to his parents when they pray for a "child who may be according to thy will' ("par ton cumandment/Amfant nus done ki seit a tun talant!"; 11. 24–25). Alexis's fundamental act, his abandonment of the world, is seen as an answer to God's call. And when he leaves Rome (and, later, Alsis), a boat is waiting for him at the water's edge, and the men land "where God wants to lead them" ("La pristrent terre o Deus les volt mener," 1. 80): Lalice. Alexis then goes to Alsis, where there is a statue of the Virgin made by angels at God's command. He gives his possessions to the poor, sits down among them, and receives alms, when God grants them to him ("reçu l'almosne, quant Deus la li tramist"; 1. 98). And so on.

In short, God is Subject here, in the sense that it is his will that guides the action, that pulls Alexis where he goes, makes him do what he does. Could we say then, simply, that God is the Subject and Alexis his servant (or *Adjuvant*), that in hagiography we have the glorification of the *Adjuvant*, and exaltation of service, submission, obedience? In part, most certainly. One of the principal elements in the Catholic definition of the saint is that he is the *servus Dei*, the servant of God. It is essential to recognize that, in profoundly religious texts, God cannot be relegated to the role of mere Dispatcher, or *Destinateur*. His will is recognized as dominant. The first verse of Psalm 127 expresses this idea perfectly: "Except the Lord build the house, they labour in vain that build it; except the Lord keep the city, the watchman waketh but in vain."

Now the text emphasizes the extreme form of Alexis's submission and service to God. Unlike Saint George, he kills no dragons. Mostly he sits: among the poor of Alsis for seventeen years; then seventeen more years on a pallet under the stairs in his parents' house, unrecognized by his family. His service takes the form of poverty, mortification, humiliation. But the text stresses not only the passive and ignominious character of Alexis's service but also the will behind that service. Alexis is not a talking statue (like the one in Alsis), not a inanimate being; and the strange things that he does, he does because he wills to serve God, because he wants to love only God, because he rejects all that is not God,

God is indeed the principal Subject in this text; and Alexis is to be considered a saint precisely because he acknowledged God as the Subject of his own life and considered himself only God's servant. He "forgot himself." (The saint is often represented as wanting to be God's "instrument," an inert and perfect tool.) But *we* are not allowed to forget that Alexis is also a Subject; without that *will*— that saintly will—there can in fact be no saint. The narrator frequently speaks of Alexis's will as turned completely to God: Alexis loves God more than all his lineage; he makes a great effort to serve God, and so on (for example, 11. 50, 180, 245, 249–50, 259–60, 541–44).

In short, we need these two Subjects to understand the concept of a saint and the narrative structure of the hagiographical text. Without Alexis, without his will, his love for God, we would simply have theophany, a manifestation of God's power. We would only have God and talking statues. And without God as Subject—with Alexis alone as Subject—we might have a hero, we can certainly have a glutton for punishment, but we cannot have a saint. (Indeed, we cannot really have any voluntary service without the notion of a double Subject—and yet the concept of willing service is fundamental to medieval literature and institutions.)

Alexis is not the most *attachant* of saints. Though he is presented as admirable and venerable, I think it is safe to say that he is not particularly lovable. The difference in appeal between Alexis and a saint such as Francis of Assisi or Nicholas (or between their respective literary representations) is altogether striking. If Alexis seems less lovable, the reason is no doubt that he is portrayed as less loving. Or to put it a little differently, Bernard describes the love of God as the "voluntary movement of the affective faculty." His title itself suggests the role of will in this notion of love: *De Diligendo Deo. Diligo*, meaning "to prize, love, esteem," comes from the verb "to choose" *(dis + lego)*.[5] One chooses to prize one love object above other possible ones. Some saints may be said to represent a balance between these two—*voluntas* and *affectio*. Others are depicted as stressing in their life—in their desire—the affective part of the equation; they are essentially "lovers" of God, and often this love spills out onto other creatures, as it did for St. Francis of Assisi, *il poverello*. But Alexis is clearly in a sterner mold; he is one of those formidable saints who specialize in will. Words of "love" do occur, and quite frequently, in the text devoted to him, but Alexis is rarely the grammatical subject of such verbs. Alexis gives all his goods to the poor, but one gets the distinct impression that he does so because he wants to get rid of these earthly encumbrances, not because he so loves the poor. In this text, it is Alexis's parents and his bride who are the subjects of the verb "love"; they love Alexis, whose "will" *(talant, volentét)* is turned to God. In short, the Alexis of this text is not a passionate saint, not a lover of God in the Bernardian sense. And it is perhaps this, even more than his rejection of his family, that makes Alexis so chilly, and to modern tastes so repellent, a saint.[6]

We should perhaps note that the representation of Saint Alexis that we find in this text is at least as revealing about the spirit of the eleventh century as it is about the historical Alexis;[7] indeed, the saint commonly referred to as Alexis appears to be a composite of two saintly individuals (see, for example, Storey's introduction, pp. 18–21). Bernard's effusions and the loving and lovable saints—the great friars and the mystics, for example—are, to a substantial degree, a new phenomenon; they begin to emerge along with that new human and literary interest in love which occurs from the mid-twelfth century on, with that new mode of Subject-Object relation. We sense in Bernard a contemporary of Tristan and Iseut, while Alexis embodies an earlier, sterner ascetic spirituality.

We have then, for the moment, two Subjects: God and Alexis. It is not that we have two stories, one after the other, each with its Subject. Rather these two Subjects, and the orientation—the frame of reference—that they project onto the text, coexist, and we cannot do without either of them without mutilating the text. But *can* a text have two (or more) Subjects? I take the Subject to be the character (or a character) with respect to whose desires we consider the events and the other characters: a Subject is he whose interests and desires we regard as the (or a) frame of reference.

Now any creature possessing an "I"—indeed the Creator Himself—can in the abstract be thought of as the (or a) Subject, in the sense that and insofar as, he, she, or it has desire. Every human Subject can be presented, or can conceive himself, in relation to an Object that he wants. Every *je*, if it wants (something), is hence a potential literary Subject. When, in fact, a literary text has a single Subject, this simply means that one will has been allowed to dominate, to orient the narrative. The Subject is then that character to whom all the other potential Subjects have been subjected—subjected, that is, by a narrator.

In short, the question of the Subject involves two separate considerations; first, there is no Subject without desire, without some sort of Object; second, there is no literary Subject without a narrative choice—a *narrator's* choice. And a narrator may refuse to make a definitive choice among a number of willful characters, to allow any one to dominate. It is, I believe, quite common for a text to have several different Subjects, at different points and/or different levels of the work.

Let me clarify this point by referring to a short children's story, "The Little Gingerbread Man":

> An old man and his wife bake a gingerbread man, and as they are taking him (it? This text clearly requires a semantic analysis of its animate/ inanimate dichotomy, as well as the one I am suggesting) out of the pan, he jumps up and runs away. They run after him and try to catch him, to no avail. A rabbit also joins in the chase, and a woodcutter. Several other characters, eventually five of them, chase as well. Finally the panting gingerbread man arrives at a stream. There is a fox in the water who offers to carry him across to safety. The gingerbread man is dubious but, of necessity, accepts a ride high up on the fox's tail. As the water gets deeper, the gingerbread man is obliged to climb first onto the fox's back, then onto his head, then to sit on the fox's nose—whereupon the fox eats up the poor gingerbread man. The story, at least the version I was reading, ends with the words "But then, that's what gingerbread men are made for."

Now in such a story who is the Subject? We thought we were reading a story about a gingerbread man who encounters various Obstacles in his desperate struggle, as Subject, for life and liberty. We were following his adventures, his interests. But at the same time, though we had perhaps forgotten, we were also following the interests of those who wanted to eat him. And in the last sentence, which provides philosophical consolation (to the children, not the cookie), the narrative shifts, and the gingerbread man, no longer the Subject, becomes the appropriate Object of desire of the various Subjects (each conceived individually) who want to eat him. He becomes, retroactively, not a man, but a piece of gingerbread.

In other words, the same sequence of events can be presented with any number of different characters as—in some sense, at some point—the Subject. We can look at the events with respect to the wishes of each of the characters in turn, even if their wishes remain unfulfilled, even if their actions are futile, even if they never get their Object. What is more, the Subject can be shifted retroactively (as in the story of the gingerbread man). We can easily discover, after the fact, that the character whom we took to be the Subject turns out to be (is turned, by the narrator, into) an Object, or whatever. In short, the identity and functioning of the Subject are far more complex issues than Greimas appears to have envisioned.

One more point is worth making briefly here, even though we will return to it later: the words "that's what gingerbread men are made for" are very significant, for they suggest the difficulty of applying a Greimasian model, based on human desires, human *fines*, to any text (even this little secular one) in which an eschatology is clearly embedded, that is, in which what matters is not so much what the characters want as what they were *made* for, by their maker (or Maker). The natural end of gingerbread men is not (alas) to be free but to be found delicious; not to fulfill themselves but to fill others.

Let us return to the *Alexis* and to the two Subjects, the two wills, that we have before us: God and Alexis. These two wills are compatible because one of them has voluntarily aligned itself with, and subordinated itself to, the other. Alexis wills to do God's will. We can therefore follow, narratively, Alexis and God at the same time; we see what God wants by watching what Alexis does. But these two Subjects are not of equal narrative importance. God, though he dominates the action, is ever absent; his Object remains in many ways mysterious; his will is manifest, not his purpose. He is rarely the subject of a verb of action; rather he acts indirectly, through waiting boats, talking statues, perfect servants. Alexis, though he does not dominate the action and does only what God calls him to do, is ever present; it is therefore he who is the protagonist, as well as the hero, of this work.

Now this concept of the hero, and of the saint as hero, needs to be examined briefly, and a couple of points should be made. But first, a question: Why bother at all with this rather fuzzy word, hero? Hasn't narratology freed us from such hopeless terms? I think not. We cannot, in point of fact, understand why Alexis is a saint unless we understand how he is a hero. (The notion of "heroic virtue" is fundamental to the Catholic definition of the saint.) [8] And yet many of us have difficulty in recognizing Alexis, that sedentary individual, as a hero. One of my students complained that Alexis was rather a "lump"; another asked, rhetorically, "This blob is a hero?" We are, most of us, used to rather more aggressive heroes. Before discussing any further the nature of the saint's heroism, we should immediately note that Alexis, like most other saints and like all martyrs, is implicitly understood to be imitating Christ; we are dealing therefore not merely with the problem of saintly heroism but with the very nature of Christian (or Christ's) heroism. To a considerable extent, Alexis's (Christ's) heroism can be integrated into most definitions of the heroic simply by shifting the locus of the familiar battle from outside to inside and/or from the physical to the spiritual or moral. Alexis never fights any glorious battles, but his various renunciations can be said to constitute heroic struggles against the temptation to become attached to things of the world, the temptation to forget God.[9] In this perspective, it is just as heroic to sit under the stairs for seventeen years as to defend the honor of *douce France*. (Alexis does perform *one* heroic, exemplary deed, as a *clerc*—glorification of the written tradition!: he writes up his life's story.)[10]

But although it is functionally just as heroic to sit under the stairs as to wield Durendal—and although saints are spiritual heroes and Alexis is a veritable athlete of asceticism and renunciation—it is no mere semantic trifle that most literary (and real) heroes do things that are more obviously heroic. They ride on high horses rather than lying low under staircases; they mortify others, not themselves. It is only in an ideological system as profoundly permeated by paradox as is Christianity—the "crown of thorns"!— that such a notion of the heroic can flourish, only in a system in which one can speak, as Bernard (among so many others) does, of Christian souls as "glorying in the ignominy of the cross." In Christian theology (and rhetoric), the lowest are the highest, the humblest the greatest, the vanquished the triumphant; or rather, the haughty will be cast down, the downcast (and the dead) will be raised up—and the "will be" is crucial. In the Christian drama we are in a fundamentally two-act drama: the first act, earthly existence, ends in suffering and death; the second act consists of earthly recognition (by the people) and paradise. It is because Alexis willingly accepted a miserable, low, poor, despised state on earth— indeed because he wanted nothing more than that, and to serve

God—that he is now buried in a bejeweled coffin and venerated, that he is now "together with God and the company of angels" ("Ensembl' ot Deu e la compaignie as angeles"; 1. 607), that now, in heaven, he "sees God Himself" ("veit Deu medisme"; 1. 615).

The first act without the second—the death without the resurrection, the abasement without the subsequent glorification—would be unthinkable, or intolerable, in a Christian perspective. The suffering is essential, but it is never allowed to end the story; for this reason medieval Christian literature is profoundly resistant to tragedy.

There is yet another will—another Subject, I would maintain—not only present in this work but essential to its function as hagiography. In the course of this text, the narrator, at several points, addresses us. For example, in the passage describing how the people of Rome honor the body of Alexis, he says:

Sainz Alexis out bone volentét,
Puroec en est oi cest jurn oneurét.
Le cors an est an Rome la citét,
Et l'anema en est enz el paradis Deu:
Bien poet liez estra chi si est alüez.

Ki ad pechét bien s'en pot recorder,
Par penitence s'en pot tres bien salver.
Briés est cist secles, plus durable atendeiz.
Ço preiums Deu, la sainte trinitét,
Qu'o Deu ansemble poissum el ciel regner. (ll. 541–50)

Saint Alexis had a good will,
For this reason he is honored this day.
His body is in the city of Rome.
And his soul is in God's paradise:
He who has his place there can indeed by happy.

Anyone who has sin may well remember him,
By penitence he can very well be saved.
This life is short, await a more lasting one.
Let us pray God, the holy trinity,
That together with God we may reign in heaven.

After describing Alexis's magnificent funeral, the narrator says of the people of Rome:

Desure[e] terre nel pourent mais tenir:
Voilent o non, sil laissent enfodir.

Prenent congét al cors saint Alexis
E si li preient que d'els ai[e]t mercit:
Al son seignor il lur seit boens plaidiz. (ll. 596–600)

Above ground they could not keep him:
Whether they will or no, they allow him to be buried.
They take their leave of Saint Alexis's body
And ask him to have mercy on them:
To his lord may he be a good advocate for them.

And he ends his work thus:

Las! malfeűz! cum esmes avoglez!
Quer ço veduns que tuit sumes desvez.
De noz pechez sumes si ancumbrez,
La dreite vide nus funt tresoblíer,
Par cest saint home doűssum ralumer.

Aiuns, seignors, cel saint home en memorie,
Si li preiuns que de toz mals nos tolget.
En icest siecle nus acat pais et goie,
Ed en cel altra la plus durable glorie!
En ipse verbe sin dimes: *Pater noster*.

                                             Amen. (ll. 616–26)

Alas! unfortunate ones! how blind we are!
For we see that we have all lost our way.
We are so burdened down with our sins,
They make us forget the right life.
By this holy man we should regain our sight.

Let us remember this holy man,
Let us pray to him that he may remove us from all evils.
In this world may he procure for us peace and joy,
And in the other, the most lasting glory!
And on this word, let us say: Our Father.

                                             Amen.

These passages define, in a significant way, our relation to the text. The narrator invites us not only to believe what he tells us but to be moved by it; and not merely to be moved but to remember Alexis and to pray to him. The narrator is reminding us that we want—we *should* want—to be saved, to be "happy" and to "reign with God in heaven," and that with Alexis's intercession we can be saved. (We are not invited, at any point in the text, to emulate

Alexis; we are exhorted, not to be saints such as he was, but to pray to him.) In other words, the narrator is inviting and entreating us, his tepid Christian public, and exhorting himself along with us—*Priuns:* "Let us pray"—to want something and to ask Alexis's help in getting it. Like the people of Rome, we are not only to venerate Alexis but also to seek to be healed and saved by him. We are not so much to admire as to use him.

Now our role is sort of an expansion of that of the people of Rome. We are the Beneficiaries (Greimasian *Destinataires*) come-aware, seeking out the Helper (or *Adjuvant*) that we want and need: Alexis. In what sense can we be said to be "in" the text? Our position here is a little like that of the donor in certain medieval religious paintings, as of the Crucifixion: he is shown to one side, but still in the picture, next to the Virgin, near the Cross. He is both inside and outside the events depicted, both present and absent as a character. Like him we are ideologically and existentially in—even if historically outside—this narrative text.

I would argue that we too—like Alexis, like God—are fundamental Subjects of this text, in the sense that our desire for salvation is made explicit and significant in the text. But our desire does more than merely frame and echo the desires expressed within the story being told: it is the very condition of the existence of this text; without us this saint's life—this hagiographical text—would not exist. In the Middle Ages, it took veneration to make a saint. The notion of an unsung saint, a saint without a cult—without believers who asked for his intercession, who sought him as their advocate, their *Adjuvant*, with God—would have seemed a contradiction in terms. The process by which a saint and a hagiographical work came into existence required three subjects: God, the saint, and the people. It is we, the people, who must recognize Alexis and pray to him. Without our veneration of him, he has no legend—from *legenda*, "those things which are to be read" on the saint's feast day—no story, no existence.[11]

To borrow for a moment a cinematographic metaphor, it is on Alexis, our saintly Subject, that this text (or more precisely the narrator) focuses: we follow him in his peregrinations and mortifications. But the sound track records primarily the reactions of those he left behind, his parents and his wife; Alexis rarely speaks. What is the function, or role, of these other characters? Now in one sense they are obviously the Obstacles to Alexis's saintly heroism, to his perfect love and service of God. And it is in this light that Alexis, so long as he is alive, sees them: he hides from them, is afraid they will recognize him, and so forth. But it is the narrator, not Alexis, who controls this text, and the narrator does not present these characters purely as Obstacles to sainthood. He not only depicts them (to us) with respect to Alexis's desires but also portrays Alexis with respect to theirs. Fully twenty-nine strophes (out of 125) are taken up with the beautiful *planctus* of Alexis's bereft family.

Is it not curious that it should be *these* characters in the *Alexis* who talk the most and whom many readers have found the most moving? The narrator never censures their grief; indeed, he says of the mother, who has just discovered that the dead beggar under her stairs is the beloved son whom she had been seeking, and mourning, for thirty-four years:

> Chi dunt li vit sun grant dol demener,
> Sum piz debatre e sun cors dejeter,
> Ses crins derumpre e ses vis maiseler,
> Sun mort amfant detraire ed acoler,
> Mult fust il dur ki n'estoŭst plurer. (ll. 426–30)

> Anyone who saw her grief,
> Saw her beat her breast and throw herself to the ground
> And tear her hair and scratch her face
> And hug her dead child to her,
> Would have had to be hard indeed to keep from weeping.

Can characters who receive such ample development—whose desires, whose longings the text so fully and so movingly records—*not* be considered Subjects? True, these characters are impotent: they can do nothing but search (to no avail) and then, for years, weep at their loss; their presence is more a lyric than an active one. Is it enough for a character to weep, to be considered a Subject? The line between who is and who is not to be thought of as a Subject is clearly a fine one, and indeed perhaps arbitrary. But since the text repeatedly presents events with respect to their concerns and desires, and since their development as anything other than Obstacles —as drags on Alexis's holiness—clearly represents a crucial choice by the narrator, it seems important to include them in the category of the Subjects of this text.

It might be argued that the function of these characters in the text is essentially an exemplary one: that they are there, not to act as Subjects, but to show the full contrast between the saint and ordinary, mistaken mortals; between the saint and those who have missed the point. But I do not think that this conception of the family's role does full justice to what we find in the text. To be sure, from a strictly theological standpoint these grieving family members are wrong to grieve; they have failed to understand that their son and husband is a saint. But our narrator is not solely a Christian writer seeking to edify; he is also a *narrator*, with narrative problems to solve. I pointed out earlier the difficulties that I take to be inherent in writing the life of a saint, especially a saint like Alexis whose heroic actions consist so largely in *not* doing things, and whose Object is hard to represent without risk of monotony. Alexis's family, as Subjects, present real advantages.[12] They have two related Objects: they want Alexis, and they want relief from their uncertainty as to his whereabouts. This grieving uncertainty, which the narrator develops and amplifies, allows him to create a suspense—a suspense that the character of Alexis rarely allows—based on the question "Where is Alexis?" This question will be answered, in a scene full of drama and pathos, when the beggar's letter is read aloud; the bereft mother will finally embrace, not a fifty-year-old dead holy man, to whose holiness she is blinded by sin, but "sun mort amfant" (l. 429; the tableau is reminiscent of the later medieval Pietà). The *spuse*'s long wait receives a happy consummation: we are assured by the narrator that she is reunited with her husband in heaven (ll. 606–10). There is probably another factor operating in the positive development accorded to the *spuse* in this text. This bride, yearning for her bridegroom, grieving but ever faithful, could surely not fail to remind Christians of *the* Bride of the Christian tradition: the Church, Christ's *Sponsa*.

In short, I believe that neither the Greimasian concept of the narrative Obstacle nor the notion (dear to medievalists) of the exemplum does justice to the richness of the family's role. The human intensity of this text—to which many readers have responded, often at the expense of its theological grounding—cannot be denied, though it should not be exaggerated either. There are in fact two points of view, two kinds of human Subject, in this text: the saintly and the merely human; though the saintly certainly receives a higher valuation, both are given full narrative development, and the tension between them is never totally resolved.

We end this paper, not with one Subject, but with six, or at least four: Alexis, God, ourselves, and Alexis's family (father, mother, bride). What can we conclude from this rather untidy group? The concept of the Subject in narrative is clearly not a neat and restful one. Is it a useful one?

Let me say first that I think it *is* useful. It provides, I believe, a tool for getting at one of the major thematic concerns of medieval literature—*desire*—and, quite probably, for defining, at least in part, the specificity of various medieval genres. The different genres in this period seem to specialize in particular types of desire: desire for particular things, desires that allow for different sorts and degrees of narrative closure. In short, different kinds of works are characterized by different modes of the Subject-Object relationship. Moreover, some genres appear to require the presence of certain necessary Subjects. To be specific, the hagiographical text requires three particular narrative Subjects; the absence of any one of these means that the text, to a significant degree, belongs outside the hagiographical genre. That is, the absence of the prayers of the faithful, inscribed in the work—the absence of a "we" desiring salvation—moves the text out of hagiography and toward either religious biography (if the emphasis is placed on the historical accuracy of the work and if the primary purpose is to inform) or toward what we might call religious romance (if the text's major function is to delight).[13] In either case, it ceases to be a "sermon,"[14] whose purpose is to edify and to move; there is a fundamental shift in emphasis. If God is then removed as well—if the saint alone remains as Subject—we are very likely to have some sort of "study in psychopathology": the saint will appear to be, not a saint at all, but a lunatic, talking not to God but to himself.

But I want to elaborate further on some of the complications presented by the notion of the Subject. I am quite aware that I have been combining, in this analysis, elements that are generally thought of as coming from different levels or aspects of the text: plot development, point of view, narrative intervention, and so on. What I am trying to show is that a medieval text such as the *Alexis* forces us to expand to a considerable degree the notion of the Subject—if we are going to use it to any profit. First, it is important to recognize that the function of the Subject in literary texts, medieval and otherwise, must often be shared by various characters. No one character is allowed, by the narrator, to monopolize this function; in this sense it is the narrator who calls the tune.

What is still more important, with respect to medieval narrative, is that we often have to be willing to consider as Subject various figures that are not characters, or even "in" the story, in the obvious and traditional sense. In particular, in many a medieval text (and in the *Alexis*) the notion of the Subject cannot be restricted to an anthropocentric definition: God is here a Subject (and not merely, for example, a Greimasian *Destinateur*, or Dispatcher). God is indeed often the primary and dominant, if absent and mysterious, Subject. Now this introduction of the concept of a Transcendent Subject is disconcerting; for one reason it is, even more that the Transcendent Object, alien to modern psychocriticism (and psychoanalysis). The only "other" that modern psychology (essentially atheistic) recognizes as being able to intrude into the realm of the individual ego is the unconscious, the id. It is a question of where one is to look for the explanation of an individual's bizarre or inexplicable behavior. In the modern period—since Freud, in particular—we are used to looking down, and within man, to the mysterious unconscious.[15] But throughout the Middle Ages, and well beyond, one looked up, and outside man, to the equally mysterious workings and will of God (or of some other transcendent being: *Fortuna, Amors*—or the Devil), which affect individuals. And there is no reason to accept the modern contention that Providence was only a metaphor for the unconscious, that it represented a pre-Freudian intuition of the unconscious. The fact remains that the Christian Middle Ages had a way of explaining the inexplicable that was *different* from the modern, secular way.

The concept of the Transcendent Subject is also disconcerting in that it requires us to shift levels,[16] and it would seem that an implicit but cardinal rule of the game of narrative analysis is that the story or plot be considered in vacuo as an autonomous, closed system. (This is, in fact, a great weakness in almost all modern analysis: its tendency to tear phenomena loose from the context in which they have their meaning and without which they are often incomprehensible.) But this is precisely how one *cannot* think of medieval narrative; one of its crucial features is that it reminds us constantly that the story, with its human characters and events, is not a closed and watertight system. The ground of being of the text, we are ever reminded, is doubly transcendent. There is, as I have pointed out, a vertical transcendence by God, or by some other Transcendent Subject, that constantly interferes in, and takes precedence over, merely human intentionalities; whatever man's *fines*, his true "end" (or *telos*) and the "last things" *(eschata)* are ordained by God. (As Augustine put it: "You have made us for Yourself, and our hearts are restless until they rest in You." *Confessions*, book I, chapter i.) But there is a horizontal transcendence, intrinsic to the locutory act, that invades no less, and no less explicitly, the autonomy of the narrative message in medieval texts: the narrator (the Jakobsonian Addressor) often clearly states his own wishes with respect to the story he is telling; he has, himself, a clear Object in telling it. And the Jakobsonian Addressee is often (as in the *Alexis*) called upon to become himself a Subject. The locutory *je* and *vous* thus invade the narrative space and break the hermetic seal that is assumed so often in narrative analysis to close the *récit* in upon itself.

In much of modern literature (since about the seventeenth century) the reader has been lulled into forgetting that the literary character is necessarily overpowered by transcendent forces, is necessarily a "creature," made by an author (or Author) and used by a narrator.[17] But medieval narrative consistently reminds us that its personages—its human Subjects—however powerful and impressive, however ardent and successful in the pursuit of their heart's desire, are set in a reality that doubly transcends and overarches them. As human beings, they are clearly presented as subject to a divine (or transcendent) will. As literary characters, they are subject to the purposes of the narrator; they exist only within a genre and a work that are not theirs. And it is to fulfill the purposes of their Maker and their narrator that they are what they are—indeed that they are there at all.

NOTES

1. Quotations of *Lor Vie de saint Alexis* are from the edition by Christopher Storey, for Textes littéraires français (Paris: Droz, 1968). Translations are mine. Although an early twelfth-century date has been argued for the *Alexis* by Storey and a few others, the consensus of scholarly opinion still appears firmly in favor of a mid-eleventh-century dating.
2. See, e.g., Greimas, *Sémantique structurale* (Paris: Larousse, 1966), 180–82. Greimas ordinarily represents the "desire" relationship with an arrow

$$\text{(} \downarrow \text{) } \begin{array}{c}\text{Objet}\\ \\ \text{Sujet}\end{array} \text{ or a line (} \begin{array}{c}\text{Sujet}\\ \overline{}\\ \text{Objet}\end{array} \text{) } = \text{(} \frac{\text{Héros}}{\text{Saint Graal}} \text{)}.$$

3. St. Bernard, *In the Love of God*, trans. Sister Penelope (London: Mowbrays, 1950). This work was composed c. 1126. Many of the points that Bernard makes (in particular, the ones to which I am referring) are not exclusively Christian, but could be made by a Jewish or an Islamic writer just as well.
4. This plot summary follows closely that provided by Urban Tigner Holmes, Jr., in *A History of Old French Literature, from the Origins to 1300*, 2d ed. (New York: Russell and Russell, 1962), 30–31.
5. Five German Academics, eds., *Thesaurus Linguae Latinae*, vol, 1, pt. 1 (Leipzig: Teubner, 1910), 1175, s.v. *diligo*.
6. Holmes, e.g., says of the *Alexis:* "This narrative is somewhat unpleasant to the modern reader because of the utter selfishness of its asceticism—a disregard of the second great commandment, man's duty towards his neighbor. Alexis sees his mother and father, not to mention his wife, sorrowing unceasingly, and yet he keeps his silence to the last" (p. 31). This tendency to side with Alexis's family, against Alexis—to be sensitive to the intense human dimension of the work more than to its ascetical and theological dimensions—is, I think, a typically modern reaction.
7. As I pointed out above (note 1), there is disagreement about the date of composition of the *Alexis*. I do take it to be a mid-eleventh-century work, but should it be in fact a twelfth-century text (which is possible), then it has a very archaic flavor indeed.
8. See, e.g., the *New Catholic Encyclopedia*, ed. Catholic University of America (New York: McGraw-Hill, 1967), 12: 352–53, 972; A. Vacant and E. Mangenot, *Dictionnaire de théoloqie catholique* (Paris: Letouzey et Ané, 1939), 14:843.
9. It must be said, of course, that Alexis is never represented as feeling tempted. In this text, to be saintly, to be superhuman, is functionally much the same as to be inhuman, antihuman. Alexis is "hard of heart." There is no suggestion, in the letter of the text, that he might have thought, for example, that a soft, warm bed might feel better than his hard and damp pallet. In short, temptations exist for Alexis only in an external sense and only to be overcome.
10. See Karl D. Uitti, "The Clerkly Narrator Figure in Old French Hagiography and Romance," *Medioevo Romanzo* 2 (1975): 394–408.
11. Although I have referred to this work as a text, it is really a song *(chanson),*

consisting of 125 strophes, each composed of decasyllabic lines. It was apparently written to be sung in church on the feast of Saint Alexis.

12. There are also hagiographical texts (or representations of saintly characters in other works) in which the Devil or evil men are extensively developed as Subjects. They often make highly satisfactory Subjects—more so than the saint himself, who may be very "undynamic," and whose only Object may be "not ot abjure" before being martyred. A case in point is the *Cantilène de sainte Eulalie*.

13. This is true of Benedeit's *Voyage de St. Brendan*, which never calls directly for prayers, or even emulation.

14. It is thus that Guernes de Pont Sainte-Maxence, for example, refers to his work on the life of Saint Thomas à Becket: *La Vie de Saint Thomas Becket*, ed. Emmanuel Walberg, Classiques français du moyen âge (Paris: Champion, 1936), ll. 22, 6156.

15. The superego has received short shrift from modern psychology. Like the id, it is seen as largely unconscious and as part of the individual; in no way is it thought of as transcendent, or even as truly "above" the ego.

16. It is also disconcerting in that it is hard to tell when such forces are really present in the text. Is there a single medieval work in which God's name and pleasure are not mentioned? *A Dieu ne plaise!* When is God truly an invisible actor, and when is he merely a figure of speech or a figment of the imagination of a character?

17. I am distinguishing here between the author (collective or individual, human or divine) who made the characters and the story, and the narrator who tells the story. In some works, of course, these different functions are combined.

CHAPTER 6

The *Lais* of Marie de France: "Narrative Grammar" and the Literary Text

One of the forms that contemporary narrative analysis has taken is the attempt, as by Tzetan Todorov, to establish a "narrative grammar"[1]—the central purpose being to account for the intelligibility of the literary work at what is called the "syntactic" level. Thus, in Todorov's *Poétique*, one section on "the analysis of the literary text" is entitled "the syntactic aspect: structures of the text." Now this word "syntactic" might seem to imply that we are dealing with, if not surface structures, at least structures fairly close to the surface of the text. But it must be pointed out that this word, whose grammatical meaning is still the primary one today, is often used in quite different senses by logicians, linguists, and narratologists. In the *Grammaire du Décaméron*, Todorov never discusses any text in any specificity or detail, but deals only with narrative synopses.[2] This fact is perhaps of particular interest to those with an interest in style and stylistics—and what literary historian can despise such matters?—because most definitions of style concern themselves at least primarily with the letter of the text. Stylistics is the study of the surface of texts, of their rhetoric, of their syntax in the literal sense—not of that supersyntax and subsyntax that are most commonly meant by narratologists when they speak of "syntax." Stylistics deals primarily not with overarching or underlying structures, but with the ones that we actually perceive and respond to on the page.

But several questions arise which are as relevant to narrative analysis as to stylistics: what *is* the relation between the kind of syntax—the kinds of structures—that Todorov is speaking of, and those words that we actually read on the page? And *do* all texts provide us with "intelligibility" at the "syntactic" level (as defined by Todorov)? I shall explore these issues with respect to Marie de France's *Lais*.[3]

Let me start by referring to Todorov's definition (in *Poétique*)[4] of the "sequence," which he postulates as the basic narrative unit, often corresponding to the short *récit:*

> An ideal narrative [*récit*] begins with a stable situation that some force disturbs. The result is a state of disequilibrium; by the action of a contrary force, the equilibrium is reestablished; the second equilibrium is much like the first, but the two are never identical. There are, consequently, two types of episodes in a narrative: those which describe a state (of equilibrium or of disequilibrium) and those which describe the passage from one state to another.

Let us postulate that this definition—which presents, I think, an *a priori* plausibility, and which resembles considerably the ideas of several other contemporary narratologists—is true of what Todorov calls "the ideal narrative" *(le récit idéal)*. (That concept "ideal" does pose some problems, but let us leave them aside for the moment.) Or more precisely, let us postulate that this definition, or model, works well when applied to *plot summaries*, from the story *given*, retroactively and as a whole. Working from the narrative synopsis of a *récit*, you can cut the *récit* into the five basic moments of which Todorov speaks: a moment of initial stability, which is disturbed by some force; a state of instability; and so on. And I will ask you to trust me when I assert that, working from plot summaries of the *Lais*, one can (often) cull from Marie's little *récits* these five canonical moments.

In this context, the question that interests me—that my attempts to analyze closely Marie's text forced me to be interested in—is this: what about when you read the work for the first time? How is

it different from the work perceived, understood from a plot summary, or retroactively? That is, the point that interests me—and
this was not Todorov's concern—is the *resistance* of the text to
being summarized, synopsized. Todorov is interested in our ultimate *knowledge* or mastery of the text; I, in our *perception* of it—
and in the gap between knowledge and perception. Let me expand
a little on the problem that I see here. Todorov is trying to identify
the basic structures of texts, structures that not only make all *récits*
profoundly similar, but which provide (these structures) for the
reader the experience of recognition—of the conformity of a text to
some internal pattern or model. That is, Todorov is trying to account, in part, for the satisfactions provided by the literary text.
And these satisfactions are seen as lying primarily in the *intelligibility* of the text, narratively speaking. His model suggests that we
say to ourselves as we read through the work: "Well, here is the
initial situation. What is going to happen? Aha, here comes the
problem . . ." (and so forth). And finally: "Here is the solution; the
story is *over*." It is probably safe to assume that all narrative works
—at least those whose purpose is primarily to delight, and not to
inform or teach—do give us, at least at some point in our experience of them, and at least to some degree—this experience of intelligibility. They fit themselves into a grid that we have ready in our
mind. (I shall not address myself to the issue of where this grid
came from, where we got it: whether it is born from experience or
rather is fundamental to the structure of our mind.)

But is it not clear that different texts become "intelligible" to us
in different ways, at different points in our experience of them—
and indeed that the very notion of "intelligibility" can be conceived
in different ways? In particular, some works (texts, but films, and
so forth, as well) deliver themselves up to us as immediately intelligible. We see immediately exactly what the problem is, for whom
this problem exists, and what sorts of solutions are possible. This is
often true of popular narrative: television situation comedy, as well
as pulp novels, and so forth: such works are often staggeringly
analyzable in Todorovian terms, even as we read (or watch) [5] them.
But this is not always the case, for other works may keep us mystified for almost the whole time we are reading, and perhaps only
make themselves intelligible at the end. And in this sense the story

we read is only intelligible retroactively, is only intelligible when we *have read* it. It is part of my thesis that Marie de France's *Lais*— insofar as they *are* "narratively" or "syntactically" speaking "intelligible" are, on the whole, "intelligible" *only retroactively*.[6]

To put all this more precisely: there is a whole set of techniques by which narrators make immediately intelligible or perceptible the underlying narrative structures—or "syntax"—of the events that they are recounting. I will try to enumerate some of them, and discuss Marie's use of them.

One of the most striking of these techniques is the use of tenses.[7] It is the tenses, more I believe than any other single factor, that help us in modern French tell the forest from the trees in narrative, help us distinguish between what the psychologists call the figure and the ground. To oversimplify a bit: when we read a long passage in the *imparfait* (imperfect), we just keep skimming along until we finally hit the *passé simple* (or the *passé composé*); this basic distinction in modern French tells us what is stasis and what is action; and, as we read along, when we find the *passé simple*, we know we are onto the track of the story, of the plot.

But the tenses were used very differently in Old French[8] narrative —at least through the twelfth century. Now this is an area of historical linguistics that has not been studied very thoroughly, and what studies have been done are somewhat contradictory, but a few basic facts do stand out. First, Old French was, by our standards, extraordinarily flexible in its use of tenses. Their usage appears to have been dictated less by an emphasis on strict chronology or by any clean distinction between stasis and action than by what we might call dramatic and stylistic considerations: how intensely or vividly the scene is to be felt or perceived; whether the narrator wishes to change the pace of his narration, and so on.

The second fundamental feature of much Old French tense usage is that, within this flexibility, the *passé simple* (also called the *aoriste*) is the fundamental tense *both* for narration and for description. It alternates frequently—more so than today, in written narrative—with the present tense; it also alternates to some degree with the *passé composé* (or *passé indéfini*). While the *imparfait* does occur in description, this usage is far from being as standard as today.

In short, one of the major tools whereby we distinguish in modern narrative between action and stasis, narrative and description, figure and ground, is *absent* from Old French narrative. If we, as readers, pass from a roughly speaking modern to a twelfth-century text, I believe that we perceive a radical and immediate drop in the intelligibility of the text—that is, according to the definition of intelligibility given above: of how any proposition fits into the narrative syntax, or movement, of the story. For example, it can mean that we have a very hard time telling where the setting—the initial stasis—ends, and where the problem begins. We are lacking one of the fundamental cues to the function of various "propositions." This verb tense factor points up a very central feature in the interpretation of narrative: we determine what is "stasis" and what is "action" not so much because we have some firm internal notion of what stasis is, or of what a problem is, or of what action is, but because our text identifies them for us grammatically—in the strict sense of that term. Our perception of *"narrative* grammar" is terribly dependent on literal, *surface* grammar (or morphology). Let me, at long last, quote from Marie. I am quoting here the beginning of her *lai* "Laŭstic" (to which I shall refer several times later).

> Une aventure vus dirai,
> Dunt li Bretun firent un lai;
> Laŭstic ad nun, ceo m'est vis,
> Si l'apelent en lur païs
> Ceo est russignol en franceis
> E nihtegale en dreit engleis.
> En Seint Mallo en la cuntree
> *Ot* une vile renumee.
> Deus chevalers ilec *manéent*
> E deus forz maisuns (i) *aveient.*
> Pur la bunté des deus baruns
> *Fu* de la vile bons li nuns.
> Li uns *aveit* femme *espusee,*
> Sage, curteise e acemme;
> A merveille se *teneit* chiere
> Sulunc l'usage e la manere.
> Li autres *fu* un bachelers
> Bien coneŭ entre ses pers
> De prŭesce, de grant valur,
> E volenters *feseit* honur:

Mut *turnéot* e *despendeit*
E bien *donot* ceo qu'il aveit.
La femme sun veisin *ama;*
Tant la *requist,* tant la *preia*
E tant par *ot* en lui grant bien
Que ele l'*ama* sur tute rien,
Tant pur le bien qué ele *oi,*
Tant pur ceo qu'il *iert* pres de li.
Sagement e bien *s'entr'amerent;*
Mul se *covrirent* e *garderent*
Qu'il ne *feussent aparceǔz*
Ne desturbez ne mescreǔz . . .   (ll. 1–32; my emphasis)

I will tell you an adventure
About which the Bretons made a lai;
"Laustic" is its name, it seems to me,
Thus they call it in their country;
This is "rossignol" in French
And "nightingale" in proper English.
    In the region of Saint Malo
There was a famous city.
Two knights lived there
And they had two strong houses.
Because of the goodness of the two barons
The city had a good name.
One had married a wife who was
Wise, courtly, and fashionable;
She had a high opinion of herself [held herself
    dear]
Within the bounds of custom.
The other was a bachelor
Well known among his peers
For his prowess, his great value,
And happily did he enjoy his honor:
He went to tournaments a lot and spent
And gave good gifts from what he had.
He loved the wife of his neighbor;
He asked her so much, begged her so much
And there was in him so much good
That she loved him more than anything,
As much for the good things she heard,
As for the fact that he was nearby.
Wisely and well they loved each other;
Greatly did they conceal and watch themselves

So that they were not seen
Or disturbed or thought ill of.

Now this goes on at some length—at more length than I can quote here. But, as you can see, we have a hard time telling where we are going. We do not know when or where the description, the setting, ends and the story proper begins; when the stasis ends and the force arrives on the scene. More specifically, we do not know whether to consider love as part of the given, as part of the initial *stability*—an ongoing adulterous triangle, with a certain stability—or as the *force* that comes to perturb the conjugal stasis. Is that "love" *(ama)* functionally speaking an adjective?: they *were* in love; they *were* lovers. Or a verb?: they *become* lovers—and therein lies a tale. A reader who was not familiar with medieval literature—especially with more or less "courtly" works—might instinctively and immediately assume that adultery is to be understood as the problem, the perturbing force. But adultery is far from reliably presented as such in this period! (Many of the various "Tristan and Iseut" stories *assume* the adulterous triangle as one of the givens, as part of the initial "stasis.")

In any case, if we approached all this from the perspective of a narrative synopsis, we could cast our summary so that there was no problem: all this passage that I quoted above would turn out to be preliminary, a description of the stasis; the force which disrupts this initial adulterous equilibrium occurs when springtime comes and the lovers get so carried away that they spend all night every night at their windows which face each other. This makes the husband jealous, and off we go. But as we read along, we cannot see where we are in the story, and we only know where we *are* when in fact we get *past* it. The use of tenses in no way helps us. We are forced to be extraordinarily passive as we read along; we are not able actively to anticipate what is coming, but are ever surprised. The fact that in a good many *lais* we know—through predictions offered by some character or by Marie herself—what is going to happen, in no way diminishes our surprise as we are reading; we are still caught unawares by the actual occurrence of the foretold events.[9]

As is clear in the case I just mentioned, we have in a great many situations and phenomena, both literary and "real," no *a priori* notion of what stability—or action—is, or of how to distinguish between them. I mentioned adultery above; but indeed what of marriage? Is it a state of stability, or a problem? That depends, *literarily* speaking, a great deal on whether a text *ends* with the marriage—"And they lived happily ever after"—or whether, after a few introductory pluperfects and imperfects, the story, and hence the problem, *begin* with the couple's marriage. The former leads us into restful bliss and the other into dilemmas and conflicts. In short, a *location* of the motif within a story is one of the clues by which we code it as to stasis or force, stable or dynamic. But, as was clear above, determining the location of something in Marie de France is difficult, and commonly can be done only retroactively. That is, a sentence or proposition 50, 100, or 250 lines "into" a story may still be part of a long introductory passage, or well into the plot, or almost at the end. This is particularly true of the *Lais*, which vary in length from 118 to 1184 lines! We only know something is "at" or "near" the end of a text if nothing, or nothing much, comes after it; and texts do not necessarily end when or where we expect(ed) them to.

But of course verb tense and spatial location of propositions are only two of the techniques by which narrators facilitate or complicate for us the experience of intelligibility. In many texts there is a whole plethora of factors which allow us readily to identify the actors that matter and the problem that is arising. Another of these techniques is the use of proper names: the hero or heroine is often he or she who stands out from the crowd by the fact—the *mere* fact —of having a name. The others may remain vague and common, as it were; in the background. But Marie de France's use of proper names is enough to baffle any reader—especially any reader who expected to be able to use them as indicative of narrative function.[10] There are *lais* where no one has a proper name—that we can cope with; there are some where both the lovers have a proper name; but there are *lais* where only one—or neither—of the lovers has a proper name, but where many of the secondary characters have one. In short, the fact that a character does or does not have a name is not merely of no use to us, it is positively disconcerting, as we read along, trying to figure out who's who and what's going to happen to whom. One of my favorite examples here is "Guigemar," the first *lai* (in most manuscripts), which after a short prologue begins thus:

> En cel tens tins tint Hoilas la tere,
> Sovent en peis, sovent en guere.
> Li reis aveit un sun barun
> Ki esteit sire de Līun;
> Oridials esteit apelez,
> De sun seignur fu mult privez.
> Chivaliers ert pruz e vaillanz;
> De sa moillier out deus enfanz,
> Un fiz e une fille bele.
> Noguent ot nun la damaisele;
> Guigeimar noment le dancel,
> El réaulme nen out plus bel;
> A merveille l'amot sa mere
> E mult esteit bien de sun pere;
> Quant il le pout partir de sei,
> Si l'enveat servir un rei.
> Li vadlet fu sages e pruz,
> Mult se faseit amer de tuz. (ll. 27–44)

> At this time Hoilas ruled the land,
> Often in peace, often in war.
> The king had a baron
> Who was lord of Liun;
> His name was Oridials,
> And he was in the king's confidence.
> He was a worthy and valiant knight;
> By his wife he had two children,
> A boy and a beautiful daughter.
> Noguent was the young lady's name
> Guigemar they call the boy,
> In the kingdom there was not a handsomer one;
> His mother loved him marvelously well
> And he was on very good terms with his father;
> When the father could bear to part with his son,
> He sends the boy to serve a king.
> The lad was wise and worthy,
> And made himself greatly loved by all.

And so on. Now the reader may well be interested in King Hoilas, in Oridials, in Noguent, in this loving mother—but, except for a quick visit that Guigemar pays his family a few lines below this passage, the reader will never hear any of them mentioned again, for the rest of the story concerns exclusively Guigemar, and soon, his ladylove, who is never named at all.[11] Now at the end, when we are competent to write a plot summary, we can hide the tracks of our early confusion and uncertainty as readers by blotting out King Hoilas, and the father Oridials, and the mother, and sister Noguent because they turn out—they will have turned out—not to matter at all to the plot. And two of the people who do matter most— though they do not have names: the lady and her husband—we will of course fit into our summary of the narrative "syntax."

Now this feature of Marie de France's *Lais*—and of many other medieval narratives—is worth commenting on. We have here a lot of Agents with no verbs or (to switch to Greimasian terminology) a great many characters hanging around with no actantial function, no role, to speak of. This is a kind of character to which the narratologists have paid no attention, since, as you can readily see, it fits in no way into their models of narrative. (Greimas would be inclined to dismiss such characters as belonging to the narrative *discours*—which does not interest him.) The only apparent function of Oridials, Guigemar's father, is that of being his father, of being necessary to his physical, human existence, but not to his narrative existence. He is humanly very real and necessary indeed—just as Guigemar's sister Noguent is humanly significant—but they are both narratively redundant, and will drop out in a narrative summary.[12] What is interesting here is that medieval narrative—again, Marie in particular—had a high tolerance for functionless characters. We are used to thinking that in a good story, a good play, all the characters have a role, a function, are there for a "reason." But medieval literature seems to *enjoy* a sense of the *functionless*—the narratively, syntactically useless—that is disturbing to us (and/or to our theories).

Yet another clue to help us pick our way through the thicket of words in narrative, to tell where we are going, what is important, what—and who—matters is the very fact that the narrator commonly focuses in on a single character or small number of characters (who, as I mentioned above, generally have names). In this sense the hero will be he upon whom the limelight falls, the character whom the narrator follows. But this is primarily and necessarily true only of long narratives—of the novels of Chrétien, for example. But in a short narrative there may never be the necessity or even the possibility for the narrator to follow intensively, exclusively one or two characters at the expense of others. No one protagonist's interests may be much more developed than those of any other. (We saw this in chapter 5 in my analysis of "The Little Gingerbread Man.") This complicates considerably a Greimasian but also in fact a Todorovian reading of certain *lais:* who is/are the character/s with respect to whose intentions or whose situation we are to read and interpret the significance of events that occur? In Greimasian terms this means that we do not know whom to cast as the Subject; in Todorovian terms we find that we keep switching Agents, and that we sometimes end up with an Agent and concerns that are not the ones we started with—though we were expecting to come, somehow, full circle. This is true of "Equitan," for example. A hasty narrative summary:[13] the king, Equitan, becomes the lover of his seneschal's wife; so that they can get married, they decide to do away with her husband. The wife has two baths prepared: one scalding, for her husband; another, just right, for her lover. But the lovers get distracted from their plans by their passion: they are making love when the seneschal opens the door. To hide his shame, the king jumps into the bath—the wrong bath—and dies a grisly death, the death intended for the seneschal. The seneschal, grasping what has happened, drowns his wife. Marie comments:

> Issi mururent amb(e)dui,
> Li reis avant, e ele od lui.
> Ki bien vodreit reisum entendre,
> Ici purreit ensample prendre:
> Tel purcace le mal d'autrui
> Dunt le mals (tut) revert sur lui. (ll. 305–10)

> Thus they both died,
> The king first, and she with him.
> Whoever would like to listen to reason
> Could take this as a lesson [example]:
> He who seeks to harm someone else
> Finds that the evil turns back on him.

Are we morally reassured to hear that justice has been done? Well, frankly, I had not realized, till I read those lines, that I was supposed to be all that interested in justice in this story. This *lai* seemed all along to be about love, and the lovers, but of course the seneschal was present all along, and we were aware that what the lovers were doing was not quite "right." At any rate, in the end we seem to have switched Greimasian Subjects or Todorovian Agents, from the lovers to the husband—and it is *he* who, finally, gets a chance to "modify the situation"! At the very least, we have switched topics and verbs: from love to punishment, from passion to retribution. But then the *lai* ends with these words:

> Issi avient cum dit vus ai.
> Li Bretun en firent un lai,
> D'Equitan, cum (ent) il fina
> E la dame que tant l'ama.   (ll. 311–14)

> Thus it happened, as I have told you.
> From this the Bretons made a lai,
> About Equitan: how he ended up,
> And the lady who loved him so much.

We seem, at the last moment, to have changed back to the lovers as the Agents whose concerns and destiny matter.

To sum all of this up: when we read the *Lais* of Marie de France, it often takes us quite a while to figure out whom we are reading about, what the problem is—and even with respect to whose interests. We often cannot anticipate what attribute—and of whom—will turn out to be "modified." We may never quite understand until the end; only retroactively can we determine what "is" (in fact: "was") a state of equilibrium, or of false equilibrium, or a force, etc. The fact that we can only perceive these elements in the text retroactively makes one wonder in what sense these structures can be said to be *in the text* at all . . . Could they not be—at least in some cases—in our *minds?*[14] Is it not altogether possible that it is we who project them backward onto the text, just as we often project, after the fact, a coherent "syntax" onto our lives, or onto history?

It is not just that certain *lais* (like many other *récits*) are intelligible, narratively speaking, only retroactively. There is another, still more perplexing, syntactical problem here. There are many elements in the *lais* that are too important to be dropped out in a synopsis, and indeed there are entire *lais*, that *remain* unintelligible in the Todorovian, or generally narratological sense of the word. To make this point more clearly let me go over the distinction that Todorov makes between syntactic and semantic meaning in the *Grammaire du Décaméron:*

> A particularly striking example of the distance between a semantic unit and a syntactic unit can be found in story IV, 7. Boccaccio summarizes it thus: "Simone loves Pasquin, they are both in a garden. Pasquin rubs a sage leaf on his teeth and dies. Simone is put in prison. To show the judge how Pasquin died, she rubs one of the same sage leaves on her teeth and she dies too." (22)

Todorov comments:

> In this story, all the actions (from the syntactic point of view) are carried out by the same action (on the semantic level): death. The crime that Simone is thought guilty of is murder (poisoning); the punishment that she must undergo is also death (the stake); the means that she finds to prove her innocence is yet again death (again, poisoning). It is therefore impossible to consider death a syntactic unit; the syntactic unit will be determined by the place that it occupies in the story. (22)

And a little later Todorov goes on to state, concerning the syntactic meaning:

> It is not merely the most abstract level of reference, as one might think. The two ways of signifying *[significations]* are different by nature: the reference is a paraphrase of the word with the aid of other words, and is therefore a paradigmatic relation; the meaning *[sens]* is defined solely by the combinations into which this unit can enter; it is the sum of its combinatory possibilities. Therefore it is impossible to establish the meaning of a unit outside of its context; the meaning of an action is determined within the sequence. Murder becomes "crime" *[méfait]* once it is integrated into a series of propositions. (22-32)

Trying to explain still more precisely just how one goes about recognizing the *sens*, or syntactic meaning, of any given verb or act, Todorov says:

> Crime *[méfait]* will be defined syntactically as an action which involves, leads to *[entraîne]* punishment (and inversely for punishment). Modifi-

cation is the action that can lead to a transformation of an attribute into its opposite. (23)

Now insofar as this definition of the syntactic, and this distinction between the semantic and syntactic, work with respect to the *Decameron*, it is for two major reasons. First, because that text operates within a single and consistent moral framework: it is easy to identify, for example, what is a "sin." The *Decameron* is, if you will, both a profoundly *moral* and a profoundly *immoral* book: sinners are rarely punished (they usually escape punishment), but at least it is clear to all what sin *is;* and sin does "call for" punishment. Second, verbs have a clear *agency* and *purpose:* to return to the example given above (in the first quote from Todorov), if Simone eats the sage leaf—and dies—it is *in* order to prove her innocence. And in most other tales, when something happens, it is *because* X or Y *did* it, and in the clear *intention* (as Todorov puts it) of *"modifying the situation."* (It is also worth noting that the *Decameron* seems characterized by a high degree of similarity in the syntactic patterns of the stories. Todorov has been able to break all the 100 tales into two major plot structures: attribute-sequences and law-sequences: that is, stories where a character changes—as from "not in love" to "in love"; and stories involving crime and punishment—or the avoidance of punishment. As I will make clearer later, the *Lais* have little of this syntactic regularity.)

But a great many of the actions in the *Lais*, while they may be *semantically* analyzable, are *syntactically* incomprehensible: *undecodable.* If the moral universe or standards of the *Decameron* were always clear, the opposite is true of the *Lais.* The whole concept of sin here is extremely complex, especially with respect to adultery, one of the major themes of the work. The husbands in the *Lais* do not like to be cuckolds any more than will Boccaccio's, and they are only too happy to have a chance to punish their wives or the lovers. But the wives and the lovers and often Marie herself have quite a different moral viewpoint, one in which adultery cannot reliably be said—as a crime (or *méfait*)—to "entraîner une punition" (involve, or lead to, punishment). And yet one cannot say that adultery is not at all, or never, seen as a sin, or as "wrong." In short, its function as narrative *méfait* and its connection to punishment are very unreliable and ambiguous. It is clear, for example, that to the dichotomy between conjugal *virtue* and adulterous *vice* or *sin* must be added at least three other major dichotomies: constraint versus freedom, loyalty versus disloyalty, and violence vs. nonviolence. That is, certain wives would appear to be justified (at least by Marie's remarks, and by their destiny in the narrative) by the fact that they had been married against their will to a jealous old husband (such as the wife in "Yonec"); other adulterous wives and husbands are, apparently, guilty because they betrayed a freely chosen bond, betrayed a spouse they had loved (for example, the wife of Bisclavret); and while adultery *per se* does not seem to bother Marie, she does appear to consider it bad form to try to do away with your husband (as does the wife in "Equitan").[15] But, in any case, it is very tricky to try to pry loose syntactic functions from complex semantic considerations in the *Lais*.

What further complicates our ability to determine syntactic meaning in the *Lais* is the fact that so many of the most important verbs in the stories have no clear agent and hence no clear purpose. Actions—verbs—happen, but (syntactically speaking) *why?* They certainly change things—they transform the situation—but *who wanted* it transformed? In several *lais*, major characters die: the "Two Lovers"; the old husband in "Milun"; three knights in "Chaitivel." But nobody killed them (at least not on purpose); and Marie does not explain to us the purposes of Providence (if we are to think of Providence as an Agent). And, as Todorov pointed out in the passages quoted above, death, as such, has no syntactic meaning; it has *sens* only as we can integrate it into some comprehensible context—and we cannot always do this. In the *Lais* a great many important things happen that the characters cannot be said to have *made* happen. The *Lais* are, indeed, less about "quests" than about "adventures" *(aventures)*: things that happen to people.[16] In short, since for acts to be analyzable syntactically they must have agency and purpose—as well as a clear effect—many of the acts or events of the *Lais* are simply undecodable syntactically; they are analyzable only semantically (thematically, symbolically, and so forth) or formally (in terms of their patterns). Our experience of the *Lais*, both as we read and retroactively as well, is in fact, at this *structural* level, very much like our experience of history: of life itself. Life is not dished up to us with the *imparfaits* and the *passés simples* neatly distinguished—nor with all the characters we meet up with fulfilling any function that we can determine; many events that we live through or read about *never* quite make sense to us. Many of them we find memorable: dramatic, compelling, surprising, unforgettable; semantically or formally rich and complex—but functionally, syntactically, ever incomprehensible. The medieval period had a high tolerance for the unintelligible event,[17] which may be just another way of saying that it had a high tolerance for life itself—for in this particular sense medieval literature is extraordinarily "mimetic." The *aventures* that Marie offers us do give us that sense of mystery—*permanent* mystery, yet an incomprehensibility charged with *meaning*—that life itself gives us.[18]

And yet, there is not just mystery, not just unintelligibility here. There are real regularities in the *Lais*—but they are not, on the whole, narratively "syntactic" regularities, but are lexical, formal, thematic, semantic. Every story concerns love and lovers; the lovers are always well born and "courtly"; and so on. But there is one important regularity that one can hardly avoid calling "syntactic": every *lai* ends with some "resolution," some sort of "closure" or "satisfaction": some stasis. What we do not know, as we begin to read, and even as we are reading along, is which characters will be the lovers, whether the story will be told from the lovers' "point of view" or "frame of reference," that is, with respect to their interests —and what *kind* of resolution there will be. The stories cannot all be said to end happily—at least for the lovers. Indeed some of the endings are rather odd—certainly hard to analyze in terms of modern narratological techniques. And it is to these endings that I now turn our attention.

I am certainly not denying that there are *lais* that end satisfactorily in the obvious and banal sense of the word: indeed, not only is there a resolution to the problem, but a happy one. The lovers may triumph over their obstacles and be reunited for good, as in "Guigemar"; Fresne (in the *lai* by the name) gets to marry her lover, once it is discovered that she is of noble birth and hence "worthy" of him; in the "Chevrefoil" the two lovers—Tristan and Iseut—get to see each other, as they had wished to do; in the "Bisclavret" the good werewolf's lands are restored to him, and his wife and her lover are punished for their attempt to get rid of him. But let us look more closely at any one of these cases, "Guigemar," for example. In what sense is the ending here satisfactory? A quick plot summary: Guigemar (this is, as you recall, the son of Oridials, and so forth) was immune to love; one day he went hunting, and shot at a white doe—a magical doe; the arrow, after mortally wounding her, turned around and flew back to Guigemar (= G) whom it wounded in the thigh. Before dying the doe warned—predicted— that G would suffer from his poisonous wound until he found a woman who would suffer for him and he for her; she alone could cure him. G finds a boat waiting at the shore, which takes him miraculously off to sea; he arrives on a foreign shore, half dead. A beautiful lady and her maidservant find him; the lady and G fall in love and soon become lovers. All goes well for a year and a half. But one day she tells him that she sees disaster coming, and she fears that if they are separated he will fall in love with someone else. As proof of their mutual love, she ties a knot in his shirt and he ties a knot in her belt—two knots that cannot be untied; and they each give permission for the other person to love anyone who can untie the knot. Soon the husband does find out about the lovers; G escapes being killed by the husband and the magical boat carries him away, back to his own country. Once home, he is encouraged to marry, but he says he will marry only the woman who can undo the knot in his shirt. The lady, in the meantime, has been imprisoned by her husband in a grey marble tower. One day she goes to the door; it is unlocked, she goes out; no one is there, no one stops her. She goes down to the shore, and there is the boat, in which she goes off. The boat takes her to the country where G lives. She lands at the castle of a lord named Meriadus. He wants to have her, but no, she will have only the man who can undo the knot in her belt. Meriadus says, in a rough modern translation: "There is a knight around here with a knot in his shirt. I'll bet you tied it!" He organizes a tournament (just why is not clear) and invites all the neighboring knights. When G and the lady see each other, neither is quite sure of the other's identity, and—of course—to make sure they untie each other's knots. But the wicked Meriadus refuses to allow G to have the lady; G is forced to defeat this rival in combat, and cuts off his head. The story ends happily, on these words: (Guigemar) "A grant joie s'amie en meine; / Ore ad trespassee sa peine" (With great joy he leads his lover away/ Now his pain is gone; ll. 881–82).

In what sense does this ending provide "narrative closure"? There is clearly a satisfaction here: something unresolved has been resolved—and indeed two quite concrete and literal knots have been untied. An obstacle—Meriadus—has been permanently eliminated. And the lovers express their satisfaction: they are joyful. But, without wishing to cast any blot on their happiness, I should just like to make two points: the lovers were very happy once before in the story, before the lady's jealous husband found out about them, so why could the story not end then? "Ah," one might reply, "Such happiness is unstable, because husbands (at least in narrative) 'always find out'; adultery is unstable." Very well; but the curious fact is this (and I feel duty-bound to point it out): at the end of this story, when the lovers have untied each other's knot and hence are free to be together (the lover has refused to marry until someone came along who could undo his knot), the lady, our heroine, is *still married*. Her husband has not died; he just is not mentioned any more. In other words, the story is over not because the intrinsic obstacle to the happiness of the lovers has been in fact eliminated, not because their situation is now intrinsically happy or stable, but (when all is said and done) because *Marie* wants it over; because she allows the lovers—and us—to be and to remain satisfied anyway. More specifically, she presents the ending in such a way that we can find it satisfying, essentially by not mentioning the husband, and by (as it were) assimilating him to Meriadus, the nasty knight who laid claim to the lady, and whom Guigemar *did* do away with.

I am inclined to think that Marie is only prepared to end her *lais* —only satisfied, herself—when something sufficiently "memorable" has occurred.[19] And what is sufficiently memorable here is the way in which the lovers recognized each other. These knots are in part a *narrative* device; and they are, indeed, the very symbolic expression of embodiment of the modern concept of a "problem" and its "resolution." But they are also satisfying esthetically and semantically: by their symmetry, their symbolic value, and so forth. (In fact, we might note a rather amusing quality to these knots—and to all *literal* knots. "Satisfying" as it may seem to untie knots, we all untie knots every day without solving any problem to speak of; shoelaces, and so on. The mere fact of untying a knot does not reliably allow for "closure!") In short, I suggest that Marie is at least as interested in what we would call "esthetic satisfaction" as in what we would call "narrative satisfaction." She is satisfied—and ready to end a tale, to call it a day for the characters—when some esthetically interesting, and hence satisfactory, event or image has occurred.

What I have just been saying of "Guigemar" is no less true of "Bisclavret" (among others): here too we are made to accept as "resolved" and even as "happy" an ending which if analyzed objectively, shall we say, is far from ideal. The Bisclavret—our hero, the werewolf—has his lands back, he is back in the king's good graces; his wife and her lover have been punished and banished. But Bisclavret still has quite a few problems: he is still a werewolf—and a werewolf's lot is not a happy one! Now he is alone, and it is not clear that he will marry again. But these problems are just not mentioned. In short, the ending can be said to be satisfactory at least in part because the protagonist is presented as satisfied; that final stability is "stable" because Marie chooses not to mention its intrinsic imperfections.

In short, what is stable, what is narratively satisfactory in the various *lais* is not stable or satisfactory so much because of its intrinsic qualities—not because it is naturally "that way"—as because it is presented as such by Marie. Most commonly this means that the ending is presented as being perceived by the major character(s) as "satisfactory"; and it means that Marie does not disturb or question (through narrative intervention, etc.) that state of satisfaction.

Now in the two cases I have just been discussing, Marie did not have a very hard time persuading us—or the protagonists—to be satisfied at the end. These endings were, intrinsically, quite easy to make us accept as resolutions to the problem. I would maintain, however, that Marie almost always presents us with a resolution that contains an *intrinsic deficiency*. But be that as it may, Marie sometimes makes us accept really surprising ends as being, truly, endings, resolutions. Let us look again at the "Laüstic," which I discussed briefly above. The wife of a wealthy bourgeois loves another man; as she is carefully guarded (why? no reason is given) she and her lover can hardly ever be together, but they talk every night from the window and throw each other little presents. As springtime comes, their nightly sojourns at the window become more time-consuming, and the husband becomes angry at his wife's absence from the conjugal bed. He inquires what she is doing at the window, and she replies that she is listening to the nightingale sing —that his beautiful song keeps her awake. The husband (who we are now told is very churlish) arranges to catch the nightingale, to solve her insomnia, as it were. In his wife's presence, he wrings the bird's neck and throws its bloodied body at her.

> La dame prent le cors petit;
> Durement plure e si maudit
> Ceus ki le laŭstic traïrent
> E les engins e laçuns firent;
> Kar mut li unt toleit grant hait.
> 'Lasse,' fet ele, 'mal m'estait!
> Ne purrai mes la nuit lever
> Ne aler a la fenestre ester,
> U jeo suil mun ami veer.
> Une chose sai jeo de veir:
> Il quid(e)ra ke jeo me feigne
> De ceo m'estuet que cunseil preigne.
> Le laŭstic li trametrai,
> L'aventure li manderai.'
> En une piece de samit,
> A or brusdé e tut escrit,
> Ad l'oiselet envolupé.
> Un sun vatlet ad apelé,
> Sun message li ad chargié,
> A sun ami l'ad enveié.
> Cil est al chevalier venuz;
> De part sa dame dist saluz,
> Tut sun message li cunta,
> Le laŭstic li presenta.
> Quant tut li ad dit e mustré
> Et il l'aveit bien escuté,
> De l'aventure esteit dolenz;
> Mes ne fu pas vileins ne lenz.
> Un vasselet ad fet forgeér;
> Unques n'i ot fer né acer:

Tut fu de or fin od bones pieres,
Mut precīuses e mut cheres;
Covercle i ot tresbien asis.
La laũstic ad dedenz mis;
Puist fist la chasse enseeler,
Tuz jurs l'ad fet od lui porter. (ll. 121–56)

The lady takes the little body;
She cries hard and curses
Those who betrayed the laustic
And made the traps and nets;
For they have taken from her a great pleasure.
"Alas," she says, "woe is me!"
I will no longer be able to get up at night,
Or to go stay at the window,
Where I used to see my lover [ami].
One thing I know for sure:
He will think that I am being deceitful;
I must take counsel about this.
I will send the laustic to him,
I will let him know about this adventure."
In a piece of rich cloth,
Embroidered with gold and covered with writing,
She has wrapped up the bird.
She has called a young servant of hers,
And has given him her message,
Has sent him to her lover.
He has come to the knight;
He greeted him on behalf of his lady,
He told him her whole message,
And presented the laustic to him.
When the boy has told and shown him everything
And the lover had listened well,
He was very sad about the adventure;
But he was not low-born or slow.
He has had a coffer forged;
Never was there any iron or steel put in it;
It was all made of fine gold with good stones,
Very precious and very expensive;
There was a well-fitting lid.
He has put the laustic inside;
Then he had the case sealed,
Every day he has had it carried around with him.

And that is it! That is the ending, our resolution; in that we are to find the lovers'—and our—narrative "satisfaction." Marie adds, as a conclusion:

> Cele aventure fu contee,
> Ne pot estre lunges celee.
> Un lai en firent li Bretun:
> Le Laüstic l'apelé hum. (ll. 157–60)

> This adventure was told,
> It could not be hidden for long.
> The Bretons made a lai about it:
> They call it "Laustic."

Quite an extraordinary ending, narratively speaking. And yet it works. The question is, why? How does Marie go about making us accept this ending as "satisfactory"? We do not get the lovers' revenge over the husband's cruelty, nor their outwitting of him, nor even their tragic or pathetic death from despair—nor indeed any of the things that we commonly think of as narrative resolutions. What is more, we have completely lost sight, at the end, of the lady, whom I think we saw as our major protagonist. We only get the lover carrying around a little box containing the body of a dead bird!

But of course this bird is not just any bird; it is a nightingale, that bird who is already part of the poetic code of love, and a perfect metonym for love. (And indeed, when the lady's husband asks her what she is up to at the window, and she replies that she is listening to the song of the nightingale, are we to "code" these words as a lie or as the truth? They are of course both . . .) In any case, what the lover does with that dead symbol, with the cadaver of that winged little metonym, is immediately of poetic, metaphoric interest.

And if this bird is not just any bird, the box the lover puts it in is not just any box, but a specially made reliquary. What the lover does, symbolically, is to turn—to transform—that bird into a martyr. Now I have found several different interpretations of the meaning and even of the "function" of this act: is it essentially an act of mourning, or an act of affirmation of the undying power of love? *Has* the husband killed their love, or not? *Has* he succeeded in punishing them? (Are we even sure that he knew what he was

punishing his wife *for?*) At any rate, the lover has really moved—
and moved *us*—out of the realm of narrative into the realm of
poetry, of symbolic language. And yet, though we cannot decode it,
his act functions as narrative closure precisely because we perceive
it as an *act* of meaning; we perceive it as changing *something*—
though we do not quite know what. Through this act of metaphori-
zation, the lover and love do have the "last word," whatever that
word means.

Marie further enhances the satisfactoriness of this ending by two
stylistic strategies. The first is a switch in the use of tenses: toward
the end of the *lai* she passes increasingly from the *passé simple* to
the *passé composé*, from the language of objective narration to
another, more vivid tense. That is, she does not tell us what the
lover *fit* but what he *a fait:* what he "did" but what he "has done."
"Un vasselet *ad fet* forgeér," "Tuz jurs l'*ad fet* od lui porter," and so
forth: "He has had a coffer forged," "He has had it carried with him
everywhere." Now it is hard to say whether, at this moment in the
development of the *passé composé*, it already carries with it the
function of the modern "perfect"—the notion of completion, accomplishment, and hence satisfaction. I am inclined to think that
it does contain an element of it here.[20] But, in any case, it is a vivid
tense, one belonging to (and which clearly arose from) the domain
that Benveniste calls *discours*—and it sets apart the lover's actions,
at the end, from the middle part of the story.

Second strategy: Marie finishes off her *lai* by the lines I quoted
above—"this adventure was widely told, it could not be hidden for
long," and so on. This particular strategy (for I take it to be such)[21]
I find very amusing. If someone says to you—as Marie so often tells
us—"I have a fantastic story to tell you, a famous story that has
been told and retold for ages;" and then ends with the words "Now
isn't that quite a story? It just had to be retold!," you are not very
likely to cough and mumble: "Frankly, I don't quite get it . . . Is
that the *end?*" We are prepared, from the beginning, to be satisfied,
and, by our ultimate satisfaction, to join the great throng of *lai*-
lovers.

What I am really arguing implicitly is that *any* "last word"—*any*
ending—can be made, by a narrator who wants to do so, to *seem* to
constitute, and therefore for all practical purposes *to* constitute,

satisfaction, stability, closure. As all verbs are or signify transformations, all that matters is for the narrator to present the text's final verb as being somehow privileged: as bringing with it closure; as being not merely a *finis* but a *telos*. And, conversely, no ending is so intrinsically, so naturally, so fully happy, satisfactory, and problem-resolving that a determined narrator cannot—by the addition of a few words—make it seem inadequate and unsatisfactory; cannot make his text seem unresolved, unclosed. While the narrator's choice is probably based primarily on semantic considerations, the strategy by which the narrator determines our response is (loosely speaking) *stylistic:* it is the words, the tenses, the figures that matter.

The above is especially true in cases, like most of Marie's *lais*, when no protagonist can really be said to have a clear "object" or "quest"; at least characters rarely articulate any clear purpose. To speak, for consistency's sake, in Todorovian terms, the major characters are not really out to modify any situation, out to change anything. (As I pointed out above, a great many of the fundamental "transformations" that occur in the *Lais* are agentless, or at least purposeless; they just *happen*.) Most lovers here just want to keep on loving; it is not really that they want to get married; and they certainly have no worldly ambitions. They just want to *love*. (This sense that there is no "end" to love—at least to more or less "courtly" love—is, obviously, extremely important to the structure of many medieval narratives.) So it is not too hard for Marie to choose when to stop her story; she can, with the aid of the techniques discussed above, present almost any moment that she finds semantically or esthetically satisfactory as providing "narrative closure."

Let us look back briefly over the three major points that I have been trying to make here:

1. In the *Lais* of Marie de France—as indeed in many other literary works, medieval and otherwise—the letter of the text is very different indeed from what is perceived through a narrative summary, and a great deal less intelligible, narratively or syntactically speaking. This means, among other things, that the sorts of pleasure that this text gives us, as we are reading, are more those of surprise than of anticipation; our state, as readers, is largely one of uncertainty and bafflement, not of comprehension and control. The experience of the text as intelligible—insofar as this experience occurs—is a retroactive one.

We must therefore ask ourselves whether it can be properly said to be a *literary* experience, or event, at all, if it is only achieved through a recollection and indeed mental reorganization (or hierarchization) of the text.

2. To an important extent, the *Lais* are never fully comprehensible, or intelligible, in syntactic terms. They are far more capable of being analyzed and comprehended in semantic and formal than in syntactic terms. At this level, in this respect, the *Lais*, like life itself, remain permanently undecodable; that is, we do not know the syntax of the *Lais* any more than we know the syntax of life.

3. Marie's *Lais* do generally provide what the narratologists would call—and what we could all recognize as—"satisfaction" or "closure," some "transformation" that allows us to perceive them as "ended," "over." But the kinds of closure that Marie's *Lais* provide are often more esthetic or poetic than narrative. And in any case Marie makes us very aware of the fact that an ending is often satisfying not so much by virtue of *what* happens, *what* is told, as by virtue of *how* it is told, *how* it is presented to us.

One final postscript—or fourth point—which is implicit in the remarks made in this chapter. There is at least one glaring difference between the syntax of sentences and the syntax of narrative utterances or works; that is, between the grammatical usage of the word "syntax" and its use by the narratologists. Any competent reader or listener can tell, in virtually any sentence, what is the subject and what is the verb, and he can tell it as he is listening to or reading the sentence, or at least by the time he has reached the end. (True, there are "ambiguous sentences"—but in fact the degree of ambiguity is generally quite low: there are usually two and only two possible "readings"; the choice of interpretations is clearly limited.) The reader's ability to decode the message grammatically into a set of fundamental functions is indeed the very definition of the sentence's "intelligibility." But in a narrative this is far from being reliably the case. As I have pointed out, the "syntax" often can be identified only by retrospective reconstruction of the text—and often *not at all*. There are many texts whose syntax ever escapes us, and yet which delight and satisfy us in other ways. The syntax of a narrative work is therefore nowhere near as fundamental to the perception of, the comprehension of, the enjoyment of the text as is the syntax of a sentence.

Given this very significant difference, it is at least worth serious consideration whether the term "syntax," as applied to the broad structures of narrative, and the terms "morphology," "function," and so forth as well, are really *useful*, or whether in fact their use tends to obscure the nature of these narrative structures and of our experience of literary texts.

NOTES

1. Such as his *Poétique* (Paris: Seuil, 1968) and *Grammaire du Décaméron* (The Hague: Mouton, 1969).
2. Nor does he claim to do otherwise. He is working at a level of analysis for which he would argue that a synopsis is adequate.
3. I will be using A. Ewert's edition of the *Lais*, by Marie de France (Oxford: Basil Blackwell, 1965) with the permission of the publisher. The translations—inelegant as ever, but I hope faithful—are mine. For general reading purposes, I recommend Robert Hanning and Joan Ferrante's translation of *The Lais*. (Durham, N.C.: Labyrinth Press, 1982).
4. Todorov, *Poétique*, p. 82; my translation, here and henceforth.
5. Henceforth, though I will speak of "texts" and of "reading," other types of works and other modes of perception can be assumed.
6. I am not asserting that the *Lais* are unique in this respect; far from it! Indeed, the modern "mystery novel" is constructed on this very principle. I will, at various points in this paper and insofar as it is possible, attempt to suggest what sets apart the *Lais* (and other medieval works) from modern occurrences of similar phenomena.
7. I am taking these techniques not in a truly theoretical order, but in order of the magnitude of their effect (as I see it) on our perception. I should also point out that I will not be discussing an important technique, but which does not attract any particular attention in the *Lais:* the *order* of presentation of events.
8. See also chapters 2 and 3 for a discussion of Old French tense usage.
9. It is worth pointing out that this is very much the way in which our understanding of "time"—and narrative "syntax"—is presented in the Bible. An example: the faithful are *forewarned* by Christ that the Judgment will come—but that they will nonetheless be *surprised*, that the Lord will come "like a thief in the night." I think that this notion that the "syntax" of events is not ours to know is a very important one, not only in biblical narrative, but often in medieval narrative as well.
10. Of course, Kafka also—among many others—uses names in a disconcerting way. In his case, as most commonly in modern cases, there is a deep irony in his nonuse and use of names, and indeed there are disturbing metaphysical or philosophical implications. Marie, on the other hand, seems to attach no profound or disturbing implications to this technique. The ambiguity of her *lais* remains charming, and is never disquieting. In modern works, often there seems to be a *horror* implicit in any threat to "syntax" (the "absurd" seems strongly linked to the disappearance of narrative syntax); whereas in Marie's work (as in

other medieval works), there is an *acceptance* of ambiguous syntax. Expectations as to what we *should be able* to know, to understand, are very different.

11. One might be tempted to account for this curious introduction by an analogy to the frequent use of genealogy (or family background) in various *chansons de qeste*—and in *La Fille du comte de Pontieu* (see chapter 4). But this is virtually the only story that Marie begins in such a way.

12. I will discuss below the applicability of Roland Barthes's notion of "l'effet de réel" to such details.

13. When we talk about narrative works—and indeed when we talk about our lives as well—we cannot get along without "narrative summary." But it is worth keeping in mind that the *telling* and the *living* are very different modes of perception (and mastery) of the same events.

14. Not of course in all cases. To return to the mystery novel: in such works the syntax, though *hidden*, is very much *present* in the text; our task as readers (and detectives) is to guess what it is—ferret it out—before the end, before it is revealed to us. But in other works, it is by no means clear that the syntax is really embedded, inscribed, hidden in the text itself; it may be we who supply— who *add*—it.

15. Here, we would have to add still another factor: revenge seems allowed: in "Yonec," the wife has her son (by her lover) kill her husband, thus avenging her lover's murder.

16. Although even many medieval texts that are organized by a quest theme, contain very strong elements of *aventure:* the hero who wants something goes off—and waits to see what will happen to him!

17. One might be tempted to dismiss as examples of "effets de réel" (as discussed by Roland Barthes in "Introduction à l'analyse structurale des récits," *Communications* 8 [1966]: 1–27, these characters and events. But it should be pointed out that this concept (the "realistic detail") only works properly in a text where we can make a clear distinction between *fonctions* and *indices;* the realistic detail belongs to the domain of the *indice* (of that which is background information, ornament, etc.). But here in the *Lais* our ability to distinguish between *fonction* and *indice*—even retroactively—is very limited.

18. As I pointed out above—in note 10—the absence here of a comprehensible syntax does not (as often in contemporary literature) lead to "nausea"; the loss of meaning (or *sens*) at the syntactic level is compensated by a high degree of semantic and formal richness. The "uncertainty" at one level is compensated by a high degree of "certainty" at the others.

19. See my discussion of "memorability" in Marie's *lais,* from a somewhat different perspective, in "Orality, Literacy and the Early Tristan Material: Béroul, Thomas, Marie de France," *Romanic Review* 78, no. 3 (May 1987): 299–310.

20. See, for example, Tatiana Fotitch's study of *The Narrative Tenses in Chrétien de Troyes* (Washington, D.C.: Catholic University of America, 1950). In particular, she points out that the "perfect" is often used to stress "important events, particularly the conclusion of previous actions or a culmination in the plot" (p. 71).

21. Whether or not the *Lais* are really taken from Celtic sources is neither here nor there. What I am speaking of is a stylistic device: how Marie refers to her "sources."

CHAPTER 7

Desire and Causality in Medieval Narrative: The *Roland*, Thomas's *Tristan*, and *Du segretain moine*

This volume has, at various points, been preoccupied with the central role—and complex definition—of desire in medieval literature, and with relations (for example, hierarchical, antagonistic) among subjects of desire in the narrative structure. In these pages I should like to return to a question that has remained unasked if implicit in earlier chapters, and to take up yet another aspect of the functioning of desire in medieval narrative: the nature of the causal relation between the characters' desires, on the one hand, and the course of events and narrative outcome, on the other.

Now causality, like desire, is a concept bound up with problems of cultural anthropology and intellectual history, among others. I will define "desire" as that dissatisfaction or need, on the part of a character, which provides narrative stimulus or "causal energy" in the text. (I will refine this definition later.) By "causal relation," I mean the literary representation of the operation of cause and effect. We shall need to compare modern concepts of causality (such as we find in contemporary narrative theorists, in particular) with medieval views on the matter. (Perhaps I should make it clear that I am concerned here not with the actual philosophical or scientific problem of causation, but with the *representation* of causality in literature. I consider that every narrative text, and every theory of narrative as well, *must*, of necessity, contain, whether implicitly or explicitly, a theory or image of causality.)

I will ask several questions of each of the texts:

- To what extent do characters "get" what they wanted? And in what sense "get"? Passively "receive," or actively "cause," that is, "procure for themselves"? Are the characters competent to effect their will, and if so, to what degree, in what mode? What, then, is the relation of desire to narrative outcome?
- As a further extension of the above: what "model or models of causality" emerge from the desire/outcome relation in the texts? What kinds of narrative causality do we have here? And how might we compare them with the models provided by contemporary narratologists, or differentiate them from standard modern representations of causality?
- Third, what is the relation between final outcome—the characters' "satisfaction," and narrative "closure"? By "satisfaction" I mean the fulfillment of a previously expressed or in any case clear desire. (Only a desire that has been made explicit or which is somehow manifest in the text can provide narrative tension: only in such a case can we and the character await its resolution, which will release the tension.) By "closure" I mean the sense, created for us by the narrator at the end of the text that it (the text) is really "over," "complete."
- Finally, what is the role or importance of desire in these works? If and insofar as desire is represented as powerless, incompetent to achieve its ends in medieval narrative, if the commitment of the medieval *récit* to "causality" is limited, then what is desire there for? What is its function or importance? Why is it so central in medieval texts?

The texts under consideration will be *La Chanson de Roland (The Song of Roland)*, Thomas's *Tristan*, and the *fabliau Du segretain moine (The Sacristan Monk)*. These works, of different genres and types, dating from the eleventh through the thirteenth century, have been chosen in the hope not of exhausting the topic but at least of suggesting something both of the range and of the consistencies to be found in works of this general period.[1]

While most recent models of narrative structure, syntax, and grammar do not explicitly concern themselves with causality, they do assume its operation (such is the case of Greimas[2] and Bremond). Todorov, however, confronts directly the issue of causality. In his discussion of narrative "syntax" in *Poétique*,[3] Todorov posits two major types of syntactical structure in literature. He considers that most works of the past are organized in terms of a combination of logical and temporal factors that can be termed "causality." Either there is an immediate causal relationship between the "units" of the text—in which case we have a "récit mythologique"; or there is a general law accounting for events—in which case the text is "idéologique." In the mythological text—which Todorov considers the most common in the past, and under which rubric he classifies, for example, the *Decameron*—the basic syntactic unit is "X wants to transform the situation." X either manages to effect this intentional transformation, or he fails, is stymied generally by a conflicting attempt to transform a situation, on the part of Y. Although Todorov does not spell this out, in the "ideological" text the true causality is, I think, understood to be of a superhuman nature, and of a mechanical rather than of an intentional nature: that is, it is the impersonal working out of some "law," some "force."

Aside from these two modes of "logical-temporal" organization of the text, Todorov envisions a third—rare in narrative, frequent in poetry—in which "the logical or temporal relations move to the background or disappear, and it is the spatial relations of elements that constitute the organization."

There is another set of reflections on causality—another concept of causality—that we would also do well to keep in mind: that provided by medieval theology. Now I do not believe for a moment that any of the narrators under consideration ever read, for example, Augustine's *De Trinitate*. And I think one must be wary of assuming that, in any given period, there is only one "world view": that everyone agrees upon and subscribes to one unopposed view of reality. Still, I think we will find it useful to compare certain elements of our texts to what is the dominant understanding of causality in this pre-Thomistic medieval period: the (more or less) Augustinian position. Here are some initial considerations to keep in mind (we will refine them later):[4]

- Causality in Augustine[5] is essentially volitional: what happens (that which is "moved," "produced," "caused," and so forth) does so by the operation of a will. We are far, here, from a modern mechanistic or logical understanding of causality.[6] And it is precisely because medieval thought was so fundamentally volitional in its view of causality that causality is peculiarly bound up with desire and narrative structure in medieval texts.

- Causality (that is, the ability to cause) is essentially a divine prerogative: it belongs to God, who alone exercises "primary causality."
- Human causality is never anything but "secondary." Men exert causality—possess causal efficiency—by and only by function of the power delegated to them by God. Their efficiency is therefore "derivative."
- Human causes, therefore, can only be "proximate" or immediate: they can never be the ultimate, or rather the first, cause of anything.
- In its derivative nature and subordination to divine causality, human causality is often merely "instrumental": human agencies are used by God for His own ends.
- Human evil does not have separate power, but can exist and exert causality only as permitted by God. (Augustine also, at times, views evil not as an effect at all, but as a defect: incapacity.) [7]
- Human ability to produce effects is limited, by the very distance that separates us from divine perfection, power, and being. In particular, we are ourselves caused, by many other causes, as well as causes ourselves; we are produced by as well as producers of causal force. God alone is uncaused—and hence the perfectly efficient—cause.

In the *Chanson de Roland*:[8] Who wants what and who gets what—who gets "satisfaction"? Let us look briefly at some of the characters whose desires and attempts to achieve them occupy our attention in the poem.

- Marsile, his henchman Blancandrin, and Baligant: they all want to get rid of Charlemagne. Marsile, as the poem opens, wants to make Charlemagne leave Spain. When deceit and false promises do not work as a strategy, he decides to try humiliating and incapacitating Charles by destroying the Frankish rear guard. (Let us note here that the *characters* in this text—and most texts—clearly believe in "causation"— that they proceed on the assumption that what they do will influence events. All strategy implies a belief in causal laws.) Later, Baligant wants to defeat and kill Charlemagne for revenge and for religious reasons.
- Charlemagne wants first to finish conquering Spain; then to avenge Roland's death by punishing all those responsible.
- Ganelon wants revenge for Roland's insults, by his death; then, to defend himself against the charge of treason.
- Roland, rather than having any one single purpose, appears to have several goals. First, generally but understatedly, to serve God and Charlemagne, to uphold Frankish honor. Then—more explicitly and repeat-

edly expressed (and less altruistically, it must be said)—to fight, not to be humiliated in battle, to die facing the enemy, to win honor, to have "good songs sung" about him. And, in blowing the horn, the *olifant*, he calls for revenge (not help!).

And so on. We could, as we meet and follow each character, establish his desires (whether clearly stated or merely implied). It is with respect to the major characters' desires (to their role as "Subjects") that we understand and encode the events in the work.

Now let us look back over the text and inquire who has gotten or achieved what he had intended. At the end of the first major segment of the text, Roland is dead; Ganelon, Marsile, Blancandrin, and all the pagans are satisfied. Of course, their satisfaction will not last long: they will all soon (in the second part) be dead themselves, punished and hence dishonored—which is worse than dead. But the question that concerns me with respect even to this short-term "satisfaction" is this: can one say that Ganelon or Marsile—or any human agent—actually caused Roland's death? The pagans were certainly the cause of a great deal of mayhem and massacre. And with respect to Roland's death, their actions are contributory: he died in the context of death they had produced. But what he actually died from was the agonizing effort of blowing the *olifant* and/or of grief at the death of his men—not from any mortal wound. Now in the text the Saracens and Ganelon are certainly considered guilty of evil intentions and evil effects. They must be punished; revenge must be exacted. But they have been "inefficient" in that there is a clear discrepancy between what they were trying to achieve and what they actually produced. They were not efficient enough actually to cause Roland's death.

Indeed, not only do the pagans not literally cause Roland's death, but he emerges paradoxically victorious as he dies. His army has been destroyed, all his men are dead, he is dying—*but* they have routed the Paynim. Roland, far from being humiliated, dies aggressively facing the enemy. These dead men are nonetheless the victors! And Charlemagne is on his way back to destroy the Saracens. This is hardly what Ganelon, Marsile, et al. had in mind! They have, in short, produced only something rather *like* what they wanted—and it is not even clearly they who achieve this partial and short-term success. (That is, Roland is dead, but they did not kill him.) Two points must be made here. First, that there is a significant gap or dissimilarity between the intended results of their actions and their actual results. To put it in theological terms: their efficiency as agents has proven defective. Shortly, the efficiency of their gods will be tested, and will be shown to be inadequate: their gods cannot protect them.[9] Second, we have here a curious representation of "satisfaction," but one which is found in many other works. The pagans do receive a very partial and short-term satisfaction here. We can belittle it, in one sense, but it is narratively very useful, in that it allows us to segment the text. We get the impression, with respect to the pagans—and, even more, with respect to Ganelon—that they "won the first round." The interesting point here is that medieval narrators often give to their characters (or allow them to cause) something *like* what they had wanted, or part of what they had wanted and striven for. But they are far from committed to giving to their characters—especially evil ones—*just* what they had wanted, on their own terms, even for a short while.

In the second part of the *Chanson de Roland*, Roland is doubly avenged, which brings some satisfaction to the grieving Charles. And this is, truly, revenge, not just an unsatisfactory approximation. But the problem of causality still remains. Is it really Charles who effects or causes this revenge? We need but think of the angelic interventions in the text. For example, Charles is chasing the pagan host as night falls, and an angel stops the sun in its course so that the emperor can catch up with and destroy the fleeing Saracens. There are, of course, several other crucial angelic interventions.[10]

One might argue that this reliance on angelic helpers in no way vitiates the normal principles of causality in these passages. One might contend that the angels are there to make it absolutely clear that God is on the side of the French. At worst—it might be argued—one would merely have to say that an angel is an Adjuvant, like any other Adjuvant; that Charlemagne, together with his angelic friends, constitutes sufficient force to produce the desired results; that together they constitute an "efficient cause." But being "helped" by an angel—in a Christian work[11]—is not like being helped by a fairy godmother or a genie in a bottle in a secular text. In particular, angels do not arrive and declare to the damsel or emperor in distress: "I am at your service," or "Your wish is my command." It is not presented on those terms: they ar not "at your service" but at God's service. They are not there to help you out, but as instruments (not Adjuvants, of course) [12] of the Almighty. And the character they help is understood to be an instrument or servant too. Angels also have a way of showing up when in fact they are not very welcome: when they are not "needed." Gabriel makes a last appearance in the Roland in the final lines of the poem, and annuls the full human closure on which the poem would otherwise end. He commands the weary and uneager Charlemagne to be off and help the Christians in Imphe.

> Culcez s'est li reis en sa cambre voltice.
> Seint Gabriel de part Deu li vint dire:
> "Carles, sumun les oz de tun emperie!
> Par force iras en la tere de Bire,
> Reis Vivien si succuras en Imphe,
> A la citet que paien unt asise:
> Li chrestien te recleiment e crient."
> Li emperere n'i volsist aler mie:
> "Deus," dist li reis, "si penuse est ma vie."
> Pluret des oilz, sa barbe blanche tiret.
> Ci falt la geste que Turoldus declinet.   (ll. 3992–4002)

> The king has lain down in his vaulted chamber.
> Saint Gabriel came to him, from God, and said:
> "Charles, summon the armies of your empire!
> You must go to the land of Bire,
> In force you will help King Vivien in Imphe,
> In the city to which the pagans have laid siege:
> The Christians call and cry out for you."
> The Emperor did not want to go at all:
> "God," said the king, "how painful is my life."
> His eyes weep, he pulls his white beard.
> Here ends the story that Turoldus relates [this is only
>   one of several possible readings].

Charles, who has avenged Roland and completed the conquest of Spain, cannot now rest, satisfied. He is reminded that he is, above all, God's servant—and that he has not yet fulfilled the service God asks of him.

We have moved here into another kind of will and causality: divine will, divine causality. And divine, or transcendent, causality—at least the Judaeo-Christian version of it—is not a bit restful as a narrative construct. First, in the Christian theological and literary tradition, it is (virtually always) understood to be mysterious, in the sense that God's purpose is often unclear; it is certainly unexplained; it may even appear inexplicable. And while it is often clear when God is acting in this work, it is never altogether certain that he is not, since divine intervention is understood to be frequently hidden: indirect, veiled. The phenomena of the *ordalie*, (ordeal), and of the *épreuve* (trial, or test), are based on the notion that God's will—justice—is made manifest *through* human actions and events. There is no reliable distinction in this period between natural and supernatural.[13]

This double mysteriousness is compounded by the concept of the omnipotence of God. That is, all ability to cause—"primary causality"—ultimately belongs to God. The anguish in the poem over the (unasked) question, Why did God let Roland and the peers and all their men die? has long been noted. It is clear that God can crush evil men at any moment He chooses; and eventually He does just that: stopping the sun in its course; picking Charlemagne up off his knees to fight, when he has been stunned in battle; intervening to make sure that Ganelon's champion is bested in combat, so that Ganelon will be punished. But why did He not crush the Saracens before they destroyed the rear guard? By not destroying them in time He allowed them to kill the Franks. There is, then, the (often troubling) notion of a permissive causality on God's part: evil can exist only as He tolerates it.

(This notion that evil men or the Devil can exercise causality only by divine permission is marvelously clear in some of the saints' lives, where it is only on the third or fourth attempt to execute the saint that the wicked men finally succeed—that God finally *lets* them make of the holy man or woman a martyr. For example, Jacobus de Voragine in his *Legenda aurea* tells the story of Saint Christine[14] whose wicked father (a judge) tried, first, to burn her to death with oil on the wheel (the flames killed 1,500 people, but she emerged safe); then he threw her into the sea with a rock around her neck (angels pulled her out); then he ordered her decapitated (he died before the sentence could be carried out). His successor had her put into a cauldron with oil, resin, and pitch: she produced such miracles on the scene that he died of fright. His successor had her put into a furnace: for five days she sang and promenaded with angels. Then asps, vipers, and other serpents were thrown on her: they licked her feet, drank from her [virgin] breasts, and licked her sweat. Her enemies then cut off her breasts and her tongue; the loss of the latter did not keep her from speaking. Finally two arrows in her heart and one in her side killed her, and she "rendered her spirit to God." In short, when God pleases—and not a moment sooner— he *allows* wicked men to be "efficient" in their production of evil. Finally, the most trivial of their means—a Trinitarian one, we might note—is allowed to be efficacious.)

The very fact—which many scholars have noted—that Charlemagne begins to weep well before he has any good reason to, and his prophetic dreams as well, both obviously point to some foreknowledge in the text, as well as to Charles's privileged position as God's elect, his special servant. But one can have foreknowledge only of that which, in some sense, is already determined. This weeping, these dreams, undermine our conviction that things happen in the text because people want them to happen or make them happen. Foreknowledge threatens our belief in the integrity of temporal sequentiality, and in the validity of human causality which depends on that sequentiality. It does not destroy our belief in causation, but merely in human causation. Only divine causality seems real—and it is incomprehensible.

Now the notion of divine causality that we have been examining presents real difficulties for modern secular theories of narrative.[15] Some of these difficulties the *Roland* shares with epic in general: the concept of destiny, in particular; that it should be determined, in advance, before the hero even begins his efforts, what he should be allowed to do. The notion of predetermination, of "fate," is automatically disturbing to an analysis of "structures of causality" if the model used assumes that time is "real": irreversible, unsuspendable. But at least in classical epic, for example, the *Aeneid*, it is generally clear what the gods and goddesses[16] want, and how they act: and they *keep* acting in order to ensure that "what will be" actually comes to be; they keep meddling in the narrative flow, sending storms, and so forth. So, in a way, they are just like everybody else, only more so: more powerful.

But what makes medieval, Christian narrative so much harder to analyze with respect to causality is that God is understood to be and represented as being invisible, mysterious, having purposes and modes of operation and inoperation that can only be guessed at—not merely by the faithful, but by the skeptical narratologist as well! It is very frustrating to the critic seeking out the causal relations in a text—the relation between desire and outcome—to realize that he simply *cannot know* what Agent is to be considered responsible for any given transformation (and to what degree, in what mode);[17] and without knowing the source and the will of the agency, we can hardly know how to interpret any modification in state.[18]

Medieval religious narrative is often a strange blend of or alternation between Todorov's three major types of narrative:

- The mythological, in which God acts like a character: here it is generally clear when and how God is acting (and when he is not), and what his purpose is. The natural and supernatural levels remain (more or less) distinct: men do their part, God does his (miracles, and so forth).
- The ideological, in which God does not intervene directly or visibly but where justice eventually obtains. But we rarely have quite what Todorov seems to have had in mind, under this rubric, since justice is, in this period, generally understood to be what God *wants*, and not an impersonal principle. The same is true of the secular "Amors," who is both a force *and* a person: a god endowed with a will.
- The spatial, in which, since causality is understood to be unknowable, the text, essentially chronological in disposition, is given structure primarily on the level of recurring features and elements of expression: at a level that one could loosely call "rhetorical."[19]

Each of these modes—and we commonly find them together—is a literary (and psychological) response to the conviction that God is the, or a, central agent in the occurrences of the text. But each one stresses one particular aspect of God: of his nature and manifestations. In short, God is not seen as bound by—as binding himself to—any one mode of causality.

It is true, in the case of the *Roland*, that the text allows itself to be read and remembered as coherent on what we might call the level of narrative syntax of the mythological variety. One can follow and retain the plot, in terms of human—and occasionally clearly divine—causality. (The two levels remain fairly distinct in this work: more so, oddly enough, than in the far less Christian texts of Chrétien de Troyes or even in some *fabliaux* where divine intervention, though frequently solicited by the characters, is neither manifest nor "guaranteed" by the narrator, but could be hypothesized from the actual outcome of events.) The text does not do away with narrative syntax, that is, with an appearance of causality, of "plot" in comprehensible human terms. Outcomes conform to, they more or less resemble—in positive or negative form—characters' (or divine) desires. They are subsequent to the expression of those desires. So we, like the characters, can believe in human causality; we can believe that people have determined or at least influenced events. After all, in causality, as the philosophers would gladly attest, there is always a leap of faith—which is surely why modern philosophy, reluctant to make *make* leaps of faith, has worked so hard to avoid the concept of causality: to replace it by "logical relations"; to replace "A caused B" (which can never be immediately observed, hence proved) by "A is reliably followed by B."

The *Roland* does not annihilate all narrative syntax. What it does do, though, is quite insidious. Not merely does it represent divine intentions and operations as in many ways mysterious, but it undermines, by prophetic dreams and intuitions (as well as by the very structures of the *laisse* and of formulaic language) our belief in the significance—in the ontological solidity—of sequentiality, of temporal order, of causality.[20] In short, we slip persistently though intermittently from the "mythological" past, the mysteriously "ideological," into a "spatial" syntax, where time does not exist (as of course, for God, it does not) and where the "plot" seems like so much *trompe l'oeil*.

In concluding our examination of the *Roland*, let us look at Roland himself. Does he get what he wanted, and does he actually cause what he gets? His situation is quite complicated. In one sense, in the *Roland*, he got everything he had wanted—if we are prepared to assume (and the text suggests it) that he had no desire to live a long life. He got to fight; he won honor and glory; he died facing Spain; he will be avenged (and he knows it); good songs will be sung about him. One complication is that he died from sorrow at getting just what he thought he wanted: battle and (for himself) glory. This is no minor complication, and it suggests[21] that even the greatest heroes do not "get" (in any sense) "satisfaction" quite on their own terms. But aside from this difficulty, it also takes quite a leap of faith to say that Roland caused the satisfactions that he does receive—which raises the whole problem of heroism and indeed of human responsibility. Characters in this work are judged, both by God and by us, not by what they do, or by what they prove competent to achieve, but by what they *strive* to do. Virtue and villainy are measured by whom one serves, what one loves. Heroism—both for good and ill—is determined by the vigor and intensity of the commitment of desire.

Now the hero does have real competence; his competence may indeed be *sans pair*. But superlative is not enough. The strongest arm is not strong enough; it is not adequate as a causal force. It would be truer to say that Roland receives what he wants from God rather than that he effects or causes it himself. The situation is very familiar in the *romans* of Chrétien de Troyes (and others, as well). The hero, who goes off—just *off*—to "search for" the solution to his problem is absolutely dependent on a narrative or metaphysical Providence to guide him on the path toward his solution, to send him the appropriate *épreuves* and with God's help (divine aid is always invoked), he succeeds in combat (and so forth). In Chrétien's novel the hero does not "solve" his problems, does not find a "resolution"; resolution, or a new happiness, finds *him:* he is, essentially, tried, then rewarded.

Men are responsible for their actions in the *Roland*, but their actions are not responsible for what occurs. Human desire in this heroic text[22] is a *moral* and not a *causal* (not, in that sense, a *narrative*) principle. Virtuous heroism will be crowned and rewarded with success by God, but it cannot, by itself, cause its own success, crown itself, reward itself. A reward (at least as I am defining it here) is not the same thing as a satisfaction. Satisfaction is when a character gets what he had wanted, on his own terms: precisely as he had defined it. (He may either cause or merely receive this satisfaction.) A reward is meted out—by God, Providence, or the narrator, or some mysterious combination of the three—according to what the character deserves. It is his "just deserts." Of course, for the reward to function as such—as pleasant to the good, and unpleasant to the bad—it must bear some similarity to satisfaction or dissatisfaction: to that which he or all men most want or do not want. But it may well be different from, less than and also more than, what the character actually desired. In the *Roland* we have the extraordinary apotheosis of the hero at his death, which is far more, and far more glorious, than anything we have any reason to believe he had desired. This passage is here not to show Roland "satisfied" but, rather, rewarded and glorified. (And the quartered Ganelon is not merely most decisively unsatisfied; he is rewarded!) In many other texts as well the virtuous characters are provided more and greater "satisfactions"—joys, rewards—over and above those they had sought (and which they also, in some measure, receive). For example, at the end of Chrétien de Troyes's *Erec et Enide* the couple is not only satisfied in that their problem has been solved (Erec's prowess has been reestablished, and they are completely reunited), but they are also crowned king and queen and lavishly honored.

In short, the distinction between a "satisfaction" and a "reward" is a major one, especially in texts involved in moral questions, and containing a transcendent agency. But do all "joys" necessarily fall into one of these two categories? Are there not pure—unsought—joys? And what is narrative to do with them, these manifestations of what would be called in theology "grace"? There is a central question here concerning, ultimately, human psychology—metaphysics as well—and, at the very least, the rules of the game of narrative analysis. Does the character have to have stated his desire (have indeed to know he *had* the desire) for the "joy" to be considered a "satisfaction?" (Are there not joys that, we discover, fill a need we had not realized we had?) [23]

Another question about the troublesome notion of "satisfaction": What of the reader? Can he receive "satisfaction" in the text? Can the narrator satisfy himself? In any case, for the concept to be very useful, the "satisfaction" must be preceded in the text, in some clear way, by a "*dis*satisfaction." And of course it is far from the case that every character or reader was ever clearly dissatisfied. (See, for example, chapter 5, on *La Vie de saint Alexis.*)

There may well be texts in which we must be prepared to let go altogether of the notion of "satisfaction": in which the characters never find anything of the kind, and in which the narrator can be said less to "satisfy himself" than to "please himself": he tells, and he terminates, his tale as it pleases *him*. And we—readers and critics alike—just have to make our peace with the *freedom* of that pleasure.

The second text on which our analysis will focus is Thomas's *Tristan*,[24] which, while very different from the *Roland*, is no less rich in its presentation of the matters that concern us. In particular, it will force us to raise the problematic relation, first between "courtly" love[25] and narrative event, and, second, between the satisfaction of desire and closure.

The most immediately striking fact about this narrative work is that it does not lend itself well to the sort of analysis we have just gone through on the *Roland*. The reason is simple: in order to determine whether a character has caused (or received) "satisfaction," we must first know what he had wanted. And the paradox is, of course, that in this work, so filled with intense desire, with obsessive, constant, and undying desire, we do not really know just what it is that the characters desire with respect to one another: What *would* satisfy them? What *is* the goal of their desire?

Let us take a concrete example: the important passage when Tristan decides to marry "the other" Yseut: Yseut aux Blanches Mains (of the White Hands)—pp. 147–67. Why does he marry her? What does he want to achieve? For several hundred lines, Thomas records for us Tristan's deliberations, but there is no easy answer to our question. Tristan is jealous of the pleasure that Yseut la Blonde (henceforth: Yseut) supposedly enjoys with Marc and he wants to know that pleasure himself, partly as revenge for her disloyalty and partly, as he says, to "saveir l'estre de la reine" (to know her condition, situation). He wants to "essaier sa vie" (to try her life). And he wants to forget her, as (he assumes) Marc has made her forget him. And Tristan desires the new Yseut, desires her because he has noted in her "le nun, la belté la reine" (the queen's name and beauty). It is because of this resemblance—and the identity of name—that he desires her.

Such are the reasons why he marries her: this is what he wants to accomplish: these goals would satisfy him. But when the moment comes for him and his new wife to consummate the marriage, he sees Yseut's ring on his finger, remembers his vows, his love, all they have been through together—and repents. But he does not tell the truth to his bride. He tells her that he cannot make love because he has a painful wound. At the end of the episode, we find a sad and frustrated Tristan lying chastely in bed with his sad and frustrated new wife.

So what Tristan has "succeeded in doing"—as we today would ironically put it—is making a complete mess of things. We may not know quite what he had wanted, but we know it was not *this*. He wanted, somehow, by his action, to be happier: both to forget the old Yseut and to know her better by loving another woman. Instead, he discovers when it is too late that he has done wrong by *two* women.

How are we to account for such a disastrous representation of the relation of desire to outcome? Thomas offers a long and rather rambling discussion of Tristan's and human behavior in general, woven into the narrative itself. He makes it clear that the "means" that Tristan has chosen to "improve his situation" (to make himself happier) are predictably only going to make matters worse; and he says:

> A sa dolur, a sa gravanço
> Volt Tristans dunc quere venjanço
> A sun mal quert tel vengement
> Dunt il doblera sun turment:
> De paine se volt delivrer
> Si ne se fait fors encombrer; (ll. 265–70)

> To his sorrow, to his grief
> Tristan wants now to seek revenge,
> To his ill he seeks such vengeance
> As will double his torment:
> From pain he wants to deliver himself
> And he will only make things worse.

This negative result is so predictable first because it is clear that Tristan's reasoning is unsound, if not preposterous. He is "d'amur en destreiz" (in love's anguish). He is going to marry one woman, not because he loves *her*, but because she resembles—by name and beauty—*another* woman, whom he does love but cannot have.

Strategy presupposes a high degree of rationality on the part of the person desiring to effect his goals, and an ability to think through plausible alternatives—and Tristan is hardly behaving rationally. But of course lovers are scarcely famous—either in literature or in life—for their rationality. All strong desire or need may well have an irrational component, but love is famous for producing *furiosi:* characters rendered narratively (causally) incompetent—mad—by passion.

Thomas's explanation of Tristan's strange reasoning in marrying Yseut aux Blanches Mains is followed by another long disquisition on human nature, which is perhaps only marginally relevant to the events under consideration, but is very significant indeed as concerns the broad problem of human irrationality and human action. Here is how it begins:

> Oez merveilluse aventure,
> Cum genz sunt d'estange nature
> Que en nul lieu ne sunt estable!
> De nature sunt si changable
> Lor mal us ne poent laissier
> Mais le buen us puĕnt changer,
> El mal si acostomer sunt
> Que il pur dreit us tuit dis l'unt
> E tant usent la colvertise
> Qu'il ne sevent quĕ est franchise,
> E tant demainent vilanie
> Quĕ il oblient corteisie:
> De malveisté tant par se painent
> Tute lor vie la enz mainent;
> De mal ne se puĕnt oster,
> Itant se solent aŭser.
> Li uns sunt del mal costemier,
> Li altre de bien noveler:
> Tote l'entente de lor vie
> Est en change e novelerie
> E gurpisent lor buen poeir
> Pur prendre lor mauvais voleir. (ll. 285–306)

> Listen to something amazing,
> How people are of a strange nature,
> In that they are never, in any place, stable!
> By nature they are so changeable
> That they cannot leave off their evil ways
> But they can change their good ways.

They are so used to evil
That they always consider it right
And they are so much given to treachery
That they don't know what nobility is,
And they behave with such villainy,
That they forget courtesy.
They are so bent on wickedness
That this is where they spend their whole life;
They cannot remove themselves from evil,
They are so generally used to the habit.
Some are thoroughly accustomed to evil,
Others are curious of new things.
All the efforts of their lives
Are bound up in change and novelty
And they waste their good powers
Following up their evil desires.

Thomas goes on in this vein for many more lines. Now what concerns us here is the concept that human beings are not "stable": that we are so fundamentally "changeable," and so used to "evil," that we neither can leave well enough alone, nor can we change evil to good. We cannot "transform" (that is, if you will: ameliorate) our situation, but only exchange one evil for another. Indeed, according to Thomas, we exchange not merely something bad for something else that is bad, but generally go from bad to worse:

Novelerie fait gurpir
Buen poeir pur malveis desir
E le bien qu'aveir puet, laissier
Pur se meisme delitier . . .
Nevelerie le deceit,
Quant no volt iço qu'aveir deit
Et iço qué il n'a desire
U laisse suen pur prendre pire.
L'en deit, ki puet, le mal changer,
Pur milz aveir le pis laissier,
Faire saveir, gurpir folie,
Car ço n'est pas novelerie,
Ki change pur sei amender
U pur sei de mal us oster;
Mais maint en sun cuer sovent change
Et quide troveir en l'estrange
Ce qu'il ne puet en sun privé:
Ce lui diverse sun pensé; . . .

E les dames faire le solent:
Laissent ço qu'unt pur ço que volent,
Asaient cum poent venir
A lor voleir, a lor desir.
Ne sai certes que jo en die,
Mais trop aiment novelerie
Homes et femmes ensement, . . .   (ll. 307–10; 323–36; 339–45)

Novelty makes people abandon
Their good capacity for evil desire
And the good that they have, they forsake it
In order to enjoy themselves.
The thirst for novelty deceives him,
When he does not want what he should have
And what he doesn't have, he desires
And forsakes what is his, to take something worse.
One should if one can, leave off evil,
In order to have something better abandon the worse,
To do what is wise, to forsake foolishness,
Because this is not novelty,
When one changes to improve oneself
Or to get rid of a bad habit;
But many a person has a change of heart
And thinks to find in something new [strange]
That which he cannot find at home:
That gives him some distraction . . .
And women have the same habit:
They leave what they have for what they want,
They try to come
To their wish, their desire.
I really don't know what to say,
But too much do they love novelty,
Men and women alike . . .

To call what such characters produce "transformations" would
be to accord such pitiful nonevents and miscarried events a status
they do not deserve. Thomas dismisses these changes as *novelerie*.

While Thomas is not exactly a Christian writer, in that Christ,
God, redemption, even a clear concept of "sin," are conspicuously
absent from his work, Thomas's understanding of human nature is
of a Christian (Augustinian) somberness. Mankind's fall from grace
is visible here not explicitly in terms of sinfulness, but in terms of
evil and incapacity: of the incapacity of men to transform them-

selves or anything else: to be efficient causal agents. They can only exchange, evil for evil. In other words, we have an Augustinian sense of evil as defect, powerlessness, impotence. (Only being, which is good, can produce being: that which is, truly, *new*.) In Thomas, to be fallen is not precisely to be "sinful," but to be weakened by evil habits.

Could we just say that in the *Tristan* we have a representation of "unintentional causality": of a causality that operates mechanically, and which is not dependent on the exercise of any will: that is, the working out of some force? I think that to interpret the text along those lines would be to read a modern idea into a text, a period that did not see reality in that way. That is, involuntary causality is essentially a modern concept—in Todorov's classification, an ideological sort of structure. It assumes that there are causes other than volitional. And, in this period, there seems to be no notion of purely ideological—impersonal, will-less—forces. What we appear to have in this text is a rather "inefficient" causality, prone, by its defectiveness, to backfiring, rather than an "involuntary" or "unintentional" one, strictly speaking.

This sort of representation of causality is not necessarily either Christian or medieval. Are Tristan and Yseut crazed by love and irrational? This would not have surprised Vergil. And Freud would agree with Augustine that the libido is not too bright—or at least is not rational in its desires, or in its attempts to satisfy them. And the impotent character, or the character whose attempts to satisfy his desires backfire, is not uncommon in modern literature either. In other words, one does not need to believe in original sin to represent man as incompetent. A literary character can be a schlemiel without being, specifically, "fallen." It is worth noting though that modern narrative theorists have had as much trouble with these texts as they do with medieval ones, since their models and theories are intrinsically not only rationalistic and antimetaphysical, but based on the notion of the protagonist as agent, as competent: as productive of transformations.

But in modern literature it is not just the power to effect events that is gone: desire is often gone as well. It is not merely the quest for visions of the Grail that we miss. Even the Tempter seems to have lost his touch: the Deadly Sins are not what they used to be.[26]

In how many modern works do we really find the great intensity of desire that is so common in medieval texts—even in those where the characters never get what they wanted?

There is in Thomas's *Tristan* a second sort of relation of desire to outcome; of causality. There are passages where the character knows what he wants and does manage to get it, and where the episode closes, more or less, on that satisfaction. For example, Tristan manages to be reunited with Yseut. He disguises himself as a leper. He chooses this strategy to come to Marc's court unrecognized. And so on. Of course, one cannot really say that Tristan "manages to see Yseut": it is, rather, Brangien who takes the helpless Tristan from under the stairs to Yseut. While he can initiate the strategy, he and it are far from adequate; Tristan needs help. Be that as it may, the lovers are reunited. Satisfaction! But this satisfaction is very curious and very typical of the Tristan story, and it warrants a closer look. (Tristan and Brangien—who had for a time been enemies, due to a misunderstanding, have just made their peace.)

E vunt en puis a la reïne
Suz en une chambre marbrine;
Acordent sei par grant amur,
E puis confortent lur dolur.
Tristan a Yseut se deduit.
Après grand pose de la nuit
Prent le congé a l'enjurnee
E si n'en vet ver sa cuntree.
Trove son nevu qui l'atent. (ll. 1991–99)

Then they go to the queen
Up in her marble chamber;
They make their peace with great love,
And then comfort their sorrow.
Tristan enjoys himself [takes his pleasure?] with Yseut.
After a night's long rest
He takes his leave at day
And goes off toward his country.
He finds his ship which awaits him.

This is a very curious little passage. Tristan and Brangien go together to the queen's marble chamber—it is not even very clear whether there are two or three subjects to the verbs "accordent sei," and "confortent lur dolur." Is this just the lovers, or the threesome? (And does it matter?) The lovers then have one sentence of pleasure —of closure, as it were to their perennial desire: "Tristan a Yseult se deduit." And, the next day, Tristan, almost automatically— without any apparent reason—leaves again. And the narrative moves on, without emphasizing this point of (theoretical) closure. As a representation of what we should expect to find a "satisfaction"— and there are not many such moments in the text—this is very skimpy and strange indeed. But it would be truer to think of it as a "relief" than as a "satisfaction." That is, it will last Tristan a few days, a few months. But this moment is understood by the narrator and the public and the lovers alike to be only a temporary relieving of their need: it is like what we would call, with respect to drug addiction, a "fix." Soon Tristan will need her again. There is no permanent satisfaction; in fact there is no satisfaction that the lovers can even *imagine* since their object is so vague and unde-fined. What do they want? What is it that they yearn for? De Rougement has declared[27] that they do not really love each other, that what they love is death, and what they want is to die. I think De Rougement is mistaken, because I do not think the text supports his interpretation. But he is quite right in saying that the lovers' desire—like that, in fact, of many lovers, in many texts—allows for no happy resolution, no satisfaction. In this sense, it can have no closure. It can have only an end; only, finally, peace; only death. Thomas does make the lovers' death function more or less *as* a closure, as a metaphor for desire satisfied: the lovers are united in death—at least more or less. (Thomas, or the legend as he knew it, does not allow them to *die* together or of the same emotion, but only to lie dead together; it is only a partial togetherness!)[28] Their problem is, in a sense, solved. Death *is* a release from desire for the lovers.

We could distinguish in this text between two modes or levels of human desire, with two different relations to the concept of narra-tive causality. First, and more superficially, there is what I will call an "itch": a chronic discomfort, which produces a restlessness and the desire for a remedy. Tristan is frequently "itching" to see Yseut. Now such a desire does set in motion a certain, somewhat feeble, chain of causality. Tristan devises strategies to get close to Yseut or to get a message to her—though Tristan alone is never sufficient to accomplish his desire. In any case, it is understood that there is no real satisfaction for an itch. Scratching an itch—going to see, to briefly be with Yseut—cannot make Tristan happy, cannot "close" an episode. It is generally this sort of itch that begins the episodes, that gets them moving. It is the itch—and its nature *as* itch—that accounts for the action that occurs and for its triviality as act; and, as well, for the triviality of the satisfactions we find. The couple manages to "comfort their grief," to spend the night together, and so forth. But we, and they, are accorded no scenes of bliss, of ecstasy —no representations of or even references to real satisfaction, psychologically or erotically speaking. This desire is like an itch in yet another way: scratching does no lasting good. Love (in Thomas) is like poison ivy: the more you scratch, the worse off you are. But underlying this fairly narrative construct is, as we saw above, another—deeply pessimistic—notion of desire and of human attempts at transformation. Underneath the itch is the fundamental unhappiness or dissatisfaction from which it arises and of which it is merely the symptom: to put it in Thomas's terms, without human *mal* there would not be that incessant and fruitless generation of *novelerie*. Desire and need are not, then, for Thomas, the "will to transform"; they are not dynamic stimuli that produce narrative events. Love is not a force, but an uncomfortable state; it is a bond, indeed bondage. Underneath all the *novelerie*—the little narrative events—is a situation which is absolutely unchanging and unchangeable. Love here is the Greimasian hyphen felt not as an arrow but as a chain. Finally, desire in Thomas is less a narrative construct or "motivator" than a theme for the *moraliste's* reflection and analysis.[29]

That a narrative so strange and so unnarrative (so short on *events*) should have been and should remain today so moving need not surprise us. After all, that which defies change is hardly less powerful, literarily and psychologically (to say nothing of theologically), than that which changes. Constancy—immutability—has great fascination as an idea, even as an ideal. And such is surely the power of the story of Tristan and Yseut, in all its versions, but in this one in particular.

We now turn, finally, to the anonymous thirteenth-century *fabliau* about the sacristan monk—*Du segretain moine*[30]—which will represent a third major strain in medieval narrative,[31] and which will allow us to examine still another sort of treatment of the relation of desire to narrative event and closure.

As this tale is probably unfamiliar to the reader (unlike the first two texts), a detailed plot summary follows, which will provide the platform for our subsequent analysis.

A monk is secretly in love with Ydoine, a bourgeoise, wife of Guillaume the money changer. Guillaume having recently been robbed of a vast sum of money, he and Ydoine are in severe financial straits. When Ydoine goes to an abbey to pray, the sacristan comes up to her and offers her 100 pounds (from the abbey's treasury); he asks only

> . . . qu'avuec moi
> Vos tenisse en un lit segroi;
> Adonques avroie achevé
> Ce que lonc tens a(i) dessiré. (ll. 111–14)

> . . . that with me
> You I may embrace in a bed in secret,
> Then I would have accomplished
> What I have long desired.

Ydoine, a good and faithful wife, thinking how she and her husband could use that money, goes off to consult him. The two decide to deceive and rob the monk. She receives the monk at night at her house. As he carries her off to bed, Guillaume, who had been hiding in the bed, jumps up and hits the monk over the head, stunning him; he then hits him again and kills him. The couple, horrified to have killed the monk, try to figure out what to do with the body.

Guillaume carries the body back to the abbey, and sets it "naturalistically" on a privy. The prior of the abbey, called by nature (he had eaten too much for dinner), comes out to the privies, sees the dead monk, and insults him for falling asleep in such a disgusting place; then (giving him a poke), he realizes that the monk is dead, and (since the two of them had had harsh words recently), fears he will be blamed if the body is found there.

He then carries the body back into town and props it up against a door which happens to be that of Guillaume and Ydoine (who he does not know are guilty).

Guillaume, hearing a noise, opens the door—and the body of the dead monk falls on top of him. He then carries the body off again to the farm of Thibaut, the tenant farmer, where he prepares to hide it in a hole in a pile of horse manure.

Narrative parenthesis: the day before, a vagabond had stolen a bacon that Tibaut had had hanging in his barn, and had hidden it, in a bag, in the manure.

When Guillaume begins to dig, he finds the bag, thinks at first that the fat black object within is another dead monk. When he realizes his good fortune, he makes an exchange, and carrying the bacon, runs home. When his anxious wife (seeing the monkish look-alike on his shoulder) inquires, "Est-ce le sougretain?" he replies:

Nenil, dame, par seint Germain,
Ainz est un bacon cras et gros,
Nos avon char, querez des chox. (ll. 570–72)

No, my lady, by Saint Germain,
But rather a big fat bacon
We have meat, go fetch some cabbage.

The thief, meanwhile, drinking with friends in a tavern, gets hungry and goes to look for his booty. He and his friends bring back the "bacon" to the tavern where an alarmed serving girl, preparing to slice it, notices that this "bacon" is wearing *hose*. The terrified thief carries the body back and hangs it up on the hook from which he had stolen the bacon.

The farmer's helper is offered a slice of bacon in payment. As he goes to cut it down, it falls on him. He and the farmer discover the monk. They put it on the farmer's horse, tie the body in place, arm it like a knight, and send it galloping into the monastery, where it rides around doing damage until the horse falls into a ditch, from which the monk is pulled "dead." And the *fabliau* ends:

Ainsi ot Guillaumes son droit
Du moine qui par son avoir
Cuida sa feme decevoir;
Le bacon ot et les cent livres;
Einsi fu Guillaumes delivres,
Que onques pui clamex n'en fu;
Ainsi ot dant Tibout perdu
Et son bacon et son poulein;
Ainsi fu morz le segretain. (ll. 808–16)

Thus did William get revenge
On the monk who with his money
Thought to deceive [seduce] his wife;
He had the bacon and the hundred pounds;
Thus was William delivered,

For he was never again accused;
Thus did mister Thibaut lose
Both his bacon and his horse;
And thus died the sacristan.

Now the questions that concern us are, once again: What do the characters want? How do they go about trying to achieve it: Do they succeed? How does the ending correspond to the "satisfaction" (the attaining of expressed desire) on the part of the characters?

First, it is absolutely clear what each of the characters wants.

- The sacristan wants to "satisfy his lust" with Ydoine. We are far here from the unsatisfiable desire of Tristan and Yseut! One general characteristic of short, *fabliau*-type narratives, is that the goal or narrative object of the desire is clear and accomplishable. The monk wants, not Ydoine in some vague and romantic sense, but, very concretely, to go to bed with Ydoine; he wants to have her, once: to have had her; to satisfy a long-term desire which he considers will then have been satisfied.
- The couple need money since they have fallen on hard times. They ask God for help; that is, for money. But their general need (their situation in life) turns into a specific, and narrative, desire for an attempt to get money when the monk offers to pay Ydoine for her favors. Since the favors are (to the faithful couple) out of the question, they will deceive the monk and rob him. They then have a second desire (which occurs twice): to get rid of the body of the monk they have killed.
- The prior is presented as a man of "needs": he needed to eat a lot; now he needs to move his bowels. But the need that concerns us narratively is that which he shares with the couple and all the subsequent characters: to get rid of the body before he is accused of the murder. A dead monk is clearly a hot potato.
- The thief, like the prior, was hungry, so he stole the bacon. (He is also a thirsty man; his thirst revives his hunger, so he goes back to get his hidden bacon.) Then he must get rid of the body.
- The farm worker and Thibaut: get rid of the body!

What do they do? Each character consistently acts with the intention of achieving his desire. Now there is a certain lack of verisimilitude in their actions. The monk knew Ydoine was going to consult her husband, but he is not worried about coming to her house. It is not clear just how the couple had intended to deceive the monk. Guillaume hits him over the head; then, seeing how big the monk is, hits him again, this time killing him. But had he really expected just to be able to hit him once and steal his money and get away with it?

At any rate, they all act in some sense toward their purpose. As for their attempts to get rid of the body, their tactics all have some energy or wit: Guillaume set it on a privy, complete with a wad of grass in its fist; the prior leans the body against the door of a pretty woman in town, whom it will be assumed that the sacristan was visiting—by coincidence, he picks the right door! And so on.

The problem is—and of course this is part of the joke—all this energetic and decisive action has very unreliable, hit-or-miss results. The success of any given action is highly unpredictable. To this we will return shortly.

Who gets what he wanted? And how does the ending correspond to the satisfaction of desire?

- The monk not only does not get what he had wanted—to "achever son désir" for Ydoine—he is soon dead. This is curious, since the prologue had declared:

  D'un moine vos dirai la vie,
  Segretain fu de l'abaie. (ll. 1–2)

  I will tell you the life of a monk;
  He was the sacristan of an abbey.

  His *vie* certainly does not last very long, narratively speaking! So, despite the prologue, we really cannot say that this story is about the life of a monk; it is (in one sense) about the monk, alive and dead. Be that as it may, the monk dies unsatisfied. (Or *does* he? More on this below . . .)

- The couple disappear from the story on line 572, well before the end of the tale (on line 816). And they disappear not merely satisfied (they have the monk's money and they have successfully shed his body), but as I have put it above, *sur-comblés:* their cup runneth over. They have a bacon as well as getting off scot-free. While the rest of the characters are struggling with that dead "bacon in hose," the devoted couple are presumably regaling themselves on real bacon and cabbage. So, though they are indeed "satisfied," the end of the story has nothing to do with their happiness: the two do not coincide.

- The remaining characters are all, at the end—or whenever they disappear from the narrative—satisfied in that they did not get caught with the body and charged with the murder. Everyone gets off scot-free, in that sense. But the thief has lost his booty ("his" stolen bacon), and the farmer has lost his bacon and his horse as well. As to the farmer—who has lost more than anyone, and who is the only completely innocent character in the tale (he has done nothing wrong)—we are not invited to feel any sympathy for his plight.

So the ending does not correspond to any significant degree to the satisfaction of the desires of any of the characters. The story is over (presumably) because the body is once and for all disposed of. The death of the monk is now public; no one has been or will be accused since it is assumed that he died when his horse fell in the ditch. The story is over and cannot be revived because the monk's body is now, finally, at rest. We (as readers) knew it eventually had to come to rest, though we did not know when, or where, or how.

Let's go back to Todorov's definition of the *"récit idéal"* quoted previously:

> An ideal narrative *[récit]* begins with a stable situation, that some force disturbs. The result is a state of disequilibrium; by the action of a contrary force, the equilibrium is reestablished; the second equilibrium is much like the first, but the two are never identical.[32]

What concerns us here is not the first four segments but the fifth—that final stasis or equilibrium (which other narratologists might call the resolution to the problem, and so forth). This final stasis is, in the "mythological" text, understood to refer to the satisfaction of some character's desire or intent. The point I want to make here is that the resolution of the problem is by no means always at the level of satisfaction of the characters, nor even of the working out of some satisfaction of the characters, nor even of the working out of some principle or force, as in the ideological text. This equilibrium may simply reflect the fact that someone or something is finally at peace, at rest. With respect to human beings, this notion of "rest" generally means that someone is dead, but of course, in this particular tale (unlike most works presumably) death and peace are by no means the same thing!

But how are we to account for what does happen in the work? What is the causal structure here? There are, within this text, four competing theories or explanations for what is happening.

1. First, normal human causality—with a twist. Characters try to produce, and sometimes succeed in producing, what they desired. The

complication is that there are many characters here who all want something, and what they want is often a cross-purposes with what the others want. All these would-be "causers" are acting and reacting with each other (unbeknownst to them). Each character's efficiency as agent is limited by the existence of others; no one of them is omnipotent.[33]

2. There is, as well, a strong random or coincidental factor—chance— which is manipulated by the narrator. That is, it is precisely at the spot where the thief has buried the bacon that Guillaume starts to bury the monk, and so forth. While it is not clear whether this factor is in any sense "meaningful," it is narratively necessary, in that it provides for the *enchaînement* of the various attempts to get rid of the body: only narrative "chance" connects all these characters to the dead monk.

Now these first two sorts of causality are not specifically medieval. They are more characteristic of a genre; of comedy—more precisely of what Northrop Frye would call "low comedy"—than they are of any particular period or theology. Low comedy is largely based on human "inefficiency," on the clash of different characters' desires and attempts to satisfy them, and on randomness as an agent of transformation. But randomness is an *absurd* agent: no narrative syntax can handle it, make sense of it. (This *fabliau* always makes me think of an Alfred Hitchcock movie, *The Trouble with Harry*, in which, just as in the *Segretain Moine*, a dead body cannot be gotten rid of: it keeps resurfacing, and being reburied or hidden by the various characters; it, too, eventually comes to rest though.

3. The first two interpretations are ours. As we have just noted, they are not specifically medieval, nor are they necessarily Christian. The characters also have an explanation for the surprising discrepancy between what they had done (thought they had "caused") and what they find to be the result. For example, Guillaume had put the monk on the privy—but finds him at the door; the thief buries a bacon—which is later wearing hose, and so forth. In each case the interpretation is that the *maufé* (the evil one) has intervened in events, miraculously as it were, and has made the switch. In two of the instances, the character suggests that his own sin has made him vulnerable to the Devil. (In *The Trouble with Harry*, the continual reappearance of the dead body of Harry—for that is his trouble: he is dead—certainly gives the characters what we call today "the creeps," but no one speaks of the Devil.) At any rate, as the thief puts it, swearing to this companions that he did not kill the monk:

Onques, par toz sainz, nel toschai;
Mais c'est déable, bien le sai,
Qui a fait moine de bacon;

Se Diex me doint confesséon,
Ce fu un bacon en guise mis
De moine por nos enconbrer.   (ll. 637–43)

Never, by all the saints, did I touch him;
But it is the Devil, I know it well,
Who has turned a bacon into a monk;
If God allows me to confess,
This was a bacon put into the form of
A monk, to torment us.

Of course, though this is the interpretation for the extraordinary events provided by the characters—a supernatural causality—we, thanks to the narrator, know better, and hence can laugh at the characters.

4. But, while we laugh at their superstitious belief in the intervention of the "evil one," there is, in the text, the discreet but serious suggestion of another sort of supernatural intervention. The couple, at the beginning of the text, have been impoverished and virtually dishonored by a theft (Guillaume was robbed in the forest of monies in his care). He takes this theft "philosophically"—or rather, like a Christian, declaring:

. . . "Ydoine, douce amie,
Por Dieu ne vos corrociez mie;
Se Nostre Sire a consentu
Que ge ai mon avoir perdu,
Encor est il la ou li sielt;
Bien nos conseillera s'il velt."   (ll. 73–78)

. . . "Ydoine, sweet friend,
For God's sake, do not be distressed;
If Our Lord has consented
That I lose my money,
Then it is where it belongs.
He will give us good counsel if He wills.

The next day

. . . endroit midi
Ala Ydoine a l'abaïe
Proier le filz seinte Marie
De quoi l'iglise estoit fondee.
Une chandoile a alumee

Que Damediex la conseillast
Et son seignor gaaing donast.
Desor l'autel mist sa chandele:
Des elz, qui resanblent estoile,
Plora, et de son cuer soupire,
Que s'oroison ne li lut dire. (ll. 88–98)

. . . about noon
Ydoine went to the abbey
To pray to the son of Saint Mary
In whose name the church was founded.
She lit a candle
That the Lord God would counsel her
And give some money [gain] to her lord.
On the altar she put her candle;
With her eyes, which were like stars,
She cried, and from her heart she sighs,
So that she was unable to say her prayer.

It is at this point that the lecherous sacristan (who has long desired her) approaches and propositions her. The events that follow can be understood as the answer to the couple's prayers for divine aid (though the narrator does not explicitly "authorize" such an interpretation). At the end the couple have exactly what they had prayed for: money—and a bonus: bacon. True, they are not exactly "good": they did murder that monk, though it was an "accident" (Guillaume did not mean to hit him so hard). When Guillaume has hit him again on the back of the head "Si li espandi le cervel" (So that his brains; spill out; l. 346), the narrator states: "Ainsi va fox sa mort querant" (Thus does the fool go seeking for his death; l. 343). The monk was "asking for it": fools *want* to die! (The dead monk *is* "satisfied"—to be dead?) We are not, it appears, to blame the couple much.

Of course, when they find that dead monk back on their doorstep, they are greatly dismayed, blame it on the *maufé*, and Guillaume blames sin:

Maleoit soit mauvais avoir
Et covoitise et trahison. (ll. 508–9)

Cursed be evil gain
And covetousness and treachery.

If he has repented, his repentance seems short-lived, however, for once he is finally rid of the body—and has the bacon—he is happy to enjoy the ill-gotten gains. And there is no further suggestion in the tale that they are "guilty" or are to be punished. As we saw above, the story ends, rather, on the note that the couple "got back at the monk" for his attempted treachery:

Ainsi ot Guillaume son droit
Du moine qui par son avoir
Cuida sa feme decevoir;
Le bacon ot et les cent livres;
Einsi fu Guillaumes delivres. (ll. 808–12)

Thus did William get revenge
On the monk who with his money
Thought to deceive [seduce] his wife;
He had the bacon and the hundred pounds;
Thus was William delivered.

So in this tale—which is in many respects so perfectly immoral!—there is the suggestion of a moral, or rather of a Christian reading: God comes to the aid of those who trust in Him, pray to Him; the wicked are punished. It must be said, however, that divine justice is represented as a bit peculiar!

We do not have to understand its causality to enjoy this tale—and it is just as well we do not. A good part of the pleasure and amusement that the story provides comes first, from the repetition of certain visual images and activities. (The dead monk is continually falling onto people, and being hoisted over a shoulder and carried around.) Second, the visual resemblance—and the suggestion of a deeper one—between the monk and the bacon provides considerable humor. In fact, the only difference that anyone notes between the bacon and the dead monk is that the latter wears hose. That is, no one says, "This is no *bacon*; it's a *monk!*"—but only, "This bacon has *hose!*"

We have been dealing with three very different sorts of texts, composed over (roughly) three centuries. But it is worth noting the important points that they have in common, and which they share with many other works of this period, with respect to the narrative functioning of desire:

- Desire is presented as a narrative motor, in the sense that it initiates the action, sets off the causal chain, in the narrative. (Of course, the theologians would say that the desire did not cause itself—just as Greimas would speak of the *Destinateur*, the Dispatcher or Initiator of the quest.) And there is no causality that is *not* motivated by desire: no nonintentional causality. But if desire begins the chain of events, human agency (motored by desire) is not represented as competent, of itself, to achieve its ends. Human desire has energy but not great efficiency.
- It is not that these texts ignore or deny human causality, but they all represent its efficiency as severely limited by the unforeseeable interactions of human causes on each other, by (what appears to be) coincidence, and by the mysterious intervention of God or Providence. In fact, causality is largely incomprehensible in these texts. We cannot follow the (hypothetical) causal chain. It is not merely the characters who are mystified; the readers are only slightly less so. This causality passes all understanding—and all narratological syntax!

   The critic cannot be more "positivistic" than the text he analyzes. Todorov's categories, though they seem very plausible, assume that the narrator presents a clear image or representation of the causal forces at work in his text, yet we are very often far from such a clarity in medieval texts. The energy is clearly stated—it is desire—but the source and nature of the actual causal agency are a mystery.
- Satisfaction is of course provided to some of the characters. But often satisfaction is only partial, or short-lived, or is granted in terms noticeably different from what the character had desired or sought. The texts are as concerned with "reward" as with "satisfaction": that is, with the fulfillment of what characters *deserve*, as distinct from what they *want*.
- Closure in the texts does not reliably coincide with the final carrying-through of some desire, with satisfaction. This is, first, because closure often corresponds merely to the fact that something is over: at peace. Often the problem, the desire, cannot truly be said—in any sense that means anything—to be "resolved." Second, because whatever satisfactions to be meted out to the characters in the text were meted out earlier, before the end. Closure is often marked by a rhetorical flourish or by a shift to a didactic mode (for example, with a moral).
- Why should medieval narrators be so interested in desire? First, no doubt, because their image of man was primarily that of a desiring and willing being. It was human nature to desire—and to attempt to satisfy that desire. But it was only in the *divine* nature to be fully efficacious.

Second, desire does provide for marvelous narrative "spectacles." What extraordinary—impressive, noble, grotesque, pitiful, amusing, and so on, and so forth—things desire makes the characters in medieval narrative do! With what energy medieval characters struggle to satisfy their quest for perfect service of God, their love of glory or of noble ladies, their need for revenge, their hunger, their avarice, their lust!

Finally, medieval texts, such as those discussed here, do indeed present considerable difficulties for the theories of narrative proposed by contemporary critics such as Todorov, Greimas, and Bremond. These theorists all make a number of implicit fundamental assumptions—assumptions both literary and philosophical—which are alien to medieval texts (as to other nonrationalistic texts); they assume that we know—that the narrator of a text knows and makes apparent—why things happen in the work: whose causal energy or power produced them, and with what intention. Their various syntaxes cannot operate unless we *do* know this. But in medieval texts, the causal agency is frequently anything but clear, as we have seen. Further, the theorists assume that the order in which things occur is essential, that things must follow logically—that is, must respect temporal sequence and human logic. But medieval narrators dealing with divine reality and action are inclined to defy both time and logic. Lastly, the theorists focus on man as agent, as producer of events, as competent; they *assume* a relation between desire and potency. But medieval narrators assume, as a matter of course, *no* such relation; they are interested in human will and desire, often in themselves, and not necessarily in terms of their potency; to these writers man is not, primarily, efficient. In short, they are readily inclined to view man as "marvelous"—but largely powerless.

NOTES

1. I am attempting to cope here with the eleventh through the thirteenth century. I will not attempt to generalize much beyond that period, though I suspect that many features even of later medieval narrative would be similar.
2. One might assume, *a priori*, that causality was central to his actantial model. And Greimas does seem to assume that efforts one the part of the Subject to achieve his Object—as well as those of the Adjuvant to aid him and of the Opposant to hinder him are, somehow, narratively fruitful. But in point of fact

there is no mechanism or concept in Greimas's theory which would allow one to pass from the Subject's desire for his Object, to any narrative efficiency. Greimas has indeed no theory of what a *narrative* structure is. Wanting things is not (alas) the same as actually getting them—which is precisely why Greimas's theory is just as applicable to lyric poetry, or to our feelings about each other, as it is to narrative literature.

The model of Claude Bremond, as articulated in *Loqique du Récit* (Paris: Seuil, 1973), does not deal directly with causality. It does speak of the "rigorous linking" of events. And it speaks of Agents, of their "program," of whether or not and "thanks to what" they accomplish their "task." But Bremond is concerned above all with what is logically possible: with what can and/or must occur, and in what temporal order. Our focus is quite different, in that we are concerned with the *energy* of individual texts: with what *makes* things happen, and with the ontological nature of the causal agencies.

3. Tzetan Todorov, *Poétique* (Paris: Seuil, 1968), 67–77. Todorov's discussion draws largely on the work of other critics, in particular Barthes.

4. In this and subsequent theological discussion on the specific problem of causality, I will base myself primarily on: Vernon J. Bourke's discussion of "Causality," in his book *Augustine's View of Reality* (Villanova, Pa.: Villanova University Press, 1964), 125–34; the articles on "Causality," "Divine Causality," "Efficient Cause," "Instrumental Causality," "Motion," in the *New Catholic Encyclopedia*, ed. Catholic University of America (New York: McGraw-Hill, 1967), vols., 3, 3, 5, 7, 10, respectively); the article on "Cause" in A. Vacant and E. Mangenot, *Dictionnaire de théologie catholique*, vol. 2 (Paris: Letouzey et Ané, 1905); and Etienne Gilson's *The Spirit of Medieval Philosophy* (New York: Scribners, 1940). The major relevant texts of Augustine are: *On the Trinity*, book III; and *The City of God*, book V.

5. This is also true of the pre-Thomistic period in general: that is, until the late thirteenth century. (Aquinas's dates are 1225–1274.) There are, of course, many similarities between Augustine and Aquinas on causality: both were, of course, orthodox Catholics—though Aquinas's orthodoxy was not immediately apparent to all! But one of the many differences between them is that whereas Augustine speaks primarily of efficient cause, Aquinas systematizes the kinds of causes along Aristotelian lines: material, formal, efficient, and final. It is worth noting that both Augustine and Aquinas are primarily concerned not with the causing of actions, but of being, of things; that is, their analysis of causality deals with the end product of the act, and is not much interested in the act itself. But of course they are theologians, interested above all in divine creation; and the greatest difference perhaps between divine and human efficiency is that, in the former, there is no gap between the divine will and the end product; whereas in the latter, it is quite the opposite! Narrative is, in one sense, the story of the very *difficulty* with which we manage to "cause" things.

6. Such as that to be found, in a literary-criticism mode, in the work of Claude Bremond.

7. This would be the more Platonic tradition, of evil as a falling away from divine light, power, and truth.

8. *La Chanson de Roland* was probably composed around the end of the eleventh century. I will be using the edition by Joseph Bédier (which provides modern

French translations on facing pages) (Paris; Piazza 1922). I will assume the reader's familiarity with this work, and provide no narrative summary. The translations are mine.

9. Cf. laisses 253, 266. Interesting detail: the existence of the pagan gods is never denied—only their ability to protect and save those who worship them!

10. The angel stops the sun in its course: laisse 180. The angel Gabriel personally urges Charlemagne up off the ground and on to victory, when he has stumbled, stunned by a blow from the emir, in laisse 261. God protects Thierry from Pinabel (Ganelon's champion) in combat: laisse 285.

11. By that I mean a work in which God's action and will play a major part. I am not saying it is always easy to tell when they do!

12. An Adjuvant is a helper. God, being understood to be omnipotent, needs no "helpers." Rather, he requires "service."

13. Not until Aquinas does this distinction become standard.

14. The *Legenda Aurea* (composed around 1260) is available in a paperback French translation by J. -B. M. Rose, *La Légende dorée*, 2 vols. (Paris, Garnier-Flammarion, 1967). The legend of Saint Christine is in vol. 2, pp. 469–71.

15. Even for those which are not immediately or directly concerned with causality at all: e.g., that of Greimas.

16. The Fates are a good deal more mysterious and disturbing, both in the nature of their will, and in the mode of their operation. But the poems focus very little on them.

17. That is, is he even the proximate cause of something (he cannot be its full cause) or merely an instrumental cause? Aquinas and the Scholastics refine greatly on the modes and degrees of causality (aside from primary vs. secondary): productive vs. conservative; being vs. becoming; accidentally vs. essentially ordered; essential vs. coincidental; free vs. natural; physical vs. moral; proximate vs. remote; univocal vs. equivocal; immanent vs. transitive; total vs. partial; principal vs. instrumental; participated vs. unparticipated. (See *New Catholic Encyclopedia*, "Efficient Causality.")

18. That is, we can identify the true Agent or Subject only when we understand whose will (whose intent to modify something; whose desire for some Object) *accounts for*, is "behind," the act that occurred.

19. I refer the reader to chapter 4.

20. This denial—or undermining—of logical order would present severe problems for Bremond's model, which assumes a "rigorous linking."

21. It suggests, of course, other things as well: Roland's (arguable) "flaw" for example.

22. It is not only of *this* text that this is so. Classical epics also frequently posit a divine permission between act and effect. But other sorts of heroic texts do often assume that the hero has full causal power.

23. We do not always know what we are looking for: what it is we desire. In psychological terms, we have the problem of the unconscious: who knows what it wants! In a Christian perspective, I return to the quote from Augustine, given earlier: "You have made us for yourself, and our hearts are restless until they rest in you." (*Confessions*, book 1, chapter 1.) The fact that we do not *know* we are seeking God does not mean we *are not*.

24. Thomas's version of the story of Tristan and Yseut was apparently composed between 1160 and 1180. I will be using J. C. Payen's convenient modern edition

of the various Tristan stories (with translations into modern French): *Tristan et Yseut* (Paris: Garnier, 1974). The translations are mine. For general reading purposes, I recommend *Gottfried von Strassburg* "Tristan with the "Tristan" of Thomas translated" by A. T. Hatto, (Baltimore: Penguin Books, 1960). Hatto's translation has guided me at various points.

25. What we will find to be the case with this text is—*mutatis mutandis*—true of many other "love" texts.

26. Or rather, only Luxuria (lust) is really left, in a strange hybrid with Tristitia.

27. Denis de Rougement, *Love in the Western World* trans. Montgomery Belgion (Garden City, N.Y.: Doubleday/Anchor, 1957). Originally published as *L'Amor et l'Occident* (Paris: Plon, 1939).

28. Tristan died "of love," not knowing that Yseut was on her way. Yseut lies down next to the dead Tristan and dies "of tenderness' *(tendrur)* (ll. 3107–77).

29. The transformations to be found in this text are less narrative than they are—in a certain, modern, sense—"grammatical" or "linguistic." That is, one might well conceive of this text as a series of transformations or operations, based on the two fundamental sentences: "Tristan loves Yseut. Yseut loves Tristan." The transformations can be operated on each of the elements of the sentence: (subject, verb, complement) and on its mode. For example, *verb:*

Tristan loves Yseut
Tristan envies Yseut
Tristan wants to forget Yseut
subject:
Tristan loves Yseut
Marc loves Yseut
Cariadoc loves Yseut
mode:
Tristan loves Yseut
Does Tristan still love Yseut?
Etc. . . .

The initial pair of sentences has a privileged status: Tristan loves Yseut and Yseut loves Tristan, and no matter what happens, we keep returning to these two basic unforgettable sentences. But all the sentences are of interest, since Thomas is primarily concerned with what we could call an analysis of love in all its modes and forms. What is the relation of love to desire, to physical possession, to friendship, to fidelity? What are the opposites of love: hate, indifference, forgetfulness? But, of course, "transformation" in this semilinguistic sense has virtually nothing to do with the word as the narratologists have used it. Some of the transformations of which I am speaking here are presented as real—as part of the plot, such as it is. But some of them are hypothetical, or posed as questions, fantasies, or fears. They explore the feelings of the various characters toward each other. But, in the narrative sense, there are no transformations—at least no intended ones—that count. The fundamental sentences are, narratively speaking, untransformable, unsatisfiable, and accounted for by no clear causality. They are mysterious and immutable.

30. This *fabliau* was composed around the middle of the thirteenth century. I will be using the text provided by T. B. W. Reid in his *Twelve Fabliaux* (Manchester: Manchester University Press [French Classics], 1958). The summary and translations are mine.

31. That is, we have looked at an epic, and at one of the earliest manifestations of romance; now we turn to a *fabliau*.
32. Todorov, *Poétique*, 82; my translation.
33. There are *fabliaux* in which a character—the leading character—is represented as efficient. And it is, I think, in this genre that we first see the rise of the "competent individual." But it is by no means characteristic of the genre! The *Roman de Renart* stories are interesting with respect to this issue. What characterizes the earliest tales in Renart's mode of action (the nature of his desire and of his attempts to satisfy it), rather than any reliable competence to carry through. But Renart soon becomes increasingly—and, at least to his fellow characters, alarmingly—competent: successful in humiliating and devouring others. We are farther and farther here from the Augustinian powerlessness of evil!

Conclusions—and Questions

In these pages I should like to draw out a few issues that emerge from this volume taken as a whole, and to raise a few new questions.

I am struck by the Christianity of the texts examined. It comes as no surprise that medieval literature is strongly religious; we all knew that. There are vast—indeed daunting—numbers of obviously religious works, belonging to the various religious genres in the medieval period. But that is not what I am talking about. After all, except for the *Alexis* and the *Roland*, we have not been looking at what one normally thinks of as "Christian literature." What is startling is not, then, how *overtly* Christian most of these works are —how didactic, how pious, how thematically religious—but rather how profoundly, how *structurally* Christian they are.[1]

To take an example: Guillaume de Lorris's part of the *Roman de la Rose*. As I said earlier, I do not share Fleming's (the Robertsonian) view that this text—indeed the entire *Rose*—is a moral, that is, a Christian, work, one that condemns, by means of irony, the folly and sinfulness of the lover. I have tried to demonstrate that, on the contrary, the narrator attempts at every turn to harmonize the potentially divergent and ironic points of view, and to draw the reader into the love of love: to initiate him. But, on the other hand, I think that the Guillaume work *is* profoundly religious in its understanding of the nature of love. That this work presents love as a kind of religion (or idolatry) is obvious. But the *Rose* is religious as well at a subtler and more structural level, in its representation of love as an infinite yearning for an inaccessible, unpossessable object; and in its image of the nature of man (of the Subject, the lover) as marked, not by internal plenitude, richness, and autonomy, but by a lack, a dependence, a need to be filled, fulfilled. (I refer the reader back as well to my discussion of Thomas's *Tristan*.)

Are these ways of conceiving of desire and the self necessarily, specifically Christian, or could they not just be vaguely religious—theocentric in some general sense? Well, "religion" exists, historically speaking, not vaguely but only concretely, and not in the singular but only in the plural—and there is hardly unanimity among the various religions on many central issues. The concepts expressed here are surely characteristic of the Judeo-Christian tradition—from the Psalms and the Gospels, for example—far more so than they are of the traditions of pagan antiquity or heathen Europe.

But if these works seem strikingly Christian in their representation of desire (and the self), they are no less striking in the sheer importance that they accord to concepts and the language of desire: words such as *amor* (love), *talent* (desire, will), *désir, volenté* (will) abound. And the centrality of this theme has considerable consequences for our analysis of medieval literature.

Indeed, I would like to argue that the basic narrative genres or types of the early medieval period—hagiography, the epic, the *roman*—can best be defined *not* formally *or* thematically, as is commonly done, but rather in terms of desire: in terms of the kind of desire being represented, and in terms of the representation of the relation between that desire and the closure of the text. For example, if we focus on the central character(s): hagiography can surely be best conceived not in terms of what its hero says or does but by the fact that he desires above all to love and serve God. (The precise formulation of what it means to love or serve God is of course susceptible to varying and evolving interpretations, historically speaking.) And while the hagiographical text is always necessarily a "comedy," in that the saint is happy at the end, still the closure of the saint's desire—his complete satisfaction—is situated beyond the reach of the discourse: it cannot fully be represented in the text.

If hagiography has a protagonist who specializes in the love of God, and who must both find and yet not quite find fulfillment in the text, the epic can be defined as a narrative in which the hero desires (whatever *else* he wants) to win renown and honor among men—and simply, to fight. The epic guarantees to its major protagonist(s) a marked measure of success in the vanquishing of adversaries; success generally corresponds pretty much to narrative closure. In the *roman*, as elaborated by its early practitioners, the central protagonist may be, wish, do, other things as well, but above all he loves; his means are those of the knight—battle—but not his primary purpose, which is love. And the end of the novel generally coincides with the definitive acquisition of that love.

A few reservations and refinements: First, the comic genres as they emerge will be far less committed to providing satisfaction for characters, but tend rather to manipulate all characters' desires, and to play the characters off against each other. Second, there are, all along, works that fit no standard category very neatly: for example, Marie's *Lais*—apparently emerging from an old Celtic genre —explore the various modes and kinds of love, but guarantee no full satisfaction to any character; closure, as we saw, is as apt to be rhetorical or poetic as narrative. Third, starting primarily in the thirteenth century there are many hybrid works, showing the coming together of several narrative traditions, different ways of representing desire and its satisfaction. For example, the first part of the *Rose* clearly exhibits the impact both of courtly love poetry and of religious language—and cannot keep the romance promise to give to the lover what he desires. (If this work is, as we all agree, "incomplete," it may well be because Guillaume himself perceived that he had no way *to* end it.) Jean de Meung's part has been influenced both by comic narrative and the philosophical-didactic tradition—but Jean keeps the old romance tradition of giving to the lover, at last, what he wanted.

It is not merely the protagonists' *amor* and *volenté* that we must factor into the definition of the narrative modes, but also the desires of the listening (or reading) public whose emotions and intentionality are solicited. The case of hagiography is no doubt the clearest: as we saw with respect to the *Alexis*, the listeners' prayers are, most commonly, explicitly invited; often—though not here!—their imitation of the saint is called for as well. Thus, if the hagiographical text is already a comedy with respect to the saint himself, it is only *potentially* one with respect to the audience: for things to turn out happily, they must pray; otherwise . . . The narrative, then, is not merely story but persuasive discourse. Is the situation so different in the other traditions? The epic is generally a call to arms, or at least to solidarity, this solidarity often containing as well a Christian, a French, commonly a male, sometimes a dynastic, overlay. As to the novel, it surely speaks not merely *of* but *to* present, past, or would-be lovers.

The role of God must be assessed as well in this definition. And this fact—as well as being one of the elements that make medieval literature so curiously, so structurally Christian—is surely one of the slipperiest parts of the problem both of the definition of genres, and of the narrative analysis of medieval texts. Sometimes God is very clearly a character: the narrator tells us so. (I assume the medieval narrator to be reliable; the "unreliable narrator" is, I think, well in the future.) God simply must be counted into the plot. He is seen as a person whose intentions matter for the development of the events; he is indeed often a Subject. So far, no problem.

But God is a character unlike any other for the simple reason that he is mysterious: even for narrators he is not merely invisible, but unknowable. The narrator may tell us *that* God acted, but not *why*, and he generally does not explain why God did not intervene elsewhere. (Why *did* God let the rear guard die?) God's ultimate intentionality is unknowable, even to the narrator. Moreover, sometimes it is not the narrator himself who tells us that God has acted, but merely a character—and there are certainly unreliable *characters* in medieval literature! One need only think of the *Roman de Renart* where some of the stupid animals believe in the "miracles" worked by "Saint" Copée the hen, "martyred" by the fox. And what of situations where a worldly if somewhat devout character in a narrative prays for something to happen and then it *does*? Are we to understand that a prayer has been answered—though the narrator does not tell us so: that God has made this happen? (We had this problem in *Du segretain moine*.) What if a character begs God to intervene and nothing happens? Does that mean that God *was not* a character—was not there—after all, or that his nonintervention constitutes a negative, a punitive intervention? Here, one thinks of Thomas's poem, and of the storm-beset, then becalmed, Iseut, who is thereby prevented from being reunited, in life, with Tristan. One does often have the impression that the narrator himself is not quite sure if God is there or not in his story—after all, it is not necessarily "his" story: he did not make it up but inherited it from tradition.

We can say that not merely is religion the backdrop of much of medieval literature, but that God does seem to hover over the narrative much of the time. We must add however that medieval narrators (not unlike their modern counterparts) know how to play effectively with the uncertainties surrounding God's existence and intervention in human affairs.

All this adds up to plots whose workings are very hard to analyze. Now this uncertainty constitutes a "problem" only to the extent that we are determined for the events of the plot to *be* comprehensible, intelligible: analyzable. Perhaps we must (re)learn how to tolerate—indeed to relish—works that we simply cannot "understand" very well. Such works provide us with characters (including God) memorable in their desires and behaviors; they provide us with strange and powerful images. But much of what we find in them is essentially, irreducibly, mysterious.

This, not merely because God is so mysterious and mystifying a figure, but also because these works give us reality—protagonists, episodes, even forces—more in *chunks*, if you will, than in *strands*. We see things: they are set before us, and we are to admire and be affected by them. We can compare and contrast them. But we cannot very often pick characters, events, forces apart strand by strand. They repel analysis, at least at the "syntactical" level. For example, we can see what the characters want and how the various subjects (their desires) come into conflict, or are subordinated one to another. (See chapter 6.) But that is a way of seeing how the chunks are set into pattern, into hierarchy—and *not* really a way of understanding how the plot operates. To put it a little differently, we can see the *what* of character and event, but not analyze the *why* or the *how*. Most of these plots are not, strictly speaking—narratologically speaking—"intelligible."

There is some character analysis provided or invited in the texts, but here too it is done largely in chunks: in terms of personifications (as in the *Rose*); or of dimensions, on which one ranks high or low, and which are set in juxtaposition to each other (as in Abelard's *Historia*); or of epithets, easily transferable from one hero (saint, warrior, and so forth) to another.

As Walter J. Ong (and others) would argue, all this is characteristic, and to be expected, of a literature that is still emerging from the oral tradition which is (as he says) "tenacious."[2] And it is true: these high-powered and highfalutin superliterate analytical tools of ours[3] simply do not work very well on "texts" such as we have been looking at: texts that, however beautifully "literary" they may be in one sense, are still strongly rooted in the old oral tradition. Most of them are still at a profound, conceptual level as well as a superficial, stylistic one, broadly "formulaic"—made of reusable (and constantly reused) blocks of discourse and thought. This is literature, but it is still discourse, discourse of a largely rhetorical nature as well: the "text" talks about characters to an audience of listeners, and calls for their response.

Perhaps it is worth introducing here one final conceptual framework, one last structural dichotomy: that between the two hemispheres of the brain, whose distinctive functioning has in recent years been studied by psychologists and physiologists.[4] (This dichotomy, being physiological in nature, is of a more concrete sort than those discussed before—which does not make it necessarily less controversial!) The left half of the brain is, generally speaking, the intellectual hemisphere. It deals with mathematics and logic, as well as with spoken and written language. Its functioning is essentially analytical, involving the manipulation of discreet symbols, especially sequences of symbols—thus specializing in the decoding of events as strings occurring in time. The right half of the brain is markedly less intellectual in that it deals not with analysis, but with synthesis: it recognizes patterns (including faces) and images. It perceives wholes, rather than processing parts or sequences. This is also, according to recent research, the hemisphere in which we experience most emotion. It is the hemisphere in which imagistic (including erotic) dreams take place. And the visual and auditory experience of such activities as music, dance, and other performance is also primarily processed in the right hemisphere, as such arts call for immediate, virtually unconscious response to a wide assortment of sensorial information.[5]

Now, obviously, most of our experience of the world—and of art —calls on the combined activities of both hemispheres, and information is generally shunted back and forth between them over a bundle of nerve fibers called the *corpus callosum*. But it is worth noting that, over the past several centuries, there has been a gradual but nonetheless dramatic shift in the extent to which the two halves of the brain are called into play in our experience and appreciation of "literature" (and the other arts as well). First let us focus on the early medieval centuries, roughly through the thirteenth century. Vernacular narrative was performed—either recited or sung (more or less) from memory, or read aloud[6]—and this performance was often accompanied by instrumental music, physical movement and gestures, and other forms of nonverbal accompaniment. The stories told were clearly intended, by the narrator/ performer, to speak directly to the heart and will of the listeners, to *move* them in some way. Even people who read to themselves, read aloud, performed the "text" in some sense to, for themselves.[7] Clearly, such narrative called less for reflection and retroactive analysis— after all, the audience could not reread a text—than for immediate comprehension and affective response. This was so even when the story was not perfectly "intelligible."

This is not to deny the importance of the left hemisphere in a listener's perception of medieval narrative. After all, just to follow a plot, however simple, calls on left brain skills—and indeed it is in that hemisphere that language is processed (and produced) with respect to its sequentiality. The left cortex is in fact often called the *verbal* hemisphere. The point I am getting at is this: medieval narrative (and other medieval arts) seems to have provided artistic experiences that were far more slanted to processing by—and to providing stimulation for—the right hemisphere than is the case today. True, narrators used words, which are, as part of syntactic sequence, processed by the left hemisphere. But words also belong to the right hemisphere by virtue of their sensory (auditory) qual-

ity, of the emotional experience that they elicit (through intona-
tion, and so forth) and of our recognition of them as familiar words
—for, interesting detail, while the right brain does not deal with
language *qua* syntax, it *can* recognize basic words such as concrete
nouns (but not abstract nouns), and memorized groups or words or
phrases. It particularly responds to, and can even produce, emotion-
laden words, such as exclamations, swearwords, and words in songs.[8]
In most early medieval narrative, syntax was highly paratactic and
rarely demanded a sustained attention span. Moreover, the vocabulary used was generally restricted and very concrete, high as well
in image value. And the lines were full of formulaic and other
standard groupings—as well as rhyme, which allows for word recognition and even anticipation by the listeners. Thus, in a variety
of ways, medieval stories clearly drew heavily on the right hemisphere's ability to recognize and respond to words, and required
relatively little processing by the syntax-handling left hemisphere.
Thus, though the left brain is the "verbal hemisphere," Old French
narrative involved a minimum of left-brain attention.

I am not, of course, arguing that there was a conscious plan by
medieval artists to appeal to—to stimulate—the right hemisphere.
After all, they hardly knew what the brain was for, and Roland can
go on dying for quite some time with his brains—it is not specified
from which hemisphere—coming out of his ears. It is, rather, presumably through intuition and from long experience of what pleases,
what *works*, that medieval narrators provided the sorts of esthetic
and affective experiences appropriate to their public: a public that
for the most part could not read or write, and was certainly totally
unused to the delights (and frustrations) of literary and other sorts
of analysis; a public to whom they *spoke* and whom they wished to
move and delight. Thus, while their stories were—*il va sans dire*—
couched in words and therefore to some degree mediated through
the left part of the brain, they still provided considerable stimulation to the right hemisphere. Needless to say, the skills that a
medieval narrator had to possess—and the hemisphere on which he
had to draw—in order to *produce* a satisfactory narrative were
quite different from those that the audience used to *respond* to his
story. This distinction has always been the case in the arts. In
particular, most musicians (especially composers) are highly spe-

cialized in left-hemisphere activity with respect to their music, whereas those who listen to the music played are more apt to be responding with the right hemisphere.

Today narrative literature provides us with few pleasures indeed that come to us through the mediation of the right hemisphere. We read to ourselves, silently—no performance of any kind. (And rarely is the discourse what we would tend to think of as rhetorically "beautiful.") Generally no affective response at all is called for; we are not even moved to admiration or contempt for the hero or heroine—and the reader is apt to feel mortified if, through some failure of his sense of irony, his emotions do become engaged. Not only are we primarily invited (insofar as invitation exists) to analyze, but frequently the dissection process has already been begun for us by the author: many a work is presented to us already in some preanalyzed, predissected state, as, commonly, in the *nouveau roman*. In a word, many of the pleasures that were provided to the listener by the medieval *récit* have been withdrawn from him in modern narrative, which speaks (or rather directs itself) primarily to the left half of the human brain, to the purely intellectual side of human life. The pleasures provided do tend (I submit, uncharitably perhaps) largely to be associated with a sense of superiority at having been able to get through, and make some sense of, the book at hand.

Since, to a substantial degree, our theories of literature—and our "universals"—have been elaborated for us by readers far more used to the latter kind of literary experience than to the former, it is no surprise that their paradigms are far more appropriate to modern than to medieval narrative literature; that they are, indeed, not infrequently irrelevant to the medieval *récit*. Such modern left-brain tools, with their exclusive concern with the analysis (rather than the synthesis) of phenomena abstracted from the world of image and affect, simply cannot be expected to account for the satisfactions of medieval narrative, or to help us understand how such works were handled, mentally, by their audiences.

And if we can safely assume that human beings relish, in art as elsewhere, stimulation of *both* parts of the mind, if indeed we can assume that art—even such verbal art as narrative—has always privileged the image, feeling, synesthetic and synthetic experience, it is not so surprising that the modern equivalent of the medieval public is now not reading literature at all, but going to the movies. Only the hyperliterate read contemporary "literary"—highbrow—narrative.

Much of modern narrative analysis turns out to be more radically modernist than I had originally anticipated—and certainly more so than its major proponents seem prepared to concede. By the fact that it is on the whole so superliterate, so left-hemisphere-oriented, as well as so unconcerned with and dismissive of the transcendent, its usefulness for the understanding of medieval literature cannot help but be seriously limited. But this does not mean that models and paradigms of a structuralist and narratological type are useless to us. In my case, the tools of narratology helped me to focus on some fundamental features—some structural features—of medieval narrative that I had simply never grasped before. The success of these models was, for me, in their failures: what they *failed* to account for in medieval literature was thrown into sharper relief. Can one really ask more of any methodology?

While I have been stressing in these pages the rootedness of the medieval *récit* in the oral tradition, and its right-hemisphere orientation, still medieval narrative *is*, to some degree, "literature"—and gets increasingly close to what is meant today by this term as we reach the latter part of the medieval era. First comes the emergence of the book, originally read aloud. Then, the move to prose—and the gradual transition toward solitary, and silent, reading.[9] To some degree, then, medieval (especially later medieval) narrative and other forms must lend themselves to what we think of as literary analysis. And while I have been struck by the impact of Christian conceptual structures on medieval narrative—by its structural theocentricity—it is also true (as noted earlier) that "Christian" came to mean increasingly something explicit and concrete by way of thematics; it is true as well that secularism had its impact on medieval literature, and increasingly so. Narrative analysis is, then, potentially of considerable valuable to us—just so long as we keep revising our theories and paradigms to fit the data (the works, the culture) and not, as is so common, the other way around.

NOTES

1. Devotional works and works with explicitly Christian thematics are more char-acterictic of the later Middle Ages—as are denunciations of earlier vernacular literature, such as Arthurian romances, as being full of lies and vanity. That is, starting in the mid-thirteenth century, works that are not overtly and indeed explicitly, even catechistically, Christian in their content, works that are pri-marily concerned with worldly honor and happiness, tend to be dismissed as worthless and immoral—however significant a structural role these works may have accorded to God, and however marked they might be by Christian thought. All this is, I suppose, part of what has long been identified as an "age of didacticism."

2. Walter J. Ong, *Orality and Literacy: The Technologizing of the Word* (London and New York: Methuen, 1982), 115–16.

3. I am thinking less here of Greimas (who originally worked on folktales and whose system, whatever its defects, is not excessively sophisticated) than of such theo-rists as Todorov, Genette, etc.

4. See Paul C. Vitz, "Analog Art and Digital Art: A Brain-Hemisphere Criticism of Modern Painting," in *Foundations of Aesthetics: Art and Art Education,* ed. F. Farley and R. W. Neperud (New York: Praeger, 1986); T. R. Blakeslee, *The Right Brain* (Garden City, N.Y.: Doubleday, 1980); Sally P. Springer and Georg Deutsch, *Left Brain/Right Brain,* rev. ed. (New York: Freeman, 1984).

5. It is worth noting that Ong's oral/written dichotomy overlaps in interesting ways but not entirely with the right/left brain dichotomy. But whereas Ong contrasts the world of sound with the world of the visual, considering the visual as "text," left brain/right brain research stresses the fact that *both* sound and image are processed in the right hemisphere which deals with all sensory material and patterns perceived in their simultaneity. This is an important nonoverlap be-tween the two, otherwise highly similar, sets of dichotomies.

6. See, e.g., Ruth Crosby, "Oral Delivery in the Middle Ages," *Speculum* ll, no. 1 (January 1936): 88–110; Paul Zumthor, *La Lettre et la voix: de la "littérature" médiévale* (Paris: Seuil, 1987), passim.

7. See Paul Saenger, "Silent Reading: Its Impact on Late Medieval Script and Soci-ety," *Viator* 13, (1982): 367–414.

8. See Springer and Deutsch, 38; Blakeslee, 136 and 161; Vitz, 3.

9. See Saenger.

Index